THE PASSION OF JESUS

And Its Hidden Meaning

THE PASSION OF JESUS

And Its Hidden Meaning

Explained and Applied to the Christian Life

by

Fr. James Groenings, S.J.

(Former Title: *The History of the Passion of Our Lord Jesus Christ)*

SIXTH, REVISED EDITION

"They have dug my hands and feet. They have numbered all my bones. And they have looked and stared upon me. They parted my garments amongst them; and upon my vesture they cast lots."

—Psalm 21:17-19

TAN BOOKS AND PUBLISHERS, INC.
Rockford, Illinois 61105

Nihil Obstat: F. G. Holweck
Censor Theologicus
St. Louis, Missouri
January 17, 1908

Imprimatur: ✠ John J. Glennon
Archbishop of St. Louis
January 22, 1908

Originally published by B. Herder Book Co., St. Louis, Missouri approximately 1908 under the title *The History of the Passion of Our Lord Jesus Christ Explained and Applied to the Christian Life.* This edition was photographically reproduced from the Sixth, Revised Edition of B. Herder Book Co., published in 1928.

Library of Congress Catalog Card No.: 82-50592

ISBN: 0-89555-189-6

Printed and bound in the United States of America.

TAN BOOKS AND PUBLISHERS, INC.
P.O. Box 424
Rockford, Illinois 61105

1987

PREFACE.

(From the foreword of the first German edition.)

"This book is not, strictly speaking, a series of sermons or meditations on the sufferings of our Redeemer, but it is rather an explanation of the history of the Passion. It consists of a description of the most important and most interesting trial which has ever come before a court of justice, on whose final decision depends the weal or woe of the whole human race. The book is also a commentary on the greatest drama which has ever been enacted. Even considered from a purely natural point of view, the Passion of our Lord is a drama with which none other can be compared as regards the character of the actors, the magnitude of the action, the importance of the intrigue and the complexity of the plot. The unities of time and place have even been preserved.

In preparing this explanation and practical application of the history of the Passion, the author has spared no pains in gathering and using with discretion the best which Catholic learning and research has to offer on the subject. In pursuance of his object he has consulted by preference the great Catholic theologians of the past and from these treasure-houses of sacred knowledge has chosen the granite blocks from which to rear his edifice. The author has thought it wise not to draw from private revelations, no matter how venerable the names connected with them may be. Since it is difficult to distinguish between what is in reality revealed in these revelations and what is merely the result of pious meditation, the author judged it more in accordance with his very calling as teacher and interpreter of the Gospel to rely solely on the Gospel narratives and the interpretation put upon them by the Fathers and by men scientifically trained for that purpose. The various personal revelations may, with due respect, be left to private devotion, pious reading and meditation.

How and to what extent exegetical matter should be incorporated in the work was determined by the double purpose in view, namely, to impart useful and interesting knowledge and to offer religious edification. The author does not pretend that he has always taken the correct stand on disputed points, but, on the other hand, he does not believe that he has made any assertion without good reason and without being able to quote, in support, authorities who command respect.

For the guidance of the reader, the passages from the four Gospels which provide the subject-matter for each chapter have been indicated. The historical sequence of the different events, as far as it was possible to determine it, has been strictly observed, except that the mysteries of Mount Olivet have been arranged from an objective viewpoint and that the wonderful phenomena observed before and at the time of the death of our Lord have been condensed in one chapter. However, care has been taken to avoid confusing the order of events. Partly with a view to furnishing an authoritative foundation for interpretations and partly for the instruction and encouragement of those who have not access to a large number of scientific works, notes on various difficult points have been added at the end of the book. They were placed there in order to avoid interrupting the text in a disagreeable manner by lengthy remarks which do not have the same interest for every one. As far as circumstances permitted, the passages quoted from the Fathers, taken over, with few exceptions, from Cornelius à Lapide and Salmeron, have been covered with exact references and have been compared with the original texts. Unfortunately it was not possible to verify all the references to the Fathers.

Although, as has been stated, the work is not a book of meditations, in the strict sense of the term, it, nevertheless, affords abundant material for meditation and may even be considered as a preparatory school for meditation, because its purpose is to introduce us to a thorough knowledge of the history of the Passion of our Lord, to reveal to us His inner life and to inspire us to apply the truths here taught to our lives. But those who propose using the book for meditation will do well to remember the advice given by St. Ignatius in his Spiritual Exercises, viz., to take thoroughly to heart, in considering the persons, the words and the actions in the history of the Passion, what our Lord suffered in His sacred humanity, especially in His Divine Heart; how His divinity withdraws into the background, as it were, in order to abandon His sacred humanity to suffering, and how, finally, Christ suffers all these things for *each one of us* individually in accordance with the words of St. Paul. (Gal. ii., 20.) It was not feasible to repeat these important and wholesome thoughts in every chapter, nor is it the intention of St. Ignatius that they themselves form the object of our meditations; they are rather to be considered, to use a comparison, as the glasses through which we are to behold the objects of our attention, i. e., the various events in the history of the Passion. It is sufficient to here remind the reader to keep these three points constantly before his mind.

As it was not practicable to indicate on every page the sources from which the various explanations were taken, we name here the chief works consulted in writing this book.

A. Salmeron, S. J., Comment. in Evangel. Historiam; Fr. Toletus, S. J., Comment. in Joannis Evangelium; Joh. Maldonat, S. J., Comment. in quatuor Evangelistas; Seb. Barradas, S. J., Comment. in Concordiam et Historiam quatuor Evangelist.; Cornelius à Lapide, S. J., Comment. in quatuor Evangelia; P. A. Scherer, Bibliothek für Prediger; Fr. Xav. Massl, Erklärung der heiligen Schriften des Neuen Testamentes; Dr. P. Schegg, Kommentare zu Matthäus und Johannes; Dr. P.

Schanz, Kommentare zu den vier Evangelisten; Dr. Joh. Nep. Sepp, Das Leben Jesu Christi (second edition); Dr. P. Schegg, Das Leben Jesu; L. de Ponte, S. J., Meditationes; L. de la Palma, S. J., Geschichte der heiligen Passion; W. Stanihurstus, S. J., Dei immortalis in corpore mortali patientis historia; R. Bellarmin, S. J., Die sieben Worte Christi am Kreuze; Ad. Fr. Lennig, Betrachtungen über das bittere Leiden Jesu Christi; Ant. Etzinger, Betrachtungen über das Leiden und Sterben Jesu Christi; Dr. M. Breiteneicher, Die Passion des Gottmenschen; Dr. N. Gihr, Das heilige Messopfer.

May by God's grace, the reading of this book help to inflame in our hearts the love of the Crucified."

The second English edition has been prepared from the fourth German edition with the addition of those improvements which are to be incorporated in a fifth German edition, should such be called for.

THE AUTHOR.

BUFFALO, NEW YORK.

Feast of the Immaculate Conception of the Blessed Virgin, December, 8, 1907.

CONTENTS

Chapter VI.

Chapter VII.

Chapter VIII.

Chapter IX.

Chapter X.

Chapter XI.

Chapter XII.

CHAPTER XIII.

CHAPTER XIV.

CHAPTER XV.

CHAPTER XVI.

CHAPTER XVII.

CHAPTER XVIII.

CHAPTER XIX.

Chapter XX.

THE PASSION OF JESUS

CHAPTER I.

THE SUFFERINGS OF CHRIST'S SOUL IN THE GARDEN OF OLIVES

The Most Holy Sacrament of the Altar had been instituted. The words of leave taking had been spoken by the Saviour. The hymn of praise, prescribed by the law, had been sung. Then Jesus, as was His wont, went with His disciples to a garden situated on the Mount of Olives. The garden was distant about half a league from the Cenacle and belonged to a farm called Gethsemane, a word meaning "Oil Press." The way led over the brook Cedron, which, fed by the rains of winter, was dry in mid-summer. The word, "Cedron" means a dark, obscure ravine, a vale of shadows. This name had been given the stream either because of the darkness spread by the thick growth of woods along its borders, or because the valley of Josephat, through which it flowed, was the valley of sin, the valley of tombs. For there, in olden times, sacrifices were offered to Moloch, there the Jews were buried. Every year, over a specially constructed bridge, which spanned this deep rock-ribbed ravine, the red cow was led to the

Mount of Olives, there to be burnt for the atonement of the people. Over the same way the scapegoat was driven out to be devoured by wild beasts, thus to give vicarious satisfaction for the sins of men. We now behold, following the same way, the Son of God, the Pure One, the innocent Lamb, Who shall take away the sins of the world. In days gone by, King David with his faithful adherents had also crossed the Cedron, in tears and his head covered in mourning, for he was fleeing from his son Absalom. Christ crossed the brook, not to flee from His enemies, but to deliver Himself to the betrayer in the Garden of Olives. For Judas, the traitor, knew the place, because Jesus had often gone there with His disciples, especially in the days just passed.

On the way, Jesus, in clear terms, again foretold the unfaithfulness of the disciples, especially of Peter; but they would not believe Him. Peter, with self-confident presumption, protested anew that, even if all the others should be scandalized in the Master, he certainly would not; that he would rather die with Him than deny Him. Extolling himself above the others by his assurances of attachment and fidelity, Peter caused them to take offense, and they began to protest in like manner. But the Lord sought to prepare them for the things to come and to console them, even then, by directing their attention to His proximate resurrection. Conversing on these themes, they at length arrived at the garden of Gethsemane.

The events in the Garden of Olives can properly be considered under the following heads: Christ plunged in sadness and wrestling with death; Christ praying to His heavenly Father; Christ calling on His disciples; Christ betrayed by Judas; Christ captured by His enemies and forsaken by the apostles.

Let us consider, the sufferings of the Saviour's soul:

I. As to their nature.

II. As to their causes.

I.

The sufferings of our Saviour's soul in their first stage are described in the following manner by the evangelists: St. Matthew writes, "He began to grow sorrowful and to be sad. Then he saith to them: My soul is sorrowful even unto death." St. Mark says, "And he began to fear and to be heavy. And he saith to them: My soul is sorrowful even unto death."

The evangelists, then, make use of three expressions in characterizing the mental sufferings of the Saviour. They speak of sadness, of fear and of heaviness which we may call repugnance. *Sadness* is the result of present evil that already has befallen one; *fear* arises from the thought of future evil, to avoid which seems very difficult; *repugnance* is felt under the pressure of present inevitable evils and at the thought of future evils which appear unavoidable and are therefore considered as already present.

At the thought of present or future evils, we

human beings are overwhelmed with sadness, fear and repugnance. For these passions or emotions do not arise in us as a result of reason's reflections or of free will. They rather have their origin in the lower powers of the soul, whence they ascend to the higher faculties, moving the will and alluring its sympathy. They run ahead of the reflections of reason, and they are present before one is aware of it. They therefore render more difficult the calm apprehension of the intellect. But thus far there is no personal fault, no sin. It is merely something human, a peculiar result of our deteriorated nature. At this point however, it becomes the duty of the intellect and will to control and to conquer these ebullitions of passion by adducing motives of reason and of faith, and also by prayer and correspondence with divine grace. But instead of acting in such a manner, our wills too often, through our own fault, yield and allow full sway to the emotions and permit us to be carried onward to sins of impatience, anger and others similar, all of which causes the reason to become still more obscured.

It was not so with Christ. All that He suffered never in the least bedimmed the clear apprehension of reason. For with full conviction and freedom He first presented to His mind the causes of sadness, of fear and of repugnance. Then, it is true, He permitted these emotions to produce their painful effects to the fullest extent upon His will and, through the will, upon the other faculties of His soul. But at the same time He presented to His soul counter-motives, which encouraged Him to patiently undergo the sufferings, and, for our example, He simultaneously addressed Himself in earnest prayer to His heavenly Father. Thus He suffered and still always retained perfect control over these inner emotions.

We are here confronted by a great mystery. On the one hand, the soul of Christ from the moment of its creation, enjoyed the beatific vision and, in consequence, untold happiness whilst in the mortal body; but, on the other, it experienced sorrows from other causes and was sad even unto death.[1] Only a most incomprehensible miracle of Divine Power and Love could bring this about and did bring it about in the case of the Saviour alone. For faith teaches us that the blessed in heaven, owing to the beatific vision, are immune from any and all sufferings and that, after the last day, their bodies shall also be impassible.

In the second stage, the sufferings of the soul of Christ increased to a real fear of death, whence they passed to a condition of agony, or death-struggle, which produced a bloody sweat. This incident is mentioned by the evangelist St. Luke in the following terms: "And being in agony," i. e., whilst struggling against the fear of death, "he prayed the longer. And his sweat became as drops of blood trickling down upon the ground."

How shall we explain the fear of death in Christ? In the rest of men, this fear usually arises

[1] Note 1.

from three causes: from the consciousness of sins committed in the past, from the uncertainty of the future lot awaiting the soul and, lastly, from the natural reluctance of the soul to leave the body. It is evident that in Christ the fear of death could not arise from the first and second causes, for He had nothing to regret in the past, and, as to the future, He knew full well that He would go to the Father. The fear of death in Him arose, therefore, from the last mentioned cause. It is to be remarked, however, that the fear of death in Him was different from that which we experience. In us the repugnance to death and its fear are felt without the consent of our will, even against its consent, while in Christ the fear of death was willed with full deliberation and freedom.

The agony of the Saviour consisted in His struggling with the whole power of His will against the fear of death which He had freely admitted, in His subduing and conquering it. It was, indeed, a most remarkable conflict in the heart of the God-Man. Christ there appears as a general who, being certain of victory, challenges and provokes the enemy to combat, but only to conquer and to slay him.

The bloody sweat, finally, which accompanied the fear of death, was the result of the struggle and not of the fear. Fear, notably the fear of impending death, does not drive the blood out of the heart, but rather back to it. Fright and fear produce a pale, not a ruddy complexion. The bloody sweat, therefore, was the result of the death-struggle, that is, of the great effort of will power to overcome the fear of death. It must, indeed, have been a powerful effort, which drove the blood, after it had rushed through fear to the heart, back through the sacred body to find vent and burst forth in great drops through the pores.

There He lies, the Almighty, the Strong One of Israel, the Shield of the Hero, the Lion of the tribe of Juda, like to a worm trodden in the dust, scarcely able to emit a sigh. Finally, with great effort, He rises. He uplifts His face to heaven, and in the calm light of the full moon that Holy Face appears covered with innumerable red drops, and these drops are the heart's blood of the Son of God, which, amid the most fearful pains, is pressed from all the pores of His sacred Body. The bloody drops fall upon the earth to free it from the ancient curse, and, like to the blood of Abel, they cry to heaven, not for vengeance, however, but for mercy. What then, we have a right to ask, were the causes which gave rise to these sufferings of the soul?

II.

The sufferings of the soul of Christ resulted chiefly from four causes. The first cause was the clear knowledge the Saviour had of all the pains He had to endure in His natural body, in His sacramental body, and in His mystic body. The images of all the terrors and of all the tortures to be brought forth by the coming day arranged themselves vividly before His eyes. He beheld the bloody scourge, the crown of thorns, the dishonor of the purple mantle, the false testimonies, the scornful and biting jeers, the altar of sacrifice on Golgotha. These dreadful images caused Him to feel all the impending pains even before the rude menial raised the fearful scourge, before the cruel nails pierced His sacred hands and feet. The mere thought of an approaching operation or of a threatened disgrace has caused many a one to swoon. Why should it be a matter of surprise that the heart of the Redeemer, at the sight of such woes, trembled in its inmost fibres and prematurely shed its blood? Add to this the foreknowledge of all the wrong and ignominy He was to suffer in His sacramental body through the various sins against the Blessed Sacrament, of all the persecutions and outrages which would be heaped upon His mystic body, the holy Church, by infidels, heretics and schismatics, by cruel tyrants, by anti-Catholic governments and from the scandalous lives of many Catholics. He knew that He could no more endure these pains after His death, therefore He drank in advance this cup of suffering in the garden of Gethsemane. In the second place, the conduct of His ungrateful disciples was to the Redeemer a source of untold sadness. One is already on the way to betray Him for thirty pieces of silver; another, a few hours hence, will deny Him; all are indifferent and given over to careless slumber. In ages to come, the example of these ingrates will be followed by millions of Christians after they shall have reaped the abundance of His benefits, after they shall have been freed, through His precious Blood, from the thraldom of Satan and nourished with His own sacred flesh. Truly the Saviour could exclaim with the Psalmist, " I am become a stranger to my brethren, and an alien to the sons of my mother. And I looked for one that would grieve together with me, but there was none: and for one that would comfort me and I found none."

The third cause was the painful knowledge that all His struggles and sufferings would be wasted on innumerable souls. Hear His plaint in the words of Isaias, the prophet: "I have labored in vain, I have spent my strength without cause and in vain." May God grant that, in these pathetic lamentations, his thoughts were not directed towards any of us! Above all, He was afflicted at the thought of the awful end of His apostle Judas, as well as the temporal and eternal ruin towards which His chosen and beloved people of Israel were drifting.

All this is, indeed, more than sufficient to break a heart, even though that heart were divine. And still St. Chrysostom says that we should err were we to think that the knowledge of all these sufferings was the principal cause of the mental grief and of the mortal anguish of Christ. For no matter how fearful these sufferings were, the Redeemer had anxiously desired them and intensely longed for them. No matter how heavy, how shameful the cross might be, no matter that to many it was a folly and a scandal, it would also bring salvation unto many; for Christ Himself it would be the foundation of His Glory; to the heavenly Father it would bring infinite honor.

It must, then, have been something else that made the soul of Our Saviour tremble; it must have been something else that could make of a God of infinite glory a God struggling with death. It was sin. "The sorrows of death surrounded me: and the torrents of iniquity troubled me." In the hour when the high priests and pharisees consulted together in the court of Caiphas how they might apprehend Jesus, the heavenly Father imposed upon Him, (the purity of His soul, however, remaining unsullied), all the injustice of the whole world, the sins of all nations, the sins of all times, the sins of all classes; the sins of kings, the sins of subjects; the sins of the rich, the sins of the poor; the sins of parents and the sins of children. Is it a wonder that this burden of iniquities, laid upon the Saviour, should press Him to the ground?

To us, indeed, who know so little of the supernatural, sin often appears in more subdued colors. We excuse it, we consider it a mere weakness, something natural, a result of youth and of temperament. We fear at most the penalties of sin threatened by God's anger. But the soul of Christ saw, clearly and distinctly, not only the entire series of sins, from the disobedience of our first parents down to the desolations of dooms-day, but also all the malice, all the abomination, the revolt, the contempt, the dark ingratitude contained in each and every sin. Even when we recognize the wrong done to Almighty God by our sins, we take it little to heart, because we love Him so little. But the soul of Christ, which sought nothing more strenuously than the glory of His heavenly Father and which loved Him with an immeasurable love greater than that of all the Cherubim and Seraphim, felt most vividly the wrong inflicted on the Divine Majesty by sin. The sorrows of David over the injustices of the chosen people, the grief and indignation of Elias at the scandals and the idolatries of Israel, the tears of the prophet Jeremiah over the infidelities of Jerusalem were merely faint figures of the sadness of Jesus when He beheld the sins of the entire world.

And if this be true, we cannot shut out from our hearts another consideration. At the sight of our sins a God is seized with painful disquiet, and we remain calm. A God is sad over our sins, and we take pleasure therein. A God sweats blood for our sins, and we never shed a tear. We sin and, instead of hesitating and trembling, we think, perhaps, "I have sinned and what harm hath befallen me?" At the sight of our sins a God-Man writhes in agony, and we, perhaps, live on in a dreadful torpor which is an insult to the agony of Christ, in a false security, which, in a way, is more terrible than sin itself. We, perhaps, shall slumber on in utter blindness until that hour in which the voice of the eternal Judge will awaken us. Oh, dreadful moment in which the Redeemer, now mute and patient in the Garden of Olives, burdened down with the mountain of our sins, will unsheathe before the sinner the flaming sword of vengeance! Oh, dreadful moment, in which the same Redeemer, who now sheds His blood for our sins, will demand of the sinner an account of the blood shed in vain! Oh, most dreadful moment, in which the heart, now tortured out of love for us, even unto death, will appear glowing with eternal wrath!

Still, however great our fault may be, even if our sins be as numerous as the grains of sand on the sea-shore, we must not despair. Now is still the time of grace, even now, from all the pores of the Redeemer wrestling with death, His precious blood is being shed for us, even now His divine Heart is beating warmly for us. Let us firmly resolve to flee the monster sin which caused a God to tremble; by means of the Precious Blood, to purify ourselves in the sacrament of Penance, and, henceforth so to live as to justify the hope that, when we shall writhe in the throes of death, the agony of Christ may bring us, not despair, but solace; not ruin, but salvation.

CHAPTER II.

CIRCUMSTANCES SURROUNDING THE SUFFERINGS OF CHRIST IN THE GARDEN OF OLIVES

"And he saith to them: My soul is sorrowful even unto death."
(St. Mark, xiv., 34.)

In considering the history of the Passion, we must, as much as possible, pass in review not only the chief events, but also the subordinate occurrences, even minute details narrated by the evangelists. Whatever, that is to say, the Holy Ghost, through the Sacred Scriptures, has made known to us concerning the person, the work and the Passion of Christ, cannot be considered small or trivial; it must be worthy of our consideration and mature reflection. These various outward circumstances are often full of deep mystery, and, when we penetrate into their meaning, they heighten the interest in the chief event itself. Furthermore, for a thorough understanding of the facts, it is also very useful to examine and investigate, with humble moderation, in so far as our limited powers will permit, their inward circumstances, i. e., the causes why they should and must have happened as they did.

We shall, therefore, stop at the subject of our

first chapter in order to impress more clearly on our minds the picture of the Saviour, sad even unto death and bathed in His blood. Let us consider

I. The circumstances of His sufferings;
II. The motives which induced Him to suffer.

I.

The outward circumstances of the sufferings of the Redeemer's soul are threefold: circumstances of place, of time and of persons.

Let us consider first the circumstances of place. Christ began His Passion in a garden, more precisely, in an olive-garden. When the Redeemer felt that the hour of His capture was drawing nigh, He left the Cenacle. He would not cause discomfort to the good man who had generously opened his house to Him for the institution of the Most Holy Sacrament. He wished to spare this friend all annoyance which might come to him, were the Lord to be seized in his house. He left the city altogether. Beyond its walls, in God's open country, He decided to begin and to end His Passion, to show that He shed His blood not for Jerusalem alone, but for the entire world. For the beginning of His Passion, He chose a wonderfully beautiful garden. How significant this choice was! In a garden the first Adam had committed the first sin, the sin of disobedience; therefore it was in a garden that the second Adam should say to His Father, "Not what I will, but what thou wilt." In a garden Adam, by an abuse of liberty, had plunged the entire human race into the most shameful captivity; in a garden, therefore, by the bonds of Christ our fetters were to be broken. In a garden God had pronounced the death-penalty upon Adam; hence, in a garden Christ would take upon Himself this judgment and this curse. In a garden the human race was lost; and usually an object is sought where it was lost. Christ had come into the world to lay out a garden wherein, amid splendor and abundance, there should thrive the violet of humility, the myrtle of mortification, the rose of love, the lily of virginal souls, the laurel of confessors and the palm of martyrs. It was necessary, then, that He should water and render fertile by His precious blood the soil of this garden. The garden of Gethsemane was furthermore an olive garden, at least it contained quite a number of olive trees, and, according to several interpreters of Holy Writ, the oil for the use of the temple was obtained here. This circumstance, again, is full of significance. "Oil illumines," says St. Bernard,[1] "it nourishes and heals." All these effects were to be produced by the blood of Christ in the Christian temple, and that in an infinitely greater degree than by the fruit of the olive-tree in the Jewish temple. For Christ is the great olive-tree, on which the heathen were grafted, according to St. Paul the Apostle. Now as the oil, before it could be used in divine service, had to be pressed forcibly from the fruit,

1 S. Bern. serm. 15. sup. Cant. n. 5.

so the blood of Christ also must be forced from His Sacred Body in His mighty agony.

Let us pass on to the circumstances of persons. Christ permitted only three of His apostles to be witnesses of His agony, namely, Peter, John and James. The reasons are easily surmised. First, Christ had specially prepared these three, and only these three, for the contemplation of this scene. "The rest," as Origen makes the Lord say, "as the weaker ones, I have invited to remain seated; but of you, as of the stronger ones, I expect that you labor with Me in watching and in prayer." Here we see how true the saying of Scripture is that God does not allow man to be tempted above that which he is able.

Furthermore, these three apostles had made greater promises than the others. Christ had asked John and James, "Can you drink of the chalice that I drink of?" They courageously answered Him, "We can."[1] And Peter had assured the Lord that it would be an easy matter for him to die with Him.

Then again, the sight of the Redeemer, praying that the chalice of suffering might pass and receiving no answer to His prayer, should show these apostles that God will not be satisfied with mere promises, but that they also must drain the same chalice. Finally, these same apostles were to be, more than the others, the supports and pillars of the Church; Peter was even to be its head. There-

[1] St. Mark, x., 38, 39.

fore it was meet that they have a greater share in the cross of Christ. For this reason, people in high positions, superiors and parents, must always expect greater tribulations, which are inseparably and especially connected with the duty of vigilance.

But, that He might be more undisturbed in prayer, Christ retired a stone's cast from these three apostles also. "He was withdrawn away from them,"[1] says the evangelist. These words show us His great love for His apostles. To leave them, He had, as it were, to make a violent effort. They also show how great His sadness was. It is natural, in sorrow, to wish to be with friends. Christ made this sacrifice also to His heavenly Father. St. Anselm says the Saviour retired to a small elevation, so that, in the light of the full moon, the three disciples could observe Him from the distance mentioned.

In contrast with His agony, the seizure of Christ which followed was to take place in presence of the whole college of apostles. They all were to witness the fact that Christ freely allowed Himself to be bound, therefore He first threw His enemies to the ground. This circumstance also precluded any possible accusation that, when alone, He was surprised in the act of some great crime and therefore arrested. The pharisees would certainly have found false witnesses to swear to such an outrage.

[1] St. Luke, xxii., 41.

There remain the circumstances of time to be considered. It was towards eight o'clock in the evening when Christ set forth to begin His passion. This is the hour when millions of people, millions of Christians, ay, millions of Catholics set forth to seek the embrace of sinful pleasures. From nine until twelve o'clock at night, Christ was sad unto death. He trembled and quaked, He fell in agony, He shed a bloody sweat. What an awful contrast this picture of the suffering Saviour presents to the noisy carousals, frivolous dances, shameless ballets, secret meetings, lustful orgies which in exactly these hours of the night, defy the blood of Christ. At the sight of these abominations the heart of the God-Man would fain lose its strength and its courage: He trembled and shrank back in fear.

Another circumstance of time is not to be overlooked. The death-struggle and agony are usually the immediate precursors of death. Why was it not thus with Our Lord? This is the reason. Had Christ undergone His agony on the cross in the last hours of His life, it would have appeared as if He died as a result of His agony or of weakness. But He wished to show the world that He suffered death of His own free will. Nevertheless, as He would not forego the pains of agony, He suffered them in the garden.

This leads us to the second part, that is, to the consideration of the motives which induced Christ to take upon Himself, although they were not necessary for our salvation, the sufferings of the soul above described.

II.

The first motive was, as the Fathers tell us, the intention of convincing us of the reality of His human nature. At the death of Christ the divine nature revealed itself more prominently. And indeed, when we reflect how the most cruel pains failed to extinguish the life of the Saviour as He hung on the cross, how, contrary to all laws of nature, He exclaimed with a loud voice, " Father, into thy hands I commend my spirit," how He then bowed His head and died, we must avow that only a God could so die. Wherefore the centurion cried out, "Indeed this man was the Son of God." The agony, however, affords the most powerful proof of man's impotence, shows that he is in truth mortal. Christ wished to convince us of this fact regarding Himself. Had His body been merely a phantom, as later heretics asserted, our redemption would not be an accomplished fact, because the blood of a God-Man was to be its price. Thus did the agony of Jesus Christ, His fear and trembling and the blood that issued from every pore of His sacred Body put to confusion in advance all these heretics.

In assuming such sufferings of soul, Christ desired, moreover, to atone for our abuse of the faculties of the soul, for all sinful thoughts, imaginations and desires; through His sadness, He wished to atone for the pleasure felt by the sinner in satisfying his passions. Especially did Christ intend to begin His Passion, the source of all weal, where sin, the source of all woe, takes its beginning. "For from the heart come forth evil thoughts, murders, adulteries, fornications, thefts, false testimonies, blasphemies," says Christ Himself.[1] For this reason, the heart of the God-Man was to be tortured and martyred before His sacred Body was cut with lashes, His head crowned with thorns and His hands and feet pierced with nails.

Furthermore, Christ intended to encourage, by His example, all those who, like to Himself, should die a martyr's death and to merit for them all the necessary graces. There is no doubt that many of the holy martyrs, notwithstanding their ardent desire for the martyr's crown, were sad in their hearts unto death, trembled and feared at the thought of approaching pains, at the thought of the wild beasts, the burning fagots, the red hot tongs and the hundreds of other instruments of torture. But then they remembered how their Saviour, who had also such a longing desire for the cross, was seized with agony at the approach of His passion. This thought dispelled all pusillanimity, all fear. It raised them out of their sadness, it filled them with confidence, so that strengthened by the grace of Christ, they heroically approached their tortures, even with greater joy than that of the bride meeting the bridegroom.

[1] St. Matthew, xv., 19.

When, again, we behold Christians on their death-bed looking death with all its terrors calmly in the face and exclaiming triumphantly with St. Paul, "O death, where is thy victory? O death, where is thy sting?"[1] must we not say that this is one of the effects of the agony of Jesus Christ?

Finally, "nowhere," says St. Ambrose,[2] "does the love and majesty of Jesus cause more admiration in me than in this sadness, in this agony. It was not enough for Him to assume my nature, He also assumed my feelings and my sensations. He who had no reason to be sad for Himself, wished to feel my sadness." And so it is. In assuming those sufferings of the soul, the Saviour thought of us. He foresaw all the mental sufferings that would be ours, and mental anguish is the greatest and most painful of all. He saw mothers mourning over the disobedience and bad behavior of their children; fathers who know not whence to obtain the daily bread for their families; the sick utterly discouraged and afflicted, and those unhappy souls who have been despoiled by calumny of their reputation.

Then there are the young who are about to lose courage at the repeated onslaughts of temptation. All ye disconsolate souls, be consoled at the sight of the Redeemer, sad unto death, and reflect that, by His bloody sweat, He has gained for you the grace to support the sufferings of your souls with

1 I. Cor., xv., 55.

2 Ambr. Exp. s. Luc. l. 10. 56.

patience and with merit. How many a great sinner has felt himself relieved when, frightened by the great number of his sins and tortured by remorse, he in spirit plunged himself into the depths of that Heart which was so cruelly frightened and tortured by those very sins; when he united his well deserved mental sufferings with the sorrow of the Saviour and offered them to God in a spirit of penance. Then the star of hope began to shine upon this sinner on the brink of despair. It was the first step to his conversion. Let us, then, have courage and confidence whenever sadness comes to us.

Especially when the last hour approaches and the agony of death seizes upon us, let us remember the Saviour sad unto death, so that in our death-struggle we may, like the saints, be strengthened and comforted at the thought of the death-struggle of Christ. But that will happen only if, while we still have health, we meditate often and piously upon the agony of Christ and impress his sorrows deeply upon our hearts. Otherwise, at the moment of death, we shall think of every thing else but of our divine model. The principal fruit, then, of this consideration ought to be the firm resolve often to reflect, with the grace of God, on the agony of Jesus Christ, especially in the season of Lent and on the Fridays throughout the year. It would also be very salutary, if the occasion should offer, to become affiliated to a confraternity having that object and to assist devoutly at its meetings and devotions.

In conclusion, let us repeat the prayer which Holy Church says at the bedside of the dying. "O Lord Jesus Christ, through Thy holy agony and Thy prayer which Thou hast offered for us upon the Mount of Olives, when Thy sweat, as drops of blood, trickled down upon the ground, vouchsafe, we beseech Thee, to present and to offer to God, the Father Almighty, against the multitude of all our sins, the abundance of Thy bloody sweat, which Thou hast copiously shed for us in fear and trembling, and to deliver us in the hour of our death from all the pains and anguish which, we fear, we have merited for our sins. Who livest and reignest with the Father and the Holy Ghost, world without end. Amen."

CHAPTER III.

THE PRAYER OF CHRIST IN THE GARDEN OF OLIVES

> "My father, if it be possible, let this chalice pass from me. Nevertheless not as I will, but as Thou wilt."
> St. Math., xxvi., 39.

The sensations of sadness, of fear and of repugnance to suffering and death, which Our Saviour had freely admitted, gradually developed into a real death-agony. The gospel further narrates[1] that during these sufferings of soul, Christ lay prone on the ground, flat upon His face. This prayer, however, as we shall hereafter more closely observe, was interrupted twice by His going to His apostles. The sum and substance of the thrice offered prayer was, "My Father, if it be possible, let this chalice pass from Me. Nevertheless not as I will, but as Thou wilt." After Jesus had offered this prayer for the third time, an angel appeared to submit to Him the will of the Father and to encourage Him to overcome His fear of death. After that, He no more returned to the three apostles, but He persevered in prayer; as St. Luke narrates, He prayed the longer. Meantime He wrestled

[1] St. Mathew, xvi, 39-46; St. Mark, xiv., 35-42; St. Luke, xxii., 41-43.

with death in such an effort that He sweat blood. Holy writ has not made known to us the burden of this last, longer prayer. But assuredly, after being strengthened by the angel, He no longer prayed that the chalice might pass from Him, He rather prayed, "Father, Thy will be done." When the struggle in which He overcame the agony was over, He returned to the three disciples. When he found them again sleeping, He said to them in mournful grief, if all my admonitions avail naught, do as you deem best, "Sleep ye now and take your rest." But as just then the clash of weapons resounded, He added, "It is enough. Rise up." In these words, He summoned the three disciples to rise and go with Him to meet the enemy.[1] Frightened by the noise of the soldiers, the eight other apostles ran as quickly as possible towards the Saviour, but whether they arrived soon enough to witness the kiss of Judas cannot be determined with certainty.

We shall now fix our eyes upon the praying Saviour. That He prayed is certainly nothing novel, for the gospel teaches us that He prayed during his whole life. But as by His prayers in the house of Nazareth and during His public career He wished to show us how we should sanctify our youth and the duties of our state of life by prayer, just so, by His prayer in the Garden of Olives, He would be our model in the hour of suffering and at the hour of death. The thrice repeated prayer

[1] Note 2.

of the Redeemer is, indeed, very instructive, if we consider

I. The circumstances,
II. The qualities and
III. The effects of this prayer.

I.

The first circumstance which makes the prayer of Christ instructive is that He prayed at a time of extreme sadness, in other words, while He was in a frame of mind in which thousands of others would say, I cannot pray. It is indeed most unfortunate that we neglect prayer in times of trouble, vexation, sadness and other depressions of the soul. Many, even, neglect their prayers when they are somewhat out of sorts or in bad humor. And still prayer is never so necessary as in times of depression. For it is in just such moments that the evil enemy attacks us with his temptations and that our natural resources are weak to resist them. And if we then seek not help from above in earnest prayer, we yield to temptation. Then follow complaints against God's Providence, curses and blasphemies. Some drown their grief in dram shops, others seek solace in the impure lusts of the flesh. And is it not a fact that many a one, urged on by discouragement and despair, has sought to put an end to a miserable existence by committing suicide? We should, then, follow the example of our divine Saviour, who being sad unto death, prayed three times over to the Father. We should say to ourselves, Christ could pray in all the anguish of His soul, consequently we can do it also. Then we shall experience what the Psalmist [1] says of himself, "My soul refused to be comforted. I remembered God and was delighted."

Christ prayed while His friends slept. It may happen that, in the midst of woe, we are entirely deserted. And if it happen not in life, it will certainly happen at the moment of death, when, all alone, we must face the tribunal of God. Then nothing remains for us but to pray and to remember that "Our help is in the name of the Lord." [2] Christ prayed while His disciples slept. We must also pray when among the sleeping, that is, when we must needs be among luke-warm and slothful Christians, in order, on the one hand, not to become affected by their example, and, on the other, to arouse them by the cry of our prayer from their dangerous sloth. So in a family, a single member who knows how to pray well, is often the greatest blessing to the rest. But if those must pray who are among the sleeping, how much more those who are among the dead, i. e., among sinners, and who must associate all day long with people whose hearts are full of malice and whose tongues are full of impurity.

Finally, Christ prayed while His enemies were banding together to take Him prisoner and to deliver Him to the most shameful death. In this

1 Psalms, lxxvi., 3, 4.

2 Psalms, cxxiii., 8.

circumstance we are shown the weapon to be used when the same Christ, either in His Bride, the Catholic Church, or in us, His brethren and members, is attacked by the dark powers of this world. This weapon is none other than prayer. When Peter incontinently wielded the sword, Christ reproved him and commanded him to sheathe it. Armed with prayer alone, joined to the patient bearing of trials, may we meet our enemies. The first Christians understood well the example and the teaching of their Master. We find them, therefore, joined together in prayer in order to obtain the freedom of the first Pope held in bondage. And thus it happened in all succeeding centuries, whenever the tragedy of the garden of Olives was repeated in Holy Church. Hence, we also, in these troublous times, should use trustingly the weapon of prayer and confidently hope that the liberation of Holy Mother Church may be brought about by Him who directs the hearts of kings as He wills and who, besides, has the power to cast down and lay low the wicked as He would the vessel of the potter.

The thrice offered prayer of Christ is, therefore, instructive when we consider its circumstances, but it is just as instructive when we consider its qualities.

II.

The prayer of the Saviour unfolds to us the consoling truth that we are allowed to pray with our whole soul for the removal of temporal sufferings. But that our prayer may have a claim to a hearing, it must have the qualities of the prayer of Christ.

In the first place, Christ, whilst praying, showed the greatest outward respect. "He knelt down and fell upon His face." This indeed must silence all those who are so prompt and decided in condemning all external manifestations of interior devotion. For if ever any man could deem himself dispensed from external marks of reverence, it was certainly the God-Man whose Most Holy Body, by virtue of its intimate union with the second Person of the Godhead, had been raised to such an immense dignity. But if, nevertheless, the Most Sacred Body of Christ lay, as he prayed, prostrate upon the ground and if the Saviour did not dare to raise His countenance toward heaven, what awe should not appear in the body of the sinner, who, laden not with the sins of others but with his own, approaches God in prayer. I do not wish to champion the cause of exaggeration and of affectation. When we pray, however, our interior respect must show itself externally. The Saviour at prayer teaches us this. Is it not remarkable that there should be Christian men who are ashamed to bend the knee to God Almighty and who believe that their dignity would be compromised were they to kneel before Him who is their Creator and their eternal Judge? But those who, in the house of God, give scandal to others by silly and impertinent behavior can only be people of thoughtless brains or of depraved morals. They are proud spirits, slaves of human respect. When we are about to pray, we should, then, be recollected and remember who we are and who He is with whom we are to converse.

Let us observe, furthermore, that childlike confidence in which the Redeemer gives expression in the words, "My Father." Although visited by God with such terrible afflictions, He calls Him His father. How differently we act! When, to punish us for sin, to furnish us with an opportunity of doing penance or of gaining merit for heaven, God visits us in affliction, the word "Father" falls from our lips only by means of a great effort, because, in our inmost heart, we are tempted to consider God, not as a father, but rather as a cruel master or a tyrant. And still, let us rest assured, we can hardly show God greater reverence than by confidently addressing Him by the sweet name of father, in the hour of affliction.

We should further learn from Christ to persevere in prayer. Christ prayed, but heaven remained closed. He prayed the second and the third time and, as the evangelist says, it was always the same prayer. Hence we must also pray with perseverance; if we would be heard, we must not grow weak or weary in repeating to God the same petition. How great must have been the anguish of soul of the Redeemer! With the most intense desire He had yearned for the cup of suffering. And now, when it is offered Him, He repeatedly begs that it may pass from Him.

We ought, finally, to admire the perfect resignation of the Redeemer to the divine will. "If it be possible. Nevertheless not as I will, but as Thou wilt." And let us here consider what tortures and sorrows were contained in the chalice to be drained by the Redeemer, and we shall, as a consequence, show more patience and more resignation to God's Holy Will in our much lighter trials.

Lastly, the thrice offered prayer of Christ in the Garden of Olives is instructive if we consider its effects.

III.

The first effect of the prayer of Christ is described in the following words of the Gospel: "And there appeared to him an Angel from Heaven strengthening him."[1] This angel, according to some interpreters, was St. Gabriel, according to others, St. Michael, the former being the angel of the Incarnation, the latter the vanquisher of the fallen spirits. The King, then, of the Holy angels, He who is Divine Power itself, the Consoler of hearts, is strengthened and consoled by an angel! It is, indeed, wonderful! We can understand how, at the birth of Christ, the angels descended with joy to intone the first gloria in honor of their Lord. We can understand also how, later on, after the Saviour had fasted forty days and forty nights, the same angels came and ministered unto Him. But that an angel should

[1] St. Luke, xxii., 43.

approach his Creator in the quality of a consoler, is strange to the last degree. Still, God had so willed it, and Christ, with an humble heart, took from one of His creatures that comfort which He might have had from and of Himself. Is this not a touching and an attractive scene? Does not such humility render the Lord infinitely lovable and dear to us? From this occurrence we learn, furthermore, that in our trials we can expect efficacious help from heaven above. It is worthy of note also that Almighty God could not in a more beautiful and impressive way show us what confidence we ought to place in the holy angels.

We now arrive at the query as to what the comfort given to Christ by the angel really consisted in. Did it consist in the removal of the chalice of suffering, as it did in the case of Abraham, when the angel commanded him to sheathe the sword raised over Isaac? Certainly not. The chalice, which, because He so willed it, contained nothing but bitterness for Him, was shown to the Saviour by the angel from another point of view and in a more favorable light so that it lost all that was abhorrent and repulsive and appeared as something desirable and precious. Above all, he showed Christ the will of the heavenly Father engraven upon the cup, and he reminded Him of His own words, "My meat is to do the will of him that sent me."[1] Then he showed Him the

[1] St. John, iv., 34.

glory of the holy Cross, how from His death there should accrue to the heavenly Father infinitely more honor and glory than from the united praises of all creatures. Then, again, he let pass before His mental vision all the millions of men who would be irretrievably lost if He persisted in His request and all the millions of souls who were awaiting in limbo the hour of redemption. He further represented to the Redeemer His passion as the foundation of His own glory and pointed out how, for all eternity, thanks would arise to Him as to the Saviour and Redeemer of the world. By means of these and similar thoughts the angel worked upon the will of the Lord in order to determine Him to accept the cup of suffering. And what a mighty result he achieved! Before this the Saviour quaked and trembled at the sight of impending woe; now he combats this fear of death with such efforts that the bloody sweat flows from His pores. Before this He prayed, howbeit with resignation, that the chalice might pass from Him; now He prays for this alone, that the will of God be done. Before this, He repeatedly interrupted His prayer, now this prayer is continuous, and His soul is entirely immersed in God. Before this, He sought solace with His disciples, and now He tells them, "Rise up, let us go," and courageously He goes to meet the enemy. That was the first effect of the prayer of Jesus Christ in the Garden of Olives.

From these last considerations three important truths are brought to our knowledge. Just as certain as it is that the prayer which we address to heaven, in imitation of the Saviour, shall be heard, just so certain is it that this will not always happen in the manner which we desire. But if Almighty God, instead of removing the bitter cup, gives us the strength to support our trials or even greater ones with patience, even with joy, should we not be grateful to Him throughout all eternity? Again, we should become accustomed to consider the cup we must drain from another point of view and in a more favorable light. We should also see engraven upon it the will of our heavenly Father. We should not forget that God's honor and our glory are increased by patient suffering, and then all our murmuring and complaining will cease. Finally, Christ made the most powerful effort to accomplish the will of His heavenly Father in a matter which was so difficult that it caused Him to sweat blood. We ought, therefore, to be ashamed of our sloth and our cowardice which cause us, at the least difficulty, to cease our struggle against evil and to destroy God's commandments. And surely, we have never yet resisted evil to the shedding of blood.

The second effect of the prayer of Christ is described in the following words of St. Leo:[1] "This word of the Head, 'Thy will be done,' hath brought weal to the whole body. The word hath enflamed all confessors, hath crowned all martyrs. For who would have victoriously overcome

[1] Serm. 2 de Pass., c. 5.

the hatred of the world, the storms of temptations and the fearful tortures of the persecutors, if Christ had not, in the Garden of Olives, suffered in all and for all, if He had not said in all and in the name of all, 'Thy will be done?' "

In all our tribulations, we should, therefore, pray with the Saviour: "Father, if it be possible, let this chalice pass from me. Nevertheless not as I will, but as thou wilt." Especially should it be our prayer on our death-bed, when mortal agony approaches to seize upon us. It is true, our heavenly Father is not likely to send us an angel from heaven in visible shape. But Christ, the King of all angels, the Son of God Himself, will come to us under the sacramental appearances. Even more, He will enter our hearts to strengthen us in our agony and mortal combat and to lead us happily from time into eternity.

CHAPTER IV.

THE REPEATED APPEALS OF CHRIST TO HIS APOSTLES

> " And he cometh, and findeth them sleeping. And he said to Peter: Simon, sleepest thou? couldst thou not watch one hour? Watch ye and pray that ye enter not into temptation."
> St. Mark., xiv., 37, 38.

Christ prayed during the sufferings of soul which He had of His own free choice taken upon Himself. The more violent they became, the more also did He strive to overcome His fear, and the more perseveringly and devoutly did He pray. All this was for our instruction. In order to control our inordinate passions, we must strive and pray. By our own strength alone we cannot obtain the victory; we must secure for ourselves God's help by means of prayer. Again, the grace of God alone will not bring us success; we must, on our part, co-operate with grace. Our efforts and our prayers must grow in earnestness and perseverance proportionately as passion increases in force.

The evangelists St. Matthew (xxvi., 40–44), St. Mark (xiv., 37–41) and St. Luke (xxii., 45, 46) state that Christ not only interrupted His prayer several times, but that He even left the place where He was praying and went to His disciples; which is indeed astonishing. It might appear that, as He was preparing for death, He would, to give us an example, devote no further thought to the world, but occupy Himself solely with God. Let us therefore consider

I. The reasons of the repeated visits of Christ to His apostles and

II. The words which He spoke to them.

I.

There were two reasons which determined the Saviour to interrupt His prayer and seek His disciples. The first reason was the desire to find some consolation in His sadness. In fact, experience teaches that the fire of mental grief is intensified by being confined to its own hearth. It has drawn many into melancholy and even into despair. It is also universally acknowledged that nothing relieves the heavy heart or consoles the sad soul as much as the imparting of one's grief to a true friend. It was, then, not only weakness freely admitted, but also the intention of instructing us which led Christ to His disciples that He might unbosom His grief to them. It must, therefore, be allowable to appeal to others for the purpose of finding solace and encouragement in grief, sadness and mental anguish. But in so doing, we must observe three rules.

What should be the nature of our complaints? This we may gather from the words addressed by the Redeemer to His disciples before leaving them to pray: "My soul is sad unto death." Here we have the model of a legitimate complaint. It contains nothing but the recital of fact in as far as it concerned the Saviour. Yet certainly Christ had cause to speak harshly against those who were preparing to do Him the greatest of all wrongs and to rob Him, the Innocent, of life. As opposed to His plaint, the plaints of men are, at times, naught else but explosions of anger, slander and calumnies.

Moreover, Christ does not unfold His sorrows to the first comer, nor even to all of His apostles. Only three were permitted to share His grief. We also, in communicating the burdens of our heart, should use great circumspection. It would, for example, be not only foolish, but sinful also, for a wife and a mother to reveal her family troubles to all her neighbors, because very often the honor of her husband and children would thereby be damaged to a great extent.

Finally, Christ does not complain solely to His apostles, but He addresses Himself chiefly to His heavenly Father. Too often in sadness and affliction we forget God entirely and seek solace and support from men alone.

But while it is allowable and profitable thus to share with faithful friends our afflictions, it becomes almost necessary when they arise from annoying temptations. In this case, however, they ought to be communicated to one of the apostles only or to one of their successors. In case it appear difficult or humiliating to reveal to another such shameful temptations, one should consider the well nigh inconceivable humiliation undergone by Christ in looking for consolation and comfort to His disciples. Does not the Redeemer, in fact, resemble a general, who, after having spurred on his troops for years to deeds of valor, gives way now to mortal fear at the sight of the enemy and feels constrained to beg for comfort and encouragement from his subalterns? Do not say that it will be useless anyway to tell this or that to your confessor. It may be that from his own resources the confessor can help you just as little as the apostles helped the Lord. But if, according to the Saviour's example, you humble yourself before your fellow-man and give yourself to earnest prayer, then God will help you even, if needs be, by sending you an angel from heaven to encourage you in the combat and to comfort you.

The second reason which urged the Lord to interrupt His prayer and seek His disciples, was His love for them. If the expression be permissible, it was the anxiety lest harm had befallen them, it was the desire to ascertain what they were doing and how they were faring. We know, of a certainty, that for three whole years Christ had cared for His disciples, had watched over them and protected them as much as any loving mother would her only child. But there are two circumstances which reveal to us in the clearest light the love of His heart for His apostles.

The first is that Christ thought of them, was anxious about them, when He lay in the agony of death. He was anxious about them while in a condition in which we, yielding to pain, would think only of ourselves and in which we certainly would refuse to think of any one else. Not only in the heat of fever but often also in slight maladies, we care nothing for our best friends and are short and indifferent in our manner toward them.

Secondly, Christ thought of His disciples and was anxious about them in an hour when their behavior made them unworthy of His love. For three years, He had done so much for them. They had on former occasions often been ungrateful for His devotion; but now they add thereunto this ingratitude that, while their Divine Master is plunged in sadness and in the agony of death, they, lacking in courage and wanting in sympathy, fall asleep. What a contrast between these sleeping disciples and friends of Jesus and the wide-awake enemies! Judas is awake to betray Christ; Caiphas and the high priests are awake to condemn Him; the menials and soldiers are awake to bind, scourge and crucify Him: but the disciples are asleep. How that must have saddened our Saviour's heart! What Christ experienced then, His Bride, the Church, experiences now. She is downcast and sad even unto death. An armed rabble threatens to deal her the death blow at any moment. And mighty governments who call themselves Christian and who even glory in the title of Catholic look on without emotion and draw around themselves more closely the heartless cloak of neutrality and non-intervention. The satellites of Satan develop a feverish, restless activity to annihilate Christianity and to wipe it from the face of the earth, and thousands of Catholic men stand by and will not move a hand to defend the good cause and the interests of Holy Mother Church.

By His appeal to the apostles under the circumstances which we have noted, the Saviour teaches all superiors and Christian parents in particular three important lessons. Nothing can dispense you, Christian parents, from the duty of watching over your children and giving heed that no harm befall their immortal souls; nothing, I repeat; neither sorrow nor affliction, nor any cross of suffering, not even, I might say, approaching death; much less work and business, much less still, lassitude or fatigue, and least of all love of ease and comfort. Think of this, Christian parents, when, returning tired from your work in the evening you would seek repose, though your older children still require your vigilant care. Nothing dispenses you from this vigilance, not even the ingratitude with which the children repay your love, nor their dullness of intellect, nor their insubordination, nor their disobedience, nor their indifference to your adverse fortunes. You may, therefore, never say: our children do not heed our commands and our wishes; let them go and do as they please. It is true that if grown children are guilty of continued insubordination or of scandalous conduct, parents have the right to cast them adrift, but as long as they tolerate them at home, they are in duty bound to watch over their conduct and morals and to see that they perform their religious duties. Learn, lastly, from the Saviour to unite vigilance with prayer. It would be wrong to be so engrossed with the care of your children, that thereby you would neglect to pray for yourselves and for them. On the other hand, it would also be wrong and it would denote a counterfeit sort of piety were you to increase your practices of devotion in such a manner as to relegate to the background the duties of watching over your children and of admonishing and instructing them. You must do the one and not neglect the other. Christ shows you how you can and must do both. Let us now listen to the words which Christ spoke to His apostles.

II.

It was with no little grief that Christ found the three apostles in sound slumber. It altered his purpose of confiding in them, and He spoke to them merely a word of reproach and a word of admonition. In the language of the evangelists St. Matthew and St. Mark, the word of reproach was: "Simon, sleepest thou? Could you not watch one hour with me?" This reproach deserves our attention for several reasons.

In the first place it was a *just* reproach. Before Christ entered the garden of Olives, He had told the apostles in express words that now the hour of temptation had arrived, that now there was danger that they leave Him and deny the faith. Again, later, He gave to the three the distinct command to watch and pray during His absence in order to overcome by these means the impending temptation. They did neither the one nor the other. They slept. They knew themselves that they deserved the reproach, for they had no excuse to offer. "And they knew not what to answer Him," says Holy Writ.[1] And what could they answer to justify themselves? When they were fishing, they could watch the whole night. "Master, we have labored the whole night."[2] But now, still early in the evening, after being refreshed by supper, they fall asleep. When the boat was about to sink and their life was in danger, they knew how to pray, "Lord save us, we perish."[3] But now, when their souls are in danger, they do not feel inclined to pray. However, we should not be too severe with the apostles; many Christians are far more reprehensible. They spend entire nights, not merely in work and affairs of business, but in dangerous pleasures and amusements, in the satisfaction of sensual lusts, in fact in anything which leads to hell. But at evening prayers or during the sermon, they are asleep. They sleep at home even on Sundays when they ought to be at mass. In afflictions and trials, in impending peril, hands are raised high to heaven; in temptation, when prayer is most necessary, prayer is omitted.

The reproach expressed by the Saviour was just also, inasmuch as he who deserved it most, received the greatest share of it. Certainly that

[1] St. Mark, xiv., 40.
[2] St. Luke, v., 5.
[3] St. Matthew, viii., 25.

was Peter. He was destined by the Saviour to be the head of the others. He had also made greater promises. For that reason, Christ first said to Peter alone what He thereafter said to all: "Simon, sleepest thou?" How this word must have penetrated the heart of the apostle! How it must have spread confusion over his countenance! Once, when Christ had appointed him to be the guardian of the apostolic college, He changed his name from Simon to Peter. Now He addressed him by his former name as though He would say: If you cannot exercise vigilance over yourself and your brethren, you are not worthy of the name of Peter. Woe, then, to all spiritual and temporal rulers, to all masters, woe to all parents especially, who, through lack of vigilance and of earnest prayer, are the cause of thousands and thousands of sins committed by their children and by their subordinates!

Secondly, the reproach of our Saviour was extremely *mild*. In the few words, earnest though they were, which He addressed to them, there was no trace of anger or of undue excitement. On the contrary, He recognized their good will. "The spirit indeed is willing, but the flesh is weak." He knew that their fault was the result of weakness, not of malice nor of grievously culpable negligence. The gospel tells us that sadness caused them to fall asleep. On that account, the Lord used a different language and spoke in a different tone to the hardened pharisees, and on the traffickers in the temple He used a scourge.

Thirdly, Christ reprimanded the apostles with prudent moderation. When at His second approach He found them again asleep, for which they surely deserved a sharper rebuke, He refrained from reproving them at all, for He saw that in that moment they were not susceptible of correction.

When our calling requires us to reprimand others, we should learn from the Saviour to punish with justice and with mildness, especially when the delinquent shows a good will. It is unreasonable and foolish when parents, for trivial faults, continually scold well-intentioned children; it is demoralizing and sinful to overwhelm them with a flood of injurious epithets. Neither should we punish when we have reason to fear that the culprit will not take the punishment in good part and that he is not susceptible of reproof. It is more advisable then to postpone the correction to some future time in order that there be not more harm done than good. In imitation of the apostles we should, when receiving the correction of superiors, preserve humble silence. We must not deceive ourselves; we must acknowledge our faults and refrain from all frivolous excuses.

The reprimand of the Saviour was followed by a word of admonition. It was the same advice He had given them before He had retired to pray. "Watch ye and pray that ye enter not into temptation;"[1] or translated more literally, "that ye

[1] St. Matthew. xxvi., 38; St. Mark, xiv., 34; St. Luke, xxii., 40.

walk not too willingly into temptation,'' and become caught and entangled therein as birds in a net. This is not the place to expound elaborately the necessity of vigilance and of prayer. I only call attention to the fact that the words given above are the last admonition of the Saviour to His apostles. We may, then, be convinced that these parting words contain the best and the most useful advice which Christ could give His apostles for their eternal salvation. They must be the summary of all that the apostles had to observe in order to avoid sin and to save their souls. And they understood their Master and kept His word. It was not by spreading admiration over the entire world as teachers, nor by working signs and wonders, nor by revealing the future, but it was by watching and praying throughout their lives that they became saints, saints of heaven.

These apostles to whom the Redeemer, in parting, so earnestly recommended vigilance and prayer, were simple, ordinary men. They had for three years lived, remote from the world and its dangers, in the immediate presence of their divine model and instructor. Hence they had an ardent love for Him. How can we, then, enter heaven without vigilance and prayer, we who are so lukewarm and cold in the love of Christ? How, without vigilance and prayer, can they, above all, hope for perseverance in grace and for eternal salvation, who live in the midst of the dangers and scandals of a godless and immoral world? We should, therefore, consider the last admonition of

Christ as addressed to ourselves, impress it deeply upon our hearts and shape our lives in accordance with it. Then we shall also receive the crown of eternal glory which is at the same time the reward of combat and the gift of grace.

CHAPTER V.

THE TREASON OF JUDAS

> "And forthwith coming to Jesus, he said: Hail, Rabbi. And he kissed Him. And Jesus said to him: Friend, whereto art thou come?"
> (St. Matthew, xxvi., 49–50.)

While Christ was speaking to His apostles, behold, Judas Iscariot, one of the twelve, came and with him a great multitude with swords and clubs, with lanterns and torches, sent from the high-priests and ancients of the people. The high-priests who played a leading role in the history of the Saviour's passion, appear now for the first time. In reality, there were not several high-priests in actual office at the same time, but several who were out of office after their removal still retained the honorary title. For, after the Roman occupancy of Palestine, the governors, whose avarice exceeded all bounds, made of the appointment to the office of high-priest a source of revenue, or at least, in their political wisdom, they sought to degrade the high-priest to the level of a tool in the hands of pagan statecraft. Hence, at times for political reasons, at times as a favor to the highest bidder, the incumbents of this office were often changed. The old custom of keeping the high-priest in office until death had ceased. The title of high-priest was also applied to those who were descendants of the first-born of Aaron and to the chief-priests of the different subdivisions of the entire numerous priesthood. Holy Writ says of Caiphas alone that he was *the* high-priest of that year.

The soldiers sent by the high-priests had no other intent than that of taking Christ captive. But the one who had prepared the whole matter was the Apostle Judas, surnamed Iscariot. The treason of this unfortunate man will be the subject of this consideration.[1]

Let us consider the betrayal

I. In the events which led up to it,

II. In its final execution and

III. In its innermost source.

I.

On the Wednesday after His triumphal entry into Jerusalem, the Redeemer for the last time denounced the high-priests, the scribes and the pharisees in the temple for their sins and abuses. He referred them finally to the day of judgment when, from the severity of their own punishment, they should recognize his own grandeur and majesty. With this forceful warning He ended His instruction, and filled with holy wrath, He

[1] St. Matthew, xxvi., 46–50; St. Mark, xiv., 42–45; St. Luke, xxii., 47, 48; St. John, xviii., 2, 3.

left the temple toward evening. Provoked and extremely angered by His denunciations, the high-priests, scribes and elders of the people met for the second time on the following day to take counsel against Him. And first, they approved the resolution taken in a former meeting [1] to remove the Saviour by force. As to the time of executing their plan of putting Him to death, they agreed that it should not be during the festivities of the Passover. Such a course would be too hazardous, as the paschal solemnity brought together many Jews, and among them would be many friends of Christ. These might organize a revolt, the people armed might liberate their victim and thus, for a long time to come, render the execution of their plan impossible. They certainly would rather slay Him before the holidays, but they knew of no scheme by which they might seize Him in secret and by stealth. To their extreme joy, Judas helped them out of the difficulty.

Judas had for a long time been an apostle in appearance only. He had become heartily tired of apostolic life with its wanderings, its burdens, its vexations and its persecutions. His former love for Christ had grown cold. In its stead, there arose indifference, then a certain irritability and disgust. The Redeemer's continual praises of poverty had become unbearable to him. Besides, his longing for a well salaried position in the new kingdom of Christ did not appear to be approach-

[1] St. John, xi., 47.

ing realization. His feelings were more embittered by the words which the Lord, who read his heart, addressed to all the apostles, after promising the Holy Eucharist: "Have I not chosen you twelve; and one of you is a devil."[1] He saw that Christ read and knew him. But instead of repenting and being converted, he was offended. The public rebuke, finally, which he received at the banquet when Christ took the part of Magdalene, increased his rancor to the uttermost. On the other hand, it did not escape Judas that a storm was brewing against Christ, and he began to fear that he, as one of His disciples, would also have to bear a part of the brunt of impending persecution. He therefore resolved to save himself and, by the same move gain both friends and money. He was aware of the council meeting of the high-priests with whom, for some time back, he had entertained secret relations and who strove to draw him over to their party by flattery and promises of money. Hence Judas hastened to offer his services to the members of the Council and to show them how, without much disturbance, they might capture the person of the Redeemer. He does not seem, however, to have been without fears as to the outcome of his undertaking, for he takes care to provide himself with an armed body of men, for greater security. To this end he discusses his plans with the temple guard, which was composed of Levites (St. Luke, xxii., 4.) To the members of the Coun-

[1] St. John, vi., 71.

cil he said, "What will you give me, and I will deliver Him unto you?"[1] They offered thirty pieces of silver, and the bargain was closed. But, O miserable Judas, is the Lord your property that you may sell Him as you would an animal or a piece of furniture? And if you think Him your property, why do you not ask as His price at least a whole kingdom? Why are you satisfied with the price of a slave? "The ointment," says St. Ambrose,[2] "with which Christ was anointed for His passion, you appreciated at three hundred pieces of silver, but do you deem the Passion itself fully paid for with thirty pieces?" "However," answers the same saint,[3] "Christ desired to be estimated at such a low price that He might be bought by all and that not even the poorest might be deterred." Where is thy self-respect, O Judas, and thy pride that thou didst not immediately turn thy back indignantly upon the high-priests who offered thee such a pittance to show their contempt for thee? But it is a peculiar fact, that hell always offers the least and that the servants of the devil are satisfied with the smallest wage. For is it not true that many a Christian sells the Lord for a much smaller sum, for a momentary, shameful pleasure?

Judas, having parted with the high priests after many expressions of gratitude, in order to ward off suspicion, again mingled with the apostles and participated in the prescribed supper which took

[1] St. Matthew, xxvi., 15.
[2] de Spir. S. I. 1. c. 18.
[3] Exp. Evang. sec. Lucam 1. 6, c. 31.

place on Thursday evening. He even permitted the Lord to wash his feet. The discovery he made on this occasion, namely, that Christ was aware of his foul plan, drove him to extremities, and he resolved to betray the Master that very evening. Then, shortly before the institution of the Most Holy Sacrament,[1] urged on by infernal powers, he left the hall never again to return to the Saviour. He hurried from house to house and made known his object to the high-priests. "Now," said he, "or never!" Afterwards there would hardly present itself a better chance for the capture. Above all, there must be obtained a detachment of soldiers from the rightful authorities in order to give the whole affair the appearance of legality and to preclude any opposition. That task was assumed by the high-priests. As the Easter festivities were often the occasion of bloody riots, Pilate had, in former years, placed soldiers at their disposition especially to protect the temple. On this occasion he did the same and allowed them one hundred and twenty-five men, according to some interpreters, even three hundred. But as the high-priests had no confidence either in the Romans or in Judas, they ordered their own servants to accompany the soldiers, and by mutual consent some of their own number went along as leaders. Magistrates of the temple, also, of whom there were many, were present. The temple furnished employment to many

[1] Note 3.

men who resided in adjoining buildings. Some supervised the constructions, others the property, others again the sacrifices and the gift offerings. All these men were now hurriedly armed with swords and clubs. The full moon was then shining, it is true. However, to avoid the obstacles of an uneven way and not to be deceived by shadows, also the more easily to find the Saviour in case He should hide Himself in the underbrush as Adam did, they took with them torches and closed lanterns. The eternal Light had hidden Itself in Its humanity to such an extent that the powers of darkness needed lanterns to find it. God permitted it in order that a brighter light might be thrown upon the dishonor of Christ's enemies, while they lay prostrate upon the ground.

After they were furnished all that was needed and were placed in ranks, Judas said to them, "Whomsoever I shall kiss, that is He." A sign was necessary. The Roman soldiers had, perhaps, never seen Christ or they had never observed Him very closely. Again, in the pale light of the moon, one is easily deceived in the features of a person. Lastly, Judas gives them this advice: "Lead Him away carefully." In itself this was certainly very good advice. We may apply it to ourselves. We ought to lead the Lord carefully, who lives in us through His grace, lest He be taken away from us. But in Judas it denoted a blindness beyond all conception.

Now this rabble, with Judas in the lead, began its march between eleven and twelve o'clock at night and wended its way by the nearest route towards the garden of Olives. Since the creation of the world such an array, such an infernal band, had never been seen. Even pagan conquerors would never have thought of apprehending a Son of God and of chaining Him to their triumphal chariots. The enacting of such scenes was reserved to Christian powers. Thus it was only recently that an outrageous band of robbers, led secretly by a Judas of their own, approached the Holy City to enchain the Vicar of Christ and to imprison him in his own house. And the end of the last and the beginning of this century beheld two pontiffs in bondage.

The God-man and His betrayer were now in each other's presence, for Jesus had gone to meet Judas. A good conscience gives courage. It makes one resolute. The sinner slinks and hides himself. A resolute attack of difficulties and temptations breaks their force and conquers them. It endows man with heroism. Then followed the betrayal. Let us consider its execution.

II.

It is probable that satanic malice and divine goodness never approached each other so closely as here. Heaven and hell struggle for the mastery. We have now an opportunity of beholding what an abyss of wickedness may be found in a human and what an abyss of love in a Divine heart.

When Judas saw the Saviour, he advanced from before the soldiery, as if he did not belong to the mob, and quickly went towards Christ. To approach Christ and do it quickly, is certainly the best thing to be done. Still the promptness of Judas had something strange and suspicious about it. It seems to me that he received from the Saviour before him another great grace. The apostle perceived the fearful depth of perdition to which he was hastening, he was amazed at the atrocity of his purpose, he shrank for a moment from the execution of his plan. But in order not to have time for reflection, to remove the possibility of a change of mind, to quickly stifle all rising qualms of conscience, he approaches Christ quickly, determined to execute his foul deed. Behold here the sin against the Holy Ghost, a complete hardness of heart, the usual result of blindness. Now Judas no longer shrinks from the most abject meanness, from the greatest outrage. Like to Joab, of murderous intent, saluting as brother Amasa, the faithful servant of his King, he says to Jesus, "Hail, Rabbi" and he kisses Him. To salute one means to wish him all that is good. But this salute was the cunning of the wolf approaching in sheep's clothing, the cunning of the serpent hiding in the grass, the cunning of the assassin carrying the dagger in his bosom. Honey is on his lips and gall and wormwood in his heart; a friendly smile is on his face and dark hatred in his soul. He inhales health and life, he emits death and perdition, and he does it under the mask of a devoted disciple. "Hail, Rabbi." O Judas, thy Master never taught thee that! Then this devil incarnate embraced the Lord in treacherous arms and kissed Him. The sign of peace was the declaration of war, the sign of friendship was the signal of attack, the sign of love was the signal of rout and murder. Such is also the cunning hypocrisy of an impious world. "O world," exclaims St. Augustine, "You traitor! You promise all that is good and you bring only what is bad; you promise pleasure and you offer sorrow; you promise rest and you prepare ruin; you promise to remain and you quickly disappear; you promise life and you give death."

Who would think ill of us, if, in a similar case, in just indignation and with a cry of horror, we should thrust far from us the traitor approaching to embrace and kiss us; if, in the strongest possible terms, we should upbraid him for his faithlessness and depravity? But our Divine Saviour not only permitted the kiss, He also returned it. The divine, the most holy mouth touched that abject mouth at which even hell was disgusted. What an incomprehensible mystery! What an incomprehensible condescension and humiliation! O Saviour Jesus Christ, how couldst Thou allow this? When Magdalene kissed Thy feet, the pharisee was scandalized and said to himself, "This man, if he were a prophet, would know surely who and what manner of woman this is that toucheth him."[1] Dost Thou not force the high-priests and pharisees who see Judas with his lips to Thine, to judge:

[1] St. Luke, vii., 39.

"This man, if he were a prophet, would know surely who and what manner of man this is that toucheth him: that he is a traitor"? Must not even Thy disciples lose confidence in Thee? May not they reproach Thee as Joab reproached David when he deplored the death of his treacherous son Absalom, "Thou lovest them that hate thee and thou hatest them that love thee?"[1] For Peter Thou preparest a cross, for John seething oil, for James a sword, but to Judas Thou givest the kiss of Thy mouth! Or dost Thou imagine Thou hast Peter in Thy arms, who desires to go to death with Thee? Or Andrew, who left all for Thee? Or the disciple who lay upon Thy breast and who now, filled with love, would approach Thy mouth? "Judas," answers the Lord, "dost thou betray the Son of Man with a kiss?"

Every one of those words was a wound inflicted to free the soul from the thralls of passion. May every sinner take them to heart. *Judas,* says the Saviour, thou, my apostle; Judas, whom I have overwhelmed with benefits; Judas, to whom I have given the gift of miracles, and who, in my name, hast cured diseases; Judas, who wast a terror to demons! Indeed, if my enemy had reviled me, I would verily have borne with it.[2] But thou my friend, my apostle! Judas, thou *betrayest* me! It is not sufficient for thee that thou repayest not my love with thine, no, thou breakest the oath of

[1] II. Kings, xix., 6.
[2] Psalms, liv., 13.

allegiance which thou hast sworn me; thou art one with my worst enemies, thou hast bargained me off to them for a mere pittance! *With a kiss* thou betrayest me! The privilege thou hast of approaching me in familiar intercourse, thou dost abuse in order to deliver me to mine enemies. If thou be my friend, why these swords? And if thou be my enemy, why these kisses? Thou betrayest the *Son of Man,* the Son of God, who now shall die for thee, but Whose sign shall appear in the clouds on the day of judgment.

And then, in order to spread balm upon the wounds inflicted by His words and to revive the courage and confidence of the disciple, with touching gentleness and divine love Jesus finally calls him friend. "*Friend,* whereto art thou come?" Reflect, Judas, and desist from thy impious undertaking. Behold the arms of thy Saviour extended to receive thee; His hands are ready to lead thee back to the right path; His heart is open to pour upon thee all the treasures of mercy. Tell thy Saviour that thou wilt be His friend, that thou art His friend, and thou shalt be His friend. Do not think it difficult, deem it not impossible. It is difficult to be a friend of the world. It means night-watches and troubles, it means fear and worry, it costs sacrifices of money, of honor, of health, it costs one's immortal soul. But if thou wilt be a friend of Christ, show a single tear of compunction in thine eye, a real sigh of thy heart shall suffice; an humble pulsation in thy breast, a word from thy mouth shall be enough. Say with David, "I have sinned,"[1] and at the same moment thou shalt be told, "Thy sins are forgiven thee."[2]

But Judas was more hardened than a rock, and he would not be converted. On the contrary, the loving words of the Saviour, which, according to St. Chrysostom,[3] would have pacified the tiger and the leopard, caused the traitor to cast aside his mask and to openly break with Christ. After having given the sign, he did not mingle with the apostles, as he had intended doing, in order to avert suspicion. Consumed by internal anger because Christ knew his heart and reproved him, he openly, before the eyes of his master, goes over to His sworn enemies. Where can a man be found who ever fell from such a height as did unfortunate Judas?

Let us then consider the innermost cause, the source of the sad fall.

III.

What started Judas on the way to ruin and finally made him a traitor was one single, inordinate passion not subdued. It was avarice. When he was received into the college of apostles, he was certainly no bad man; he must have had many good and praiseworthy qualities. Especially must he have been irreproachable in regard to the purity

[1] II. Kings, xii., 13.
[2] St. Luke, vii., 48.
[3] Hom. 22 in ep. ad Rom. 1, 12.

of his morals. For that reason the Lord trusted him to the extent of making him the treasurer whose duty it would be to take care of the alms received by Him and to defray therefrom the living expenses both of the Lord and of the apostles. With all his good qualities, Judas had in his heart one evil inclination to curb which, however, he had the best possible guidance and help in his association with Christ. This was the inordinate love of money. In the beginning it was unimportant and of small consequence; he scarcely took notice of it; it was not a matter of grievous sin. But because he did not pay sufficient attention to it, it gradually developed in his heart until it finally spread into quite a poisonous growth. He began to love money more and more, to rejoice in its possession, to measure everything by its standard. At first he kept for himself some of the money confided to him and the surplus of which was destined for the poor. It appeared to him that his services ought to have some little recompense. Like our modern church despoilers, he judged it better to put money in circulation and employ it in other useful ways, than to allow it to remain, as dead capital, in the church treasury; besides, Christ would not need it; He knew how to help Himself in need, and He certainly would not let the apostles starve. Soon Judas began to steal without the least scruple, and finally the words of Paul, the apostle, were fulfilled in his case: "They that will become rich, fall into temptation and into the snare of the devil, and into many unprofitable and hurtful desires, which drown men into destruction and perdition. For the desire of money is the root of all evils; which some coveting have erred from the faith."[1] For the repeated thefts, which in the beginning were possibly small and venial sins only, made this apostle indifferent to sin in general and brought him to the condition of luke-warmness. At the same time, the growing love of money stifled in him the love for Christ and for his apostolic vocation. He fell into mortal sins, became filled with aversion to Christ and even lost faith in His Divinity. His formal apostasy was only a matter of time. Then happened the incident in connection with Mary Magdalene, who was so lavish in her use of costly ointments. It vexed Judas that such a chance for a splendid stroke of business should slip by him, and the reprimand he received vexed him still more. As indemnity, he resolved to sell the Son of God himself.

From this dreadful event let us draw some conclusions for our own instruction. It is absolutely necessary to combat *all* passions, to pamper none, least of all the dominant passion which has the deepest roots in the heart. Let no one say: I am not a drunkard, I am not impure, I harbor no enmities. A single passion which you do not resist is capable of bringing on your ruin. And these passions must be combated *early*. When the fire is still small, a little water suffices to extin-

[1] I. Tim., vi., 9, 10.

guish it. But when the flames appear all over the roof, all the engines in town may not be enough. These passions must be resisted by *every one*, even if one be an apostle or a saint. Avarice led Judas to his ruin. With how much more reason must one begin early to combat the far more dangerous passion of impure lust which in a very short time easily develops into an all-consuming fire.

Furthermore, we should take heed not to trifle with venial sins, not to commit hundreds and thousands of them with a smiling countenance as if they were not offensive to God. We should guard against fatal luke-warmness. Peter, who otherwise was zealous, in an unfortunate moment, fell woefully. But touched by the grace of Christ, he was converted immediately. Not so Judas. Although the Saviour had overwhelmed him with love, still, on account of his numerous infidelities and his disregard of venial sins, he gradually drifted into the state of mortal guilt.

But from the Divine Redeemer we may learn generously to pardon our enemies, unceasingly to follow the lost sheep, to hope against hope. Let us furthermore have the firmest confidence in the love and mercy of Christ. And indeed, what sinner ought to despair? Return to Christ in sorrow, and the Saviour in whose embrace we now behold the traitor, will hail thee as His friend and give thee the kiss of peace.

CHAPTER VI.

THE SEIZURE OF THE SAVIOUR

"Then the band, and the tribune, and the servants of the Jews took Jesus, and bound him."

(St. John, xviii., 12.)

The betrayal of Judas was followed by the taking of the Saviour. The Holy Scriptures describe the event in the following terms: "Jesus, knowing all things that should come upon him, went forth and saith to them: I am he. And Judas also, who betrayed Him, stood with them. As soon therefore as he had said to them: I am he, they went backward and fell to the ground. Again therefore he asked them: Whom seek ye? And they said: Jesus of Nazareth. Jesus answered: I have told you, that I am he. If therefore you seek me, let these go their way. That the word might be fulfilled which he said: Of them whom thou hast given me, I have not lost any one. And they that were about him, seeing what would follow, said to him, Lord, shall we strike with the sword? And one of them that stood by, Simon Peter, drawing a sword, struck a servant of the high-priest and cut off his right ear. And the name of the servant was Malchus. But Jesus answering said: Suffer ye thus far. And when he had touched his ear, he healed Malchus. Then Jesus said to Peter: Put up again thy sword into its place, into the scabbard. For all that take the sword shall perish with the sword. The chalice which my Father hath given me, shall I not drink it? Thinkest thou that I cannot ask my Father, and he will give me presently more than twelve legions of angels? How then shall the Scriptures be fulfilled that so it must be done? In that same hour Jesus said to the chief-priests, and magistrates of the temple, and the ancients that were come unto him: Are ye come out as it were against a thief, with swords and clubs? When I was daily with you in the temple, you did not stretch forth your hands against me. But this is your hour and the power of darkness. Now all this was done, that the Scriptures of the prophets might be fulfilled. Then the band and the tribune and the servants of the Jews took Jesus and bound him. Then the disciples all leaving him fled."[1] Such is the description given by the evangelists of the seizure of the Redeemer.

Let us consider the miracles that Christ then worked, namely,

I. Miracles proving His Divine Power and

II. Miracles proving His Divine Love.

[1] St. Matthew, xxvi., 50–56; St. Mark, xiv., 46–50; St. Luke, xxii., 49–54; St. John, xviii., 4–12.

I.

To prove His Divine Power, Christ performed two miracles. The first consisted in bringing His enemies to a halt and the second, in causing them to fall to the ground.

The kiss of Judas and with it the sign for the attack had been given. But why do they not advance? Why do they hesitate? What keeps back these villains thirsting for the blood of the God-Man? They need certainly not fear greater numbers. On the one side stand Christ and the apostles with two swords, on the other a numerous band fully armed with swords and clubs and lances. Still, there they stand, as if rooted to the ground, and they cannot advance one step. Was there perhaps some doubt as to the person to be taken, notwithstanding the kiss of Judas, the light of the full moon and the lights they had with them? There truly was such a doubt. The enemies of Christ, and Judas too, were so stricken with blindness that they did not recognize Him, although He stood before them. Had they recognized Him, then surely when He asked them the second time, "Whom seek ye?" they would not have answered, "Jesus of Nazareth," but "We seek thee." It would then have been an easy matter, had Jesus so willed, to escape His enemies, notwithstanding the cunningly laid plan and the treachery of Judas. But Christ goes towards them and asks, "Whom seek ye?" And they answer, "Jesus of Nazareth." He responds, "I am he."

At these words, as if struck by lightning or overturned by a whirlwind, they fall back to the ground, Judas with them. "The voice of the Lord breaketh the Cedars."[1] Poor Judas! If you know of no way out of the difficulty now, your pieces of silver are gone. The enemies of Christ fell backwards to the ground, not like penitent sinners upon their faces; and he who falls backwards is apt to damage his head.

Finally, Christ restored to them their powers. Filled with shame, struck with amazement, but burning with anger, they arose. For the second time the Saviour asked them, "Whom seek ye?" Again they answer, "Jesus cf Nazareth." They, therefore, did not yet recognize Him. That they might understand that it was He who threw them to the ground, Christ now said to them: "I have told you that I am he." And, as the proof was now furnished that He began His Passion of His own free will, He permitted them to seize Him, by saying, "If therefore you seek me, let these go their way." The evident demonstration, then, of His Divine Power, did not bring these hardened culprits to their senses. They are hardly on their feet before they continue their impious work, advance toward Christ and seize Him.

When, in later centuries, tyrants saw hungry lions and tigers in the arena crouch at the feet of innocent lambs as were the holy martyrs, when they witnessed how these sufferers came forth, un-

[1] Psalms, xxviii., 5.

harmed, from burning furnaces and how missiles glanced from their persons, and nevertheless kept on inventing new pains and tortures, was not this scene similar to the one described above? When entire parishes and whole countries are on account of their sins, as it were, stricken to the ground by Almighty God, by wars, earthquakes or disease, and when, as soon as the visitation is over, they return to their former dissipated and shameless ways, is this not the enactment of the very same scene? When, lastly, God chastises the sinner and he heeds it not, when He crushes him and he refuses the punishment, do we not behold a scene from the Garden of Olives?

"Whom seek ye?" asked Christ. "Jesus of Nazareth." "I am he." And they fell to the ground. What will He do as Judge, who, as the accused, in a state of greatest weakness and impotence, displays such power? How the high-priests and scribes will be confounded, when on the day of judgment from His seat in the clouds, Christ shall cry out to them, "I am he!" How all deniers of the Divinity of Christ shall then wither away from fear and terror! What will then be the sentiments of skeptics, of all sinners, especially those who have unceasingly plotted evil against Christ and His holy Church. Let us console ourselves in present tribulations. One word of the Lord, one breath of His mouth is sufficient to cast the enemies of the Church powerless into the dust.

May it be our privilege, when on the last day

Christ shall say these words to us, to greet Him with joy and exultation and to look up to Him with confidence. But we can entertain this hope only if now, truthfully and with our whole heart, we can answer His question, "Whom seek ye?" by saying, "Jesus of Nazareth, none other but Christ Crucified."

Let us now pass on to the miracles wrought by Christ in the Garden of Olives to demonstrate His Divine Love.

II.

Christ wrought two miracles for the following purpose: He wished to convince His friends of the greatness of His love by the first miracle, and His enemies, by the second.

Above all things the Saviour had at heart the welfare of His disciples, for whose steadfastness in the faith He had reason to fear, if they also, according to the undoubted intent of Christ's enemies, should be taken captives. "If ye seek me," He therefore said, "let these go their way." By these words He commanded and effected the freedom of His disciples. After that, they dared not even touch Peter who, by wounding Malchus, had excited to the highest degree the ire of the high-priests and their associates. Their hands were tied. Thus were fulfilled the words of Christ: "Of them whom thou hast given me, I have not lost any one."[1] It is true Peter soon afterwards committed a grievous sin, but it was

[1] St. John, xviii., 9.

owing to his own fault and not to his being taken captive. "Let these go their way," we ought also to say in trials and difficulties and not continually take the burden off our own shoulders to lay it on the shoulders of others.

A second miracle was wrought by Christ to convince His *enemies* of His Love and to invite them to conversion. After the last words of Christ they laid hands on Him. One of them, Malchus, the servant of Caiphas the high-priest, made himself conspicuous by pulling and tugging at the person of Christ. He desired the honor of binding Him. It would recommend him to his master. But this was more than the disciples would tolerate. They all cried out together, "Lord, shall we strike out with the sword?" Without awaiting the answer of Christ, Peter drew his sword and wielded it with a strong arm. His aim missed. He did not intend to cut off an ear, otherwise, as he used his right arm and stood opposite to Malchus, he would have struck his left ear. He meant to cleave the head of the irreverent scoundrel. But his head being covered with a helmet the sword glanced off and took with it the right ear. Peter then raised his sword the second time, and the other disciple with a sword prepared to use it. Then Christ said, "Suffer ye thus far," and, touching the ear of Malchus, He healed him. Thus did Christ take revenge on His enemies. Then turning to Peter, He ordered him to put up his sword into its place, into the scabbard, and He rebuked him. Whoever uses the sword, without legal warrant, of course, merits that his own blood be shed. He addresses Peter in holy indignation, because he would hinder Him in fulfilling the Scripture and in drinking the chalice offered Him by His heavenly Father. Peter's help, besides, would be entirely superfluous, as twelve legions and more of angels would, if He so wished, at any moment be at His disposition. However, Peter, on that occasion, committed no grievous sin. He had misunderstood a former command of the Saviour to buy swords,[1] that is, to prepare for combat with the weapons of the spirit, and what he did he considered done in justifiable self-defense. Moreover, his ardent love for Christ and his anxiety lest harm befall Him rendered him incapable of calm deliberation. If such were not the case, how could he have been imprudent enough to attempt to resist a hostile force so vastly superior?

We should learn from Christ what Christian revenge truly is, namely, the rendering of good for evil. But from Peter we may also learn something, even if it be not how to wield a sword. Were it allowable to cut off the right ear of all who sin against Christ, very many people would be in a condition to show only the left one. Blind, excessive zeal can do but harm. But to have no zeal or very little zeal for the honor of Christ and of His Church and for the preservation intact of faith and morals is another fault. In this re-

1 St. Luke, xxii., 36.

gard the civil authority, in whose hands God has placed the sword, ought to have more of the disposition of Peter. Then religion and faith would not be ridiculed and insulted as they are, and Christian morality would not be trampled under foot to such an extent. Then innumerable houses of ill repute would not exist, many public scandals would cease, bad theatres would be closed, shameless pictures would disappear from store-fronts and billboards, and the many poisonous productions of an impious and immoral press would no more be spread among the people. How persons in such responsible positions, who do nothing for religion and morality but who allow all sorts of wickedness, committed under their very eyes, to go unpunished, how such persons, I say, can render an account of their stewardship on the last day is something very difficult to imagine. Many parents, too, and masters ought to have more of Peter's disposition. Then family life would be more orderly and Christian, and many innocent souls would be saved. In fact, Peter's nature would be of advantage to us all; then, in the fight against evil, we would not in a cowardly manner throw down our weapons and surrender at the first attack of temptation.

Finally the moment arrived when Christ, to convince *us* also of His Love and to free us from the fetters of sin and hell, was to allow Himself to be bound. But first He makes one more effort to deter the high-priests and the ancients of the people from their nefarious project by holding up to them, on the one hand, the unworthiness of their act in treating as a murderer One Who had often spoken to them in the temple and Who had shown Himself a benefactor of the people, and by assuring them, on the other hand, that with all their swords and clubs they could not seize Him, if it were not their hour and the power of darkness. For the third time He finally reminds them of the Holy Scriptures to make them understand that they were instruments in the hands of God to fulfill the sayings of the prophets. "We owe you no thanks, O Jews," says St. Leo,[1] "nor thee, Judas. No doubt your impiety has served to our salvation; no doubt through you was done what lay in the counsels of God, but it was against your will. The death of Christ liberates us, it accuses you. You alone, by right, lack that which, according to your wishes, should be lost to all."

Now they began their work. Like wolves, the enemies of Christ fell upon the Lamb of God, as robbers upon their prey. The band and the tribune and the servants of the Jews took Jesus and bound Him. It was done with an ardor worthy of a better cause. And they must have fastened the ropes tightly and secured them by many knots, for Judas had told them: "Lead Him away carefully." Certainly the bands in which His Blessed Mother had wrapped Him when He still lay in the crib were sweeter and more pleasant. But He rejoiced in these bonds, otherwise

[1] Serm. 1 de Pass. c. 5.

He would have torn them asunder more easily than Samson could have done. He loved to be a captive. For that reason He had taken proper measures, on the eve of His Passion, for dwelling among us as our captive unto the end of days in the Sacrament of the Altar.

Happy, thrice happy, those who even in our days have been found worthy to carry the shackles of Christ. St. Paul had many glorious titles of which he might boast. He was an apostle, the teacher of the world, the teacher of nations. Still, he finds all his glory in chains and ropes and bonds. "I, Paul," he says, "the prisoner of Jesus Christ." As for us, it should be our pride and our glory to be bound with the bonds of His law, with the bonds of His Commandments, with the bonds of His Divine Love.

Then, dismayed at what had happened, the disciples fled, and nobody dared to hinder them. Another disciple of the Saviour, however, probably the son of the gardener,[1] who was not among the number of those of whom Christ had said, "Let these go their way," almost fared badly.[2] He escaped captivity only by leaving in the hands of the soldiers the linen cloth, which, when awakened from sleep by the noise, he had hurriedly thrown about his shoulders, and by hurrying away in his night garments or perhaps with only a cloth about his loins. From this incident we can judge that the position of the disciples was very dangerous,

[1] See note 4.
[2] St. Mark, xiv., 51.

that the terror of the enemies of Christ was great, that they were fully decided to apprehend the disciples also. The flight of the latter it is easy, therefore, to understand.

When we consider the event calmly and without prejudice, we must avow that, under the circumstances, the apostles could not well have acted differently. Full of courage, they would strike with the sword. That was forbidden them. From the words of the Saviour, "Let these go their way," they understood that they were not to follow Him into captivity and death, but that, as He further intimated, they were to relinquish Him to the powers of darkness, whose hour had now arrived. So nothing remained for them but to go away. For another reason it was the most reasonable and the most advisable thing to do, for they would not be exposed to the danger of denying Christ by close contact with His enemies. They committed a fault, however, by *running* away instead of *walking* away, because, thereby, they showed a lack of confidence in the Lord. Christ permitted this weakness in the apostles in order thoroughly to humble them and to divest them of all rash self-confidence. Perhaps while they were running, all their boastful promises came back to their minds. Peter's ears, especially, must have kept ringing with the words, "Although all shall be scandalized in thee, yet not I." How ashamed they must have felt!

Let us, then, sympathize with the poor apostles and, instead of condemning them, examine our own consciences to see whether or not we have ever abandoned Jesus from motives of human respect. As a matter of fact, the apostles really believed their lives in danger, whilst we need fear neither bonds, nor prison, nor death. A little slur, a sarcastic smile, a cutting remark on the part of some impious profligate leads many a Christian to abandon the Lord and to neglect the most sacred duties. In small matters we are all less faithful than the apostles were on this occasion. Let us then in sorrow strike our own breasts.

The weakness of the apostles which led to their salvation will then be to us a source of strength; their flight, a source of courage and consolation. When we again meet them on the day of Pentecost and see them go forth like heroes to conquer the world, we shall be encouraged by the thought that, notwithstanding our misery and cowardice, we may also become saints. For that purpose, however, we must pray to the Saviour that He attach us inseparably to Himself in the bonds of His love, so that we may remain faithful to Him even unto death.

CHAPTER VII.

THE EVENTS IMMEDIATELY FOLLOWING THE SEIZURE OF CHRIST

> "And they led him away to Annas first, for he was father-in-law to Caiphas, who was the high-priest of that year. The high-priest therefore asked Jesus of his disciples, and of his doctrine." (John xviii., 13, 19.)

After the seizure of the Redeemer, St. Matthew, St. Mark and St. Luke proceed at once to tell of His being led to Caiphas. St. Matthew and St. Mark then describe the trial proper before Caiphas and the chief-priests, which ended in the condemnation of Christ; all three evangelists then mention the triple denial of Peter in the vestibule of the palace of Caiphas. But they tell us nothing of the appearance before Annas, nor of the preliminary trial in which Annas[1] questioned Jesus concerning His disciples and His doctrine, nor of the blow upon the cheek dealt Jesus after this interrogatory. All of this is supplied in the narrative of St. John, who also tells us that the first denial of Peter occurred during this preliminary trial. However, we know that the evangelists were

[1] See note 5.

neither commissioned nor did they intend to write of *all* that happened.

Let us now consider [1]

I. The march from Mount Olivet to Annas;

II. The preliminary trial before Annas.

I.

St. John tells of Our Lord's going from Mount Olivet to Annas in these simple words, "And they led him away to Annas first." This march, in the first place, was very *painful* to the Saviour. Owing to the great loss of blood in the Garden of Olives, He was in a state of extreme exhaustion. The fetters with which the caution of His captors had loaded His Sacred Body made it very difficult for Him to walk. The rabble, drunk with victory, beat, pushed, pulled, in a word, maltreated Him in a manner of which only a violent and enraged multitude were capable. It is not improbable as some commentators opine, that on the way He repeatedly fell to the ground, even into the brook Cedron itself, whence the ruffians dragged Him as if He were some wild beast.

Again, this march was extremely *humiliating* to His Divine Heart. He was bound, as if He were a murderer and robber. The disgrace was the greater because of the high prestige formerly enjoyed by Him. It was immensely increased by the infernal laughter, the grinning faces and the

[1] St. Matthew, xxvi., 57; St. Mark, xiv., 53; St. Luke, xxii., 54; St. John, xviii., 13, 19–24.

jeers and curses of His enemies. But this ignominy reached its height at the entrance into the city. Christ was led through the Golden Portal, also called the Sheep's Gate, through which, amid the applause, the felicitations and the joyful acclamations of all the inhabitants of Jerusalem, He had, on Palm Sunday, made His triumphal entry. He was led through the same street where He had passed over palm branches and spread garments, greeted the while with solemn hosannas. The noise of the troop awoke the people from their sleep; every one ran into the street; the low characters of the city crept out of their dens; they all leered at Him in curiosity or malice; they all exulted at His capture. All this caused incomprehensible shame to the Divine Heart. It was still more incomprehensible that Almighty God did not repeat the punishment once inflicted upon the Bethsamites who, in sinful curiosity and irreverence, had dared to gaze upon the ark of the Old Testament.

It is true indeed, that the Saviour knew Himself to be innocent. But this knowledge could not remove the shame felt by His human heart. What would be your feelings, Christian man, if, amid the hisses and the jeers of a curious multitude, you were to be dragged, bound and fettered through the streets of the city to the door of the jail? Although convinced of your own innocence, you still would wish that the earth might swallow you, and the fact of your respectability would merely intensify this wish. Whether or no we shall have the honor of following Christ, Who is "the Way," on this way of disgrace, we cannot tell. We ought, however, to accustom ourselves to support patiently and joyfully lesser humiliations; then, with the grace of Christ, we may heroically bear greater ones whenever it pleases God to inflict them on us.

Meanwhile they arrived before Annas, who lived in the same house with Caiphas, his son-in-law. This man, Annas,[1] by bribing the Roman governor, had obtained the dignity of high-priest in the sixth year after the birth of Christ. Later on he had to yield the place to a certain Ismael; but, by means of money, he again succeeded in obtaining the dignity for his son Eleazar and for his son-in-law Caiphas when, one year after his installation, Eleazar had been supplanted by Simon. In the course of time, four more of his sons were made high-priests, the youngest of whom obtained the high office when Annas was ninety years old, for which reason Annas was called the happiest of men. He owed his continued influence in the appointment of high-priests not only to his money, but also to his energy and to the firm grasp by which he kept together the party of the Sadducees to which he belonged. Annas is indeed an apt illustration of an impenitent sinner, who will not desist from evil even in hoary old age and on the brink of the grave.

But what caused the soldiers or rather the chief-

1 **Flavius Jos., Aut. l. 20 ch. 9. n. 1. 2.**

priests and elders who commanded the troop, to lead Christ to Annas, who, not being in office, had no jurisdiction over Him? St. John gives us the first reason. Annas was the father-in-law of Caiphas. Such consideration for the father-in-law could not fail to recommend the chief-priests to the son-in-law. Then, to avoid being charged with neglect, they were impelled to please the old man himself. In this particular matter his claims were too numerous to be slighted. According to St. Cyril of Alexandria,[1] he was the very soul of the whole conspiracy against Christ. In fact, the Acts of the Apostles (iv., 6) show him to have been the spiritual head of the entire anti-Christian party. Therefore, the chief-priests led the captured prey, in triumph, into the house of Annas to present Christ that he might feast his eyes upon Him, a thing he had long desired. Judas, also, insisted upon this, because he had made the bargain with Annas, and he wanted his money. Finally, as St. Augustine writes,[2] Caiphas, to honor his father-in-law, had instructed the chief-priests to lead Christ to Annas first. But throughout all, Caiphas was secretly following out other purposes. However bold and confident he appeared during the entire proceedings, he still greatly feared lest Christ escape him again by means of sorcery or diabolical craft, which, of course, would destroy his prestige as high-priest. Whether or not this attempt would be successful must therefore be ascertained by

[1] In Joan. 1, 11 (Joan. 18, 13).
[2] Tract. in Joann. 113, 1.

the inquiry of some one else who held no official position. He thought that his father-in-law was just the proper person to try the experiment, so slender often are family ties among the godless. Whenever private interest demands it, one member of a family is ready to sacrifice another. Besides this, Caiphas, who was the first to propose the death of Christ in grand council, wished as much as possible to remove from himself the odium of the affair. Nothing, therefore, would please him more than that Annas, who to his high standing joined uncommon shrewdness, should by a preliminary examination discover matter for accusation, and prepare the way for the trial proper, in short, be the plaintiff in the case before him, the high-priest. Christ, then, stood before Annas. How the latter must have rejoiced to see, bound before him, the irksome preacher of penance. Christ had so often scourged the band of pharisees and unmercifully laid bare their malice and hypocrisy. There He now stands fettered. But how short-lived is the joy of the impious! Even death's bonds shall be severed after three days.

Let us now turn our attention to the preliminary hearing before Annas.

II.

Annas was an ex-high-priest. He therefore had no right whatever to hold an enquiry. But that mattered little to him. It was of more concern to him to gather from the Redeemer's answers points to form a basis of accusation in a subsequent legal trial. Annas, therefore, questioned the Saviour first about His disciples, their number, the reason why He had as many apostles as there had been patriarchs, as many disciples as there were elders, why He had gathered to Himself entirely uneducated, ignorant people from among the common herd. He wished to know whether Christ had bound them to Himself, like modern free-masons, by secret oaths, what were the purposes of His nomadic wanderings, whether or not He had political ends in view. His aims could hardly be proper ones or His disciples would not have abandoned Him. They had probably reached the conclusion that He had falsely claimed to be the Messiah and that He was an impostor. Annas also questioned the Saviour about His doctrine. He wished to know in what school of law He had been trained, which of the tendencies current among the scribes He followed, whether He had a rightful mission to teach, and, if so, from whom He had received it. For whoever would publicly teach either law or doctrines of faith was required to receive from an authorized teacher a proper commission which was usually given by the imposing of hands. Therefore, besides claiming a direct, divine call and attestation of His right to teach, Christ had formerly also appealed to the testimony of John the Baptist.[1] Furthermore, as Annas was aware from previous investigations[2] that Christ agreed with none of the existing and violently conflicting

1 St. John, v., 33.

2 St. Matthew, xix., 3.

schools regarding the interpretation of the Mosaic Law and the traditions of the teachers, he undoubtedly put some very pointed questions to the Redeemer. The answers of Christ were expected to stamp Him as a despiser of the law of Moses, or at least to embitter and excite against Him one or the other of the various parties. No matter how the accused might reply, he would, Annas thought, hurt His own cause.

Christ did not answer the first question relating to His disciples. Had He named them and declared them to be His disciples, a warrant for their arrest would probably have been issued at once. Besides, just at this time, He could not say anything very laudatory of them, and He would not mention their faults and weaknesses, their pride and vanity, their drowsiness and sloth in the Garden of Olives and their hasty flight at His seizure. It is a point we ought to remember in our conversations. Furthermore, an answer to this question was not necessary. Owing to the intention of the high-priest in putting his question, it was necessary to give an answer regarding the doctrine only. For if the doctrine was good and from God, Christ could not have gathered the disciples about Him for any ignoble purpose. Christ, therefore, gave an answer concerning His doctrine to show Annas that He would not withdraw jot or tittle from it. His answer, however, was again so prudent that He avoided the trap set for Him. He did not enter into an explanation or a confirmation of His teachings. He knew that He had before Him hardened rascals who cared naught for truth. For this reason, He avoided all manner of dispute and religious discussion—all of which He meant for our instruction. For although it is certainly good and laudable to silence malicious doubters and scoffers with a clean-cut, sound answer, still it is not advisable in most cases to enter into religious controversies with them. We ought rather to tell them that every Sunday sermons are preached in our churches on doctrines of faith and morals and that they ought to go there for enlightenment. In order, then, to defend His doctrine, Christ merely appealed to the fact that He had always preached in public and often in the Temple, whence it could be inferred that He never desired secretly to spread false teachings. He said that He had taught nothing secretly, that is with the intention that it should remain secret. He had indeed often spoken to the apostles alone and had initiated them into many mysteries. But He imposed upon them at the same time this injunction: "That which you hear in the ear, preach ye upon the housetops."[1] "Ask them," Christ continued, "who have heard what I have spoken unto them." It would verily be more in keeping with legal procedure were they to present definite charges regarding my doctrine before requiring me to speak in my own defence. Truly, Annas, thy proceeding is not only unlawful but also very foolish. For what reasonable judge would expect an accused to freely furnish him, by an open avowal, material for a charge?

[1] St. Matthew, x., 27.

It seemed to one of the servants that Christ looked especially at him, just as Christians sometimes assert positively that the preacher of the Divine Word, at this or that passage of his sermon, gazed directly at them. The servant therefore believed that Christ wished him to testify in favor of His doctrine. To vent his rage and anger, but mainly to please the high-priest and to deter others from taking sides with Christ, this man rushed upon the Redeemer and gave Him such a fearful blow upon the cheek that He staggered. At the same time, he feigned respect for the high-priest by saying, "Answerest thou the high-priest so?" A blow, alas, upon the cheek, a blow of the fist, a blow of an iron-clad fist upon the Holy, heavenly beautiful, Divine Face which the angels yearn to behold! Ah! how is it that his hand did not wither, that savage beasts, rushing out of the desert, did not tear the offender in pieces, that fire did not fall from heaven to consume him, that the earth did not open to swallow him! Is it not barbarous to thus maltreat an accused man who is not yet sentenced and who therefore may possibly be innocent? Since when has a court servant been given the right to deal a blow to the accused who is defending himself in open court? But the high-priest was silent. Had his dog been beaten, he would have had something to say.

However, the blow of the servant was aimed less at the Person of the Redeemer than at His doctrine. The man intended thereby to bear witness to the objectionable character of Jesus' teachings and thought to deal them a death-blow. For which reason, and also to show us that even blows should not deter us from professing the truth, the Saviour did not remain silent. He most decidedly denied that the defense of truth could be an offense to the high-priest. But regarding his former teachings he demanded of the servant proof that they were false and harmful. "If I have spoken evil, give testimony of the evil: but if well, why strikest thou me?" Christ spoke these last words to bring home to the servant the full injustice of his act and, as he probably raised his hand to deal another blow, to deter him from further sins and bring him to his senses. Wherefore he is likely to have spoken them with winning mildness and gentleness.

Meanwhile no one was in more uncomfortable straits than Annas. Had he not lost all sense of shame, he would have blushed with confusion. For it was clear to the witnesses present that the answers of Christ had rightly branded the conduct of Annas as unlawful and foolish. To get out of his awkward position and to rid himself of the odious affair, Annas hurriedly paid Judas the traitor's price and sent the Saviour, bound as He was, to Caiphas.

"Why strikest thou Me?" said the Saviour to the servant who had maltreated Him. He can say the same to every sinner. *Why* strikest thou Me? Give me the reason. Why? Is it because I created thee when thou wast not? Or is it because I saved thee when thou wast in the chains of Satan? Or is it because I have restored lost grace to thee an hundred times? Why? Name the crime which I have committed against thee. Thou *strikest* Me! Is this thy gratitude for all my benefits? It is *thou* who strikest Me, thou, the privileged one among thousands. *Thou* strikest me, a vile menial, a fault-laden sinner, thou, My creature, the work of My hand, thou, for whom I am about to shed My blood! Thou strikest *Me,* Me, thy Friend, thy Brother, thy Protector, thy Consoler, thy Judge, thy greatest and most precious Good! Indeed, these reproaches of the Saviour may well bring the blush of confusion to each of us.

Nevertheless, the blow received by the Redeemer has obtained honor. Whenever a pious artist represents the instruments of the Saviour's sufferings, the iron-clad fist is never missing. The holy confessors and martyrs suffered joyfully the blow upon the cheek. But for us it has become the accolade of knighthood in the sacrament of Confirmation. With knightly courage, then, let us profess our faith and make our lives accord with it. As true warriors of Jesus Christ, let us battle against the enemies of our faith. And may we, as true warriors of Jesus Christ, fall some day upon the battle field, for then, in death, the Saviour will give us the palm of victory.

CHAPTER VIII.

THE TRIAL OF CHRIST BEFORE CAIPHAS

> "Then the high-priest rent his garments, saying: He hath blasphemed: what further need have we of witnesses? Behold, now you have heard the blasphemy: What think you? But they answering said: He is guilty of death."
>
> (St. Matthew, xxvi., 65–66.)

Whilst the Redeemer stood before Annas, the members of the Sanhedrin assembled with Caiphas. Caiphas was the high-priest of that year. In fact, he was clad with this dignity during the entire public life of Christ. After the death of Christ, Pilate's successor deposed him. It is said that grief at his removal caused him to commit suicide. The composition of the court was unique in its way. "It presented," says St. Chrysostom,[1] "only the appearance of a court, in reality it was an assault of robbers." Where in the wide world was a man ever allowed to be the judge in his own cause? How is impartiality possible where the judges are at the same time the accusers? No

[1] In Matth., hom. 54 (al. 53) n. 2.

other assembly equaled the Sanhedrin[1] either in outward splendor of holiness or in divine prestige. It was, so to speak, the oracle of the world, the decisions of which were considered binding in conscience and irrefragable. Before this assembly which was extolled as harboring the seat of Justice, which was modelled after the fundamental outlines of the old Mosaic constitution and which once had counted among its members such prophets as Aggeus, Zacharias and Malachias and the great friends of God such as Esdras, before this "high synod" stood Jesus Christ, Who was to perfect that Law, to fulfil the predictions of those prophets and the expectations of all those just men. There He stood as an accused criminal—He, the Son of the Eternal Father, the Judge of the living and of the dead, stood there to be judged and to hear His condemnation to death. Let us listen to the proceedings of the trial. And if we are seized with terror and dismay on entering, in spirit, into the house of Caiphas, thither we shall, nevertheless, follow the Redeemer for His solace and for our own instruction. Let us, therefore, consider:[2]

I. The testimony of the witnesses;
II. The condemnation of the Accused, and
III. The unlawful maltreatment of the Condemned.

[1] See note 6.

[2] St. Matthew, xxvi., 59–68; St. Mark, xiv., 53–65; St. Luke, xxii., 63–65.

I.

The preliminary trial before Annas was barren of results. Nothing had come to light that might form the basis of an accusation, and thus Caiphas had to begin without having before him any charge. After the judges had taken their seats, the signal for the opening of the trial was given. According to custom, the Saviour was released from His bonds as a sign that He had full liberty to defend Himself. Everybody was now intent to hear the accusation, but no accuser opened his lips. As if awakening from a profound sleep, the judges collect their wits and find themselves in a bad predicament. They will not and cannot condemn Christ without a definite charge and without accusers; for they must above all, preserve the appearance of a legal, juridical trial. So, as a last resort, the high-priest requested those present to testify against Christ and to bring charges. Thereupon some complied and related what the pharisees among the crowd had hurriedly whispered to them. But, to the great dismay of the high-priest, they contradicted themselves. Here, indeed, the usual cunning of the pharisees had played them false, inasmuch as they could not train a few men to give unanimous testimony. Now was the word of the psalmist verified: "Unjust witnesses have risen up against me; and iniquity hath lied to itself."[1] Finally two more false witnesses arose, similar to the two sons of Belial, who were suborned by im-

[1] Psalms, xxvi., 12.

pious Jezabel to testify that "Naboth hath blasphemed God and the king." It is indeed a terrible thing to allow one's self to be used as a witness against the Eternal Truth. The testimony of the one was this: "This man said, I am able to destroy the temple of God, and after three days to rebuild it."[1] The testimony of the other was as follows: "We heard him say, I will destroy this temple made with hands, and within three days I will build another not made with hands."[2] These testimonies were false, because they distorted the words of Christ. Christ had said, "Destroy this temple," that is, if *you* destroy it, not *I* destroy it, "and in three days I will raise it up."[3] Christ had therefore attributed to Himself the Power and the will not of destroying but of *reconstructing,* and this only *conditionally* upon their having destroyed this temple.

Neither did He then refer to the temple of Solomon, but to the temple of His own body.[4] These testimonies were irrelevant in any case, even if Christ had spoken of the temple of Solomon in the sense attributed to Him. They furnished no cause for a death penalty, which usually can be imposed for criminal acts only. Now, of these two witnesses, one accused Christ of boastful words and the other, of an internal act of the will. The words of the Saviour, no matter to what extent

1 St. Matthew, xxvi., 61.
2 St. Mark, xiv., 58.
3 St. John, ii., 19.
4 St. John, ii., 21.

their sense was perverted, could at most justify the opinion that He was either a braggart or a fool, but not a criminal. Such an immense building as Solomon's temple could not be quietly torn down over night. And if Christ had really torn it down, but rebuilt it in three days, the damage done would be very trivial indeed. But the intention was to represent the words of Christ as being a crime against God, the Lord of the Sanctuary, and against the Temple, the center of worship.

Therewith closed the comedy of hearing witnesses. They took good care not to admit testimony for the defense, as is the custom in all trials. And they had their reasons. For were Christ to bring forward all the hungry whom He had fed, all the sick whom He had healed, all the dead whom He had raised to life, the infernal scheme of the mob would be foiled. As it was, the accusers contradicted themselves. This was truly a glorious triumph of eternal truth which the Catholic Church has also achieved in every Christian century. Everything that opposes her and contemns the mass of testimony showing her Divinity, exposes its own contradictions and makes itself unqualifiedly ridiculous.

It would have been the duty of a just judge to call, like a second Daniel, the attention of the witnesses to the contradiction in which they were entangled, to brand these witnesses as perjurers and to punish them. The high-priest, however, arose hastily and advanced. Approving by his actions the false testimony and taking its truth for granted, he nevertheless fairly boiled with anger at the inept statements as well as at the calmness with which the Saviour seemed to despise the charges, and he hurled at the latter these words: "Answerest Thou nothing to the things which these witness against Thee?" that is, "Hast Thou no remark to make upon this testimony, hast Thou nothing to say in Thine own defense?"

This question gave Christ leave to speak and challenged Him to a defense. It was undoubtedly the shortest defense ever made. The Gospel describes it in these words: "But Jesus held his peace." But for all its brevity, this defense of the Redeemer had its effect. It found enthusiastic admirers; it was repeated by thousands of saints and pious people after they had been outrageously caluminated, and it still works prodigies even to our own day.

But it threw Caiphas into shameless and unrestrained fury. Wherefore the miserable wretch sought, by a question of devilish cunning, to lay a new snare for Christ, Whom he otherwise would have to release for want of incriminating proof. He had no doubt but that the answer of the Saviour would furnish sufficient points to warrant a death-sentence.

Let us pass on to the sentencing of the Accused.

II.

It was decreed of God from all eternity that, on this day, at three o'clock in the afternoon, Christ should enter upon His functions as High-

Priest, with which act was inevitably connected the extinction of the office of high-priest of the Old Law. In a manner, therefore, the Redeemer owed it to His honor to present Himself before Caiphas in order to prove and to confirm by oath the validity of His title. Otherwise evil tongues might charge Him with having unlawfully assumed this dignity. The declaration of Christ must be placed on record and preserved in the archives of the synagogue. Now this solemn moment had arrived. Christ stood before Caiphas, the high-priest of the Old Law. In presence of the entire court and of the assembled multitude, Caiphas said with a loud voice, "I adjure Thee by the living God, that Thou tell us if Thou be the Christ the Son of God." Every one waited for the answer. The silence of death was spread over the room. Then the Redeemer opened His mouth and said, "Thou hast said it. I am."

Rejoice, O Caiphas, and be glad! How is it possible adequately to praise the honor and distinction conferred upon thee! Since the days of Malachias, thy predecessors in office have yearned for Him Who, as the High-Priest of the New Law, was to do away with the bloody sacrifices of animals and offer a sacrifice worthy of the Divine Majesty. What they longed in vain to see was reserved for thee, O Caiphas. Before thee stands the Expected of nations, the Redeemer of the world, the Son of God Himself. To thee has been given the honor of receiving Him, investing Him with the insignia of His dignity. Throw thyself, then, at the feet of

Christ, adore Him, tender Him thy congratulations! But ye, chief-priests and scribes, ancients and menials, crave His pardon in tears. Tell Him how that it was only through an unfortunate misunderstanding, never sufficiently to be deplored, that His hands were bound and He Himself maltreated and placed in the dock of criminals. Then send messengers through Jerusalem and over the entire land. Shout it from the house tops and from the pinnacle of the Temple, carry the glad tidings even into the lowliest hut, announce it to the shepherds in the field: "Christ, the Saviour, is here." "Then the high-priest rent his garments, saying: He hath blasphemed: what further need have we of witnesses? Behold, now you have heard the blasphemy: What think you? Who all condemned Him to be guilty of death, and said: He is guilty of death."

Let us cast another glance upon this scene. Let us consider especially the snare which the high-priest, by his question, prepared for the Saviour. Christ could hardly escape. He was undone. Had He answered in the negative, he would have been charged with blasphemous fraud in that formerly He falsely claimed to be the Son of God. Silence was the only escape. Christ however spoke, first, out of reverence for the Name of God by whom Caiphas had adjured Him; then, in humble obedience to the high-priest who had a right to ask the question; lastly, in order to deprive his judges of all excuse on the day of judgment. Had He not answered at all, or given only an evasive answer, they might say to justify themselves, "We asked Him officially and in the name of God, but He gave us no answer. Had He then admitted the truth, we would not only not have put Him to death, but we would have believed in Him."

Then let us admire the divine dignity, majesty and love with which the Lord says to His judges, "Now, indeed, you behold Me in extreme weakness and humiliation. But the day is coming and is not far distant when, sitting on the right hand of God, I shall appear in the clouds to pronounce upon you the sentence of eternal damnation unless you now confess Me before men."

Let us also thank the Saviour for this luminous proof of His divinity. The high-priest adjured Him by the living God to say whether He was the Son of God or not. Christ answered, "I am," and He sealed this testimony with His blood. The Son of Man is therefore the Son of God and the Judge of the living and the dead. Foolish, therefore, and contradictory is the assertion of modern pagans that Christ is not God, but that He was the wisest and holiest of men. Whoever does not recognize in Christ the Son of God must consider Him either a fool or the most shameless deceiver. Common sense must acknowledge this.

Meanwhile the alleged blasphemy made the pious heart of Caiphas heavy with anxiety and sadness. To give vent to his sorrow and indignation, this miserable hypocrite tore his garment and bared his shameless breast. Thereby was the garment of the Old Law rent for all time. "Thanks be to

God,'' he then exclaimed, ''we now have what we want; we need no more witnesses; the blasphemy is evident.'' But cunningly assuming the role of a plaintiff, he left it to his colleagues to pronounce the sentence of death. They all cried out at once, ''He is guilty of death,'' this being in perfect consonance with the law of Moses. ''He that blasphemeth the name of the Lord, dying let him die.''[1]

Meanwhile, the sentence of death was not legally valid. Setting aside the fact that it had been illegally pronounced at night time and probably only by the minor council; that, in a criminal case, the judgment was never to be pronounced on the day of the trial, and, least of all, on the eve of the Sabbath; that according to ancient custom, the condemned had the privilege of a new trial if an attorney undertook his case, it was necessary, besides, as we shall see later on, that the Roman governor give his approval. All this must increase our astonishment at the unlawful maltreatment heaped upon the condemned Redeemer.

III.

Whenever a criminal is condemned to death, no matter how great his crimes may have been, at the moment when judgment is pronounced, sympathy begins. The proximity of death is, in our estimation, atonement, to a certain extent, for the crime committed, and it reconciles us with the un-

[1] Levit., xxiv., 16.

fortunate one. And the thought of his agony, of the pains resulting from the execution and of his unnatural death, excites in every generous heart pity and sympathy. After sentence has been pronounced, even judges are sometimes found to assure the poor victim of their sympathy and of their regret that inexorable law forced them to put aside all forbearance. It is, therefore, a custom, among all peoples who make any kind of pretension to civilization, to alleviate the last days of the condemned and to gratify, as much as possible, all their desires. On the other hand, it would be considered brutal cruelty and inconceivable meanness to maltreat, aggrieve, insult or ridicule them.

But as soon as the sentence of death had been pronounced upon Christ, amid a storm of applause, the servants and menials and—who would think it possible?—several of the judges, scribes, pharisees and priests fell upon Him and vented their fury and hatred in blows, in buffeting and dragging Him hither and thither, pulling His hair and reviling Him in most bitter sarcasm.[1] Thus it happens. When prominent people abandon religion and morality, they become viler than the common rabble. The members of the court then arranged for a second full meeting in the morning to take the proper measures for the execution of the sentence. Thereupon, probably soon after two o'clock, they retired to take a well-earned rest.

Meanwhile the Redeemer was left to the servants

1 St. Mark, xiv., 65.

and court-menials. They dragged Him out of the palace, through the court-yard, past Peter, into a small prison next to the guard-room. In this prison the indicted were kept under lock and key during the intervals of their trial and at night. The Saviour was tired almost to death when He reached His cell. But sleep and rest were denied Him; for the servants and menials continued to treat Him as they had done in the court-room. What the innocent Lamb of God had to suffer until morning from these wild beasts in human form was so terrible and dreadful that the evangelists could not help but record it in detail. It was so terrible and dreadful, that, as St. Jerome writes, its horrors shall be made known only on the last day. "On that night," says St. Chrysostom, "all the pits of the nether world were opened, and, after breaking their chains and the bars of hell, Lucifer and all his satellites rushed to Jerusalem, entered into and took possession of the bodies of all Jews and pagans to pour out through them upon Christ their long pent-up hatred, envy and anger, their rage and all their fury."

In the first place, these hired inferiors tortured the Redeemer, now branded as a blasphemer, by all sorts of bodily injury. Some struck Him in the face with their fists, others tore His face with their finger-nails, others pulled Him by the hair in order that the words of Isaias the prophet might be accomplished: "I have given my body to the strikers and my cheeks to them that plucked them."[1]

[1] Is., l., 6.

"But," exclaims St. Athanasius, "Know ye not that ye are merely wounding your hands, while striking the corner-stone?" Then they heaped contempt upon Him. Vile and shameless beings threw their dirty and loathsome spittle in His Holy Face, into His Sacred Mouth; in that Holy Face before which the waves of the sea had done reverence and from which, when Christ hung upon the cross, the sun hid its rays; into that sacred mouth from which only words of blessing and of love had ever issued. It was usual among the Jews to spit upon the blasphemer. "I have not," says Christ by the mouth of Isaias, "turned away my face from them that spit upon me." It resembled the face of a leper. They further loaded Him with contumely and ridicule, by calling Him vile names, hissing at Him and caricaturing Him. The climax was reached when, blindfolding Him, they buffeted and smote Him, saying, "Prophesy, Christ, who is it that struck Thee? Who struck Thee first? Who was the second? the third? Who struck Thee now? Who at this instant spat upon Thee?" It would wound religious feeling to qualify, in proper words, the conduct of these wretches towards the thrice holy God. A greater and more abominable ridiculing of Divine Majesty, Omnipotence and Omniscience cannot be imagined. It was indeed proper first to veil the Face in Which was resplendent the glory of the Father. Ah! Let us beware of ridiculing an omnipresent and all-knowing God, lest we fall victims to His Justice.

The Jews covered the Face of the Saviour. They would no longer look upon it. They shall no more look upon it. Only once more will He show it to them—on the day of judgment. Oh Divine Redeemer! We will not cover Thy Holy Face! No, we will look upon it! Show it unto us, turn it not away, show it unto us in life, in death! By all the sufferings which thou didst undergo in the house of Caiphas on the part of Thy unjust judges and Thy bloodthirsty jailers, be merciful unto us! We pray Thee to be merciful when we, one day, shall appear before Thy judgment seat. Grant unto us that we may behold Thy face, the Face of the Son of God, for all eternity!

CHAPTER IX.

THE THREE DENIALS OF PETER.

> "Then he began to curse and to swear that he knew not the man. And immediately the cock crew. And Peter remembered the word of Jesus which he had said: Before the cock crow, thou wilt deny me thrice. And going forth, he wept bitterly.
> (St. Matthew, xxvi., 74, 75.)

At the seizure of Christ the eleven apostles beat a hasty retreat. When Peter recovered from his first fright, he felt as one who had awaked from a profound sleep. He was bewildered. His hopes for a temporal, Messianic Kingdom and for a prominent position therein seemed now entirely futile. From afar, he followed the procession,[1] to see, as the Gospel mentions, what they would do with his beloved Master. It would, it is true, have been more prudent not to follow. The more distant he remained from the menials, the further would he be removed from a fall. On the way he was joined by another disciple[2] of the Saviour, who, according to most commentators, was St. John.[3]

1 St. Matthew, xxvi., 18; St. Mark, xiv., 54; St. Luke, xxii., 54.

2 St. John, xviii., 15, 16.

3 See Note 7.

Peter and John noticed that they led Jesus through a portal facing the street, into the court-yard in front of the palace of Caiphas. Whilst Peter dared not enter, John asked the portress to admit him and she politely acceded to his request. The humility of John in describing this, is truly touching. It ought not, he says, to be attributed to his superior courage, nor to his greater love for Christ, nor to his more intense desire of defending the Saviour that he entered the court-yard whilst Peter remained in the street. It happened merely because he was better acquainted than Peter in the house of the high-priest. Now John was better acquainted in this house either because in times past he had sold fish there or because one of his relatives was employed by Caiphas or, again, because in exchanging his small possession in Galilee for a house belonging to Caiphas in the neighborhood of Mount Sion, he had been brought into frequent contact with the latter. It is said that it was this house in which Christ instituted the Blessed Sacrament, to which the apostles retired on the day of the Resurrection, in which they received the Holy Ghost and into which St. John brought the Mother of Jesus. According to this tradition, the man in whose house Christ ate the Paschal lamb and with whom we are already acquainted would have been merely a lease-holder.

When John arrived in the court-yard, he missed Peter. He therefore went back to the entrance and spoke kindly to the portress, whereupon Peter also gained admittance. This, undoubtedly, was afterwards the cause of much regret to St. John, inasmuch as thereby he had to some extent brought about the occasion for Peter's sin, albeit without knowledge or evil intent. It behooves a person indeed to be careful before introducing any one into a house or a society or before allowing one's self to be so introduced, and this applies even to the apostles and their successors. Andrew was certainly more fortunate when he introduced his brother Peter to the Saviour, and also Peter himself, when he led John to the sepulchre.

The other disciple went into the house and there saw the Redeemer. But he probably left very soon to tell the Blessed Virgin of the beginning of the trial. Peter, however, remained in the court-yard and joined the servants and menials who, owing to the cold weather, had started a fire and were conversing about the recent happenings. After a while, they all sat down by the fire. Peter, therefore, was "*outside,*" as the Gospel says, in relation to those who were in the palace; he was "*inside*" in relation to those who were on the street before the main entrance. It was there, in the court-yard, that Peter thrice denied his Master. According to the narrative of St. John, he denied Him the first time while Christ stood before Annas. The other two denials took place whilst Christ was before Caiphas and the Sanhedrin.[1]

[1] St. Matthew, xxvi., 59, 69–75; St. Mark, xiv., 54, 66–72; St. Luke, xxii., 55–62; St. John, xviii., 17–18.

Let us consider

I. The story of the denial,
II. The causes of the same and
III. The subsequent contrition.

I.

The first denial, which occurred toward one o'clock, soon after Peter's entrance into the court-yard, happened in the following manner. One of the maid-servants of the high-priest, the portress, who had admitted Peter, saw him sitting at the fire among the men-servants. She had probably often seen him in the Saviour's company, and his features were not unfamiliar to her. As, moreover, at his very entrance, he made himself conspicuous by his uneasy manner and his timid and embarrassed look, the maid grew suspicious and, impelled by curiosity, she asked him, "Art not thou also one of His disciples?" Peter answered, "I am not." But she replied, "Surely, thou also wast with Jesus of Nazareth in Galilee, that notorious and rebellious country." Peter, however, denied it and said, "I know Him not, neither do I understand what you really mean. I know so little about Him that I understand nothing of what you say." But looking at him more closely in the glare of the fire, she declared very politely to those who stood around, "This man was also with Him." And Peter denied Him saying, "Woman, I know Him not." Ah! Peter, just now Annas is questioning the Redeemer about His disciples. What is He to answer?

The words of the maid-servant caused much embarrassment to Peter. They represented him to the servants as an adherent of Jesus. In terror and fear lest these servants do him harm, he arose and walked towards the vestibule, which was a gallery supported by pillars inside of the main entrance. Perhaps he intended to use the first opportunity which offered to reach the street. Had he only done so!

Then the cock crowed. It is said that in the Orient the first crow of the cock is heard soon after midnight. But if even that were not so, it ought not to surprise us that in this night the cock crowed sooner than usual, because the dreadful noise of the soldiers had awakened from sleep not only the human inhabitants of the city, but also the animals.

Peter meanwhile, did not leave the vestibule. He returned "that he might see the end"[1] and he approached the fire. There another maid-servant, to whom his conduct had seemed strange, furnished him with the occasion of the second denial. Pointing her finger at Peter, she said to the surrounding group, "This man also was with Jesus of Nazareth. He is one of them." Vexed at the maid and wishing to remove all suspicion by acting resolutely, Peter went close to the fire, right among the servants and soldiers, who mean-

[1] St. Matthew, xxvi., 58.

time had risen from their seats. The attention, however, of the by-standers had been aroused by the words of the maid and they asked him, "Art not thou also one of His disciples?" On Peter's denial, another who knew him better, cried out, "Surely thou art one of them." But Peter answered, "O man, I am not." And with an oath he declared, "I know not the man." And thus it is. "Sin," says St. Gregory,[1] "when not removed by penance, by its own weight soon draws down to another sin."

About one hour afterwards, or soon after two o'clock, the third denial occurred. "Of a truth," said one of the by-standers, "this man was also with Him: for he is also a Galilean." When Peter denied it and acted as if he understood him not, they all shouted together, "Surely thou art also one of them; thou art a Galilean; thy speech doth discover thee." The continued denying of Peter angered especially one of the high-priest's servants, a kinsman of Malchus, whose ear Peter's sword had severed. He therefore added: "Did not I see thee in the garden with him?" In terror and dismay lest this servant take revenge, Peter began to curse and to swear that he knew not the man of whom they spoke. Then the cock crowed a second time and the guards came with Jesus out of the door of the palace to lead Him through the vestibule into a prison cell.

Peter, then, had really thrice denied the Sav-

[1] Moral l. 25, c. 9.

iour before the cock had crowed twice. He did not reject faith itself, but he sinned against the duty of *professing* it. In addition to this he cursed and perjured himself. There were, indeed, some mitigating circumstances such as Peter's excitement, his fatigue and his fear of revenge on the part of Malchus' kinsman and of the enemies of Christ. The sin, however, was mortal and must have grieved exceedingly the Divine Heart. For it was Peter who denied the Lord; Peter, the witness of the miracles of Jesus Christ; Peter, who had so solemnly declared, "Thou art Christ, the Son of the living God;" Peter, who a few hours before had, with the most lively faith, received his Redeemer under the sacramental appearances. Peter, besides, had been especially privileged by Christ. It was to him, that the Lord had said, "Thou art Peter, and upon this rock I will build my Church."[1] It was to Peter that He had addressed the words: "I will give to thee the keys of the kingdom of heaven."[2] Now this rock is shaking, now Peter is closing upon himself the gates of heaven which he is to open unto others.

To what language did this apostle give utterance before the sworn enemies of Christ at a time when, in the court-room, they were busy inciting false witnesses to brand Christ as a deceiver and blasphemer! How opportune, perhaps, the declarations of the apostle were to the Saviour's enemies!

1 St. Matthew, xvi., 18.
2 Ibid., xvi., xix.

How quickly it was spread about that he who was known to be His disciple had abandoned Him and would have no more to do with Him.

But how shall we explain the fall of the apostle? We can readily understand that Delilah overcame Samson, the strong hero, for he had confided his secret to her. Just as easily we can understand the victory of Judith over Holofernes. She found him asleep and drunk, and with a powerful arm she wielded a mighty sword. But that the prying question of a maid-servant could vanquish the prince of the apostles borders on the incredible. Let us examine the causes of his denial.

II.

To begin with the remote causes, the excessive *self-confidence* of the apostle was the first. Peter had forgotten what the Saviour had often told him, "Without Me ye can do nothing." He believed that he himself possessed the power necessary to withstand all temptations and dangers. He considered himself firmer and stronger than the others. He could, therefore, not even understand how it was possible that anything could make his faith and love waver, notwithstanding the fact that the Redeemer had warned him and had very distinctly foretold his threefold fall. At the last Supper Christ had said to His apostles, "Whither I go, you cannot come." "Whither goest thou?" asked Peter. "Whither I go," replied Jesus, "thou canst not follow me now, but thou shalt follow hereafter." Then Peter said to Him, "Why cannot I follow Thee now? I will lay down my life for Thee. Lord, I am ready to go with Thee both into prison and to death."[1] Truly, this is not the language of humility. "You will all," continued the Redeemer, addressing Himself again to all the apostles, "be scandalized in my regard this night; for it is written, I will strike the shepherd, and the sheep shall be dispersed." Whereupon Peter replied, "Although all shall be scandalized in Thee, yet not I." Then Jesus, turning directly to Peter, said to him, "Amen I say to thee, today, even in this night, before the cock crow twice, thou shalt deny me thrice." Peter replied, "Although I should die together with Thee, I will not deny Thee."[2] Nay, Peter, that will not do. Pride goeth before a fall and God resists the proud.

In this regard those Christians resemble Peter who are conceited about their real or imaginary virtues, who find pleasure in thoughts of self-adulation and who, therefore, in their hearts prefer themselves to others whom they despise. Those especially resemble Peter who waive aside all admonitions and counsels of parents and of superiors and who, with proud disdain, care naught for them. They have all set their foot upon the way that leads to a denial of faith.

The other more remote cause of Peter's fall was

1 St. John, xiii., 33, 36–38; St. Luke, xxii., 33, 34.
2 St. Matthew, xxvi., 31–35; St. Mark, xiv., 27–31.

his *neglect of prayer.* This cause is most intimately connected with the preceding one. Whosoever confides too much in himself cannot easily be convinced of the necessity of prayer. Christ had urged Peter in definite terms to watch and to pray because otherwise he could not help but fall into approaching temptations. This was laying upon him a serious obligation. It is true, as we have already considered, that Peter's negligence in prayer was not a grievous sin and, therefore, would not of itself, without the other concurrent causes, have entailed his sad fall. Nevertheless, neglect of prayer, lukewarmness in its performance and the omission of prescribed prayers, are always a step in advance on the way to perdition. A man without prayer is like a soldier without weapons, and nights not begun with a good evening prayer are often fraught with danger to the soul.

The proximate cause was the *sinful occasion* to which Peter exposed himself. Why did he associate with Christ's enemies, with the impious? Why did he talk and chat with them? The Saviour had not bid him to do so. Neither was it zeal for souls or for Christ's glory that led him to mingle with the servants and guards. In the beginning indeed, this was not a sin. It was the result of thoughtlessness and imprudence. In sadness and trouble, the disciple entirely forgot the admonition of the Master. For this reason, we must not charge the apostle with having rushed of his own free will into a sinful occasion, as far as the first denial is concerned. Weakened by pride and lukewarmness, he fell into an unforeseen temptation, to overcome which, however, the grace of God was at his command. But he failed to co-operate with it. But why did Peter return to the godless, after his sad experience, and after having started to leave them? Why did he remain in surroundings which he knew to be dangerous? After that, a maid-servant sufficed to make him deny his faith a second time, turn perjurer and curse and execrate himself.

This fall of the prince of the apostles is a most forcible sermon on the necessity of carefully avoiding sinful occasions. The company of the godless shook the powerful rock and uprooted the mighty cedar of Lebanon. "In the presence of the servants of the high-priests," writes venerable Bede,[1] "Peter denied knowing Him as man whom he had confessed to be the Son of God when among his fellow-apostles." What then should they not fear who, without necessity, are continually mingling with outsiders and enemies of the faith, yea who even prefer to choose their friends from among them. They are indeed Catholics who bear a close resemblance to the reed, as far as their firmness in the faith is concerned. What have they not to fear who join societies in which Jews and Gentiles, Protestants and Catholics walk together arm in arm. Finally how dangerous it is to the faith, or at the very least, to

[1] In Marc. 1, 4, c. 14 in fine.

its profession and to a Christian life in accordance with it, to obligate one's self in contracting matrimony to associate most intimately, as long as life lasts, with one outside the faith, with an apostate Catholic or with a Free-mason. Undoubtedly, God at times works miracles of mercy; some mixed marriages have been the occasion of splendid conversions and, in particular cases, such marriages have brought forth not merely good Christians but even heroes of the faith. Still, these cases are and always will be exceptions. Whoever is about to take such a step, would act presumptuously were he to expect such a miracle from God. On the other hand, we may count thousands of persons of both sexes who once were pious, full of faith and well grounded in their religion, but who, after contracting mixed marriages, gradually became negligent of their spiritual duties, fell deeper and deeper, until finally they publically joined the number of infidels or non-Catholics. Ah! how sad and woeful and terrible is the death, the funeral and burial of Catholics who in one or other of the above mentioned ways have fallen away from the faith. Have we not been witnesses of it very recently? Instead of the De Profundis we heard the muffled sound of Turkish drums; instead of the Miserere, a melancholy dirge; instead of the Requiem, an apotheosis delivered by a Protestant preacher; instead of the Libera, a sentimental funeral song, rendered by a vocal chorus just returning from a masked ball.

Peter frequented bad company and denied his

faith. Now, if every sinful occasion is dangerous to the soul and therefore to be shunned, it is much more necessary to avoid the occasion of impurity, because man is naturally more inclined to this vice than to any other. The avoidance of dangers leading to impurity is even a most important factor in preserving the faith. For impurity is a wide roadway leading to infidelity. Oh, Christian youth, whose soul is still resplendent in its first innocence, who still treadest the path of purity and chastity, it needs not a wild beast to tear the garb of thine innocence, it needs not a cyclone to cast thee down! No; one woman can accomplish it. Christian man, who livest faithfully according to thy holy faith and rulest thy family with exemplary conscientiousness, it needs not a band of robbers to destroy the happiness of thy home; it requires not the sophistical arguments of a teacher of errors nor of an impious philosopher to make of thee a fool, a maniac, an unbeliever. One woman can accomplish it. And thou, venerable old man with silvery hair, thou who hast to thy credit a long life filled with virtue and merit,—remember Solomon! Thou hast not yet perfect assurance of dying in the grace and charity of God. And hell need not arise from its depths to plunge thee into eternal perdition. One woman can accomplish it. There is only *one* woman, *one* maid whom we may approach without fear and full of confidence. It is the handmaid of the Lord, the always pure and immaculate Virgin Mary. This strong Woman has even the power to uplift those who have fallen and to shield us all from the fall.

But let us return to Peter. We have considered the causes of his denial. Let us now consider the sorrow he felt for it.

III.

The enemies of Christ were already rejoicing at having won over a second Judas in the person of Peter. Hell was glad that the foundation upon which the Church was to be built was already wrecked. Hell triumphed already over the downfall and ruin of the whole edifice. Then the cock crowed, and the menials led the Saviour through the court-yard past Peter. The Lord turned and looked at him. At once Peter remembered the word spoken to him by the Redeemer, "Before the cock crow twice, thou shalt deny me thrice." And going out, he wept bitterly.

We may here clearly distinguish a two-fold grace: an exterior and an interior grace. The crow of the cock was to remind the disciple of the Saviour's warnings as well as of his own presumption and unfaithfulness, whilst the look of grace was to touch the disciple's eye and his heart and wound his soul in its inmost depths. Meantime, as the Gospel intimates, Peter understood the cock's crow only after receiving the inward grace. The heavenly sun alone can melt the ice crust that encompasses the heart of the sinner.

In the midst, therefore, of His sufferings and overwhelmed with sorrows, the Redeemer still thinks of his ungrateful and unhappy apostle and does everything to convert him. He could not well speak to him. But He gave him one look, turning toward him a face disfigured, bespewn and bloody, but divine and full of heavenly mildness. And Peter going forth wept bitterly. If even the eye of a mother has power to conquer hearts, St. Jerome rightly thinks that it was "impossible for him to remain in the darkness of denial, who had gazed upon the light of the world."[1]

Let us now take notice of the qualities of this sorrow. It was a *quick,* an instantaneous contrition. The reason why many a sinner lives on and dies in sin is not to be found in a lack of exterior and interior graces. God has spoken to him often through the voice of parents, of priests, of missionary fathers, of good friends and by means of various accidents. God has looked into his heart, urged and encouraged him to conversion by inner lights and impulses. But the sinner spurned the grace and put off repentance to a future time, to the hour of death.

Peter, the Apostle, did not act thus. To receive the grace and to follow it were on his part simultaneous acts. The Redeemer had scarcely looked at him, when he began to shed tears.

His contrition was *sincere* and serious. He went forth and hid himself until evening in a cavern, as the legend has it, in order to bewail his sin. He also repaired the scandal he had given.

[1] In Matth. 26, 75. Migne 26, col. 203.

He recanted his error. On the day of Pentecost, before thousands of people, before the whole city, before the whole world in fact, he loudly proclaimed that he had known the Risen One. Besides, he rendered more than sufficient compensation. He had strengthened the enemies of Christ in their unbelief. He therefore hastened from town to town, from country to country to preach the doctrine of the Crucified, and to win over all men to the faith of Christ Risen. Now, indeed, after having come to a knowledge of his own weakness and after confessing so humbly, "Lord, thou knowest all things: thou knowest that I love thee"[1] he became the proper man to confirm in the faith even his brethren. Now, taught by sad experience, he had learned to pity poor sinners and was able to lead them to the love of Jesus Christ. To strike with the sword and to cut off people's ears has never converted anybody. The case of Malchus illustrates this.

Finally Peter's contrition was *lasting*. Tradition tells us that at every crow of the cock the tears broke forth anew and rushed down the furrows on his manly face. Eventually Peter went to Rome. There, shedding his blood in acknowledging Christ, he was finally to blot out the fault which by his tears he had striven to wash away during life. Now that he had humility, he could keep the promise, which he had, in proud self-elation, once made to his Master, "I am ready to

[1] St. John, xxi., 17.

go with Thee to death.'' With joy and exultation he greets the holy Cross and presses it lovingly to his bosom; rejoicing and triumphant, he extends his arms upon it. The honor, however, of dying in the same manner as his Master he humbly declines, in consideration of his past sin.

Ah! how good and loving Our Redeemer is! Why should we fear or tremble on account of our sins? How carefully He seeks the lost sheep! How joyfully He takes it in His arms! How generous Our Saviour is to those who sincerely turn to Him, no matter how great and deplorable their fall may have been! Christ harbored no animosity against penitent Peter. He recalled no promise made to Him. He kept every promise even to the minutest detail. He made Peter the foundation of His Church and raised him above all the other apostles. He even established for him a throne in the capital city of the world. He gave him a kingdom over which the sun should never set. He adorned him with the crown of martyrdom, with the crown of eternal life. For our benefit, however, He gave him the keys of heaven in order that through his mediation not only the innocent but all penitent sinners might enter therein.

CHAPTER X.

THE DEATH OF THE TRAITOR

"And casting down the pieces of silver in the temple, he departed; and went and hanged himself."
(St. Matthew, xxvii., 5.)

After this night of suffering, so full of sorrows and of humiliations, Christ had a second hearing before Caiphas and the Council, the members of which—seventy-one in number—were all present with the possible exception of Nicodemus and of Joseph of Arimathea. Many of them had taken but little rest and were still fatigued from the night's vigils. But because the time was employed in persecuting the Son of God, they had willingly sacrificed their sleep. The session of the great Council again took place in the mansion of Caiphas. Since he had lost the power of adjudicating criminal cases, the court-room proper, situated in the south-western corner of the inner court of the temple, was no longer used. If, as some think, Christ had been led from the house of Caiphas first to the court of the temple and then to Pilate, St. John, who mentions the walk to Annas, would have filled out his narrative by mentioning this also, as none of the goings and comings to which Christ submitted out of love for us, was to be abandoned to oblivion.

The object of this assembly was, according to Holy Writ, "that they might put Him to death."[1] It was not, then, convened for the purpose of a just inquiry, or of a second conscientious examination of witnesses, but in order to legitimize through the grand Council, the only rightful authority, the death-decree pronounced at an illegal time and, as seems probable, by the minor Council only and thus to preserve before the public the appearance of a legitimate transaction. Then they deliberated as to the most feasible means of inducing Pilate to approve and execute the judgment. It appeared advisable to drop the accusation of blasphemy as likely to make little impression on the unbelieving pagan, and, in its stead, to urge the plea of treason. The judges, therefore, asked, "If thou be the Christ, tell us,"[2] which according to their idea, meant, "If thou be that descendant of David, who, according to the promise, is to re-establish the kingdom and to rule as king, temporal king, of course, then tell us." They pretended to be ready for an impartial examination of His legitimate claims, but their purpose was to gather up any expression of His which might compromise Him before the tribunal of the pagan. Jesus, understanding this plan, advanced no more explanations. "If I shall tell you," said He, "you will not believe me. And

[1] St. Matthew, xxvii., 1.
[2] St. Luke, xxii., 66–71.

f I shall also ask you—*i. e.*, try, by questions, to induce you to acknowledge the truth—you will not answer me." He alluded to the question He had put them three days before, relating to the baptism of John, which question they had not yet answered him. "But," He continues with Divine authority, "although my death be agreed upon, although the Son of Man, at your mercy, now waives His defense, from now on, from the time of His death, caused by you, He shall sit on the right hand of God and then he shall be *your* Judge."

Thus, in a few words, Christ tore aside the veil of deceit woven by His enemies, and, while thundering into their souls a last warning, He at once brought back the discourse to the main question, to the subject of His Divinity. Together they all interrupted Him by exclaiming, "Art thou then the Son of God?" He replied, "You say, that I am." In these words, testimony of the Divinity of Christ is given to the entire great Council, and it was clearly established, in these repeated hearings, what really was the sole cause of the Saviour's condemnation and of His death. The judges then said, "What need we any farther testimony? For we ourselves have heard it from his own mouth." This closed the hearing before the grand Council and the condemnation was not renewed. The trial must now begin before the Roman governor.

Whilst Christ was being led to Pilate, and whilst He was before him, one of the principal personages disappeared forever from the scene. "Judas," says Holy Writ, "who betrayed Him, seeing that He was condemned; repenting himself, brought back the thirty pieces of silver to the chief-priests and ancients, saying: I have sinned in betraying innocent blood. But they said: What is that to us? look thou to it. And casting down the pieces of silver in the temple, he departed and went and hanged himself with a halter." As the high-priests did not deem it proper that the money, the price of blood, should be deposited in the temple, they bought with it a potter's field for the sepulture of pagans. Thus the prophecy of Jeremias was fulfilled.[1]

There are three scenes, three pictures which here merit our attention. They represent

I. Judas penitent,

II. The heartless and hypocritical high-priest and

III. The despair and the death of the disciple.

I.

There is no doubt that Judas was sorry for his treason. Holy Writ tells us that he repented himself. However, let us examine both the *occasion* and the *quality* of this repentance.

The occasion leading Judas to repentance was the sight of the terrible effects, entirely unforeseen, of his treason. "Judas who betrayed Him, seeing that He was condemned, *repenting* himself." It

[1] St. Matthew, xxvii., 3–10.

appears clearly from the Scriptures that when Judas betrayed the Lord, he neither foresaw nor intended the awful results that ensued. He had no idea that his act would cause the Lord such terrible outrages and the loss of life. He had often witnessed how Christ walked unharmed through the midst of His enemies who sought to kill Him, how He often found ways and means to escape them. He hoped that now He would escape in like manner. It will not harm the Lord much, thought he, at most it may cause Him a little annoyance and I shall have thirty pieces of silver more. Now he sees how everything turns out differently. He beholds how Christ is dragged from one high-priest to another. He witnesses the terrors of the passion. He hears Him condemned to death in the house of Caiphas. The sight of the results of his deed makes its weighty import clear to him. "He repents himself." He would fain have his deed undone; he runs after the high-priests on the way to Pilate to cancel the abominable contract; filled with loathsome disgust, he throws the money down in the temple at the feet of the priests offering the morning sacrifice.

From this incident we may draw a two-fold lesson. When Satan tempts us to grievous sin, he shows us some good or other to be had by committing it. To one he offers money, to another vain honor, to another sensual pleasure, and he would make us believe that, if we obtained this one good, our happiness would be complete. All that, however, is vain deception. As soon as the sin is committed, we experience what Judas experienced and what our first parents experienced long before. Our eyes are opened. It is only by resisting temptation and by despising the seeming goods of earth that we secure to ourselves true happiness.

We should, furthermore, carefully avoid the sin of scandal, not only in serious things but also in minor matters. Even if harm to one's neighbor is neither intended nor foreseen, who can determine results? The bad example given to one's neighbor in small matters only and in the commission of merely venial sin, may be to him the first link in a long chain of serious errors.

Let us now see whether the quality of the sorrow of Judas was such that, on its account, his sin could be forgiven. For that purpose, it was required in the first place that his contrition be perfect, as the sacrament of penance was not yet established. But the contrition of Judas was, at most, imperfect only. Judas bewailed his sin because he had shed innocent blood, that is because of its own atrocity. Had he considered this atrocity of his sin not only with the eyes of reason, but also with the eyes of faith, his sorrow would have been supernatural, it is true, but nevertheless only imperfect and not sufficient for justification. However, according to the commentators of Scripture, the sorrow of Judas lacked every reference to God; he measured the enormity of his treason by its natural, sad results only and from a purely natural point of view, and thus it was solely a natural sorrow. This appears more credible from the fact that the apostle, as we have seen before, had lost all faith in the divinity of Christ. He saw in Christ nothing more than a man.

Furthermore, to render the forgiveness of sin possible, the hope of pardon must be united with contrition. But Judas despaired. Finally, to obtain pardon, he should have had the earnest determination to make reparation and to undo, as far as possible, the unhappy results of his treachery. Freely and with full deliberation, he had gone to the high-priests and had asked them, "What will you give me and I will deliver him unto you?" It was, then, not enough to cast the thirty pieces of silver at their feet. He should have gone to the house of Pilate, he should have forced his way through the crowd to the very seat of the judge, he should there publicly and solemnly have sworn that Christ was the victim of intrigue and of foul calumny. Instead of all that, he took his departure.

Oh, that Catholics would never approach the tribunal of Penance with the contrition of a Judas! The betrayer of innocence affirms that he is sorry for his abominable deed. But is not the disgrace which he brought upon himself and others the only motive for his sorrow? Whilst trembling in his whole body, many a drunkard, many a libertine affirms his compunction for past excesses. A shattered nervous system, a squandered fortune, the unhappiness wrought in a family may be the only motive of such sorrow. Many parents bewail, with bitter tears, the sad effects of a misguided education of their children. Would that they deplored their own negligence by which they offended God grievously. Nor should it be forgotten that, to be reconciled to God, one must necessarily have the will to repair any damage done to the honor, to the property, to the bodily health and to the soul of one's neighbor.

We shall now examine the second picture. It shows us the heartless and at the same time hypocritical high-priests.

II.

As we have already remarked, Judas, in his despair, rushed after the high-priests, in order that, by returning the thirty pieces of silver, he might cancel the contract made with them and liberate the Saviour. How great was his disappointment! In his boundless sorrow he finds no sympathy among his old friends. They cast him aside with contempt as they would a dog. Not a word of pity, not a word of solace. Nothing but the contemptuous heartless answer, "What is that to us? Look you to it." O ye obdurate miscreants! You would still pretend to be innocent. What is it to us if thou hast committed a crime? Listen to St. Chrysostom: "You purposely hide your eyes behind a veil of feigned ignorance." You have hired the traitor; you will answer for it before the judgment seat of God.

Many a deceived person can complain of similar

heartless treatment. Before the deed they hear naught but great promises. Afterwards they are told, "What is that to me? Look you to it." And when driven to extremities, the culprit will even perjure himself in court and swear that he had nothing to do with the case. Many a free-thinker, who formerly was a Catholic, may experience like heartlessness. "Call a priest," exclaimed Voltaire on his death-bed, "I want to confess." "What is that to us? Look you to it," was the answer of impious friends. The same harshness has been shown many a Catholic wife. The pact was signed and a solemn promise given that the Catholic party should enjoy the free and untrammeled practice of religion and that the children of either sex should be reared in the Catholic faith. But when it comes to putting into practice what has been promised, the Protestant too often says, "What is that to me? Look you to it." It happens at times that men also meet with rebuffs of the same sort. When they sought admission to societies forbidden by Holy Church, they asked, "What will you give me, and I will deliver unto you my Catholic faith, I will abandon my Church?" The bargain was made. But when it comes to dying, the fellow lodge-members and, what appears almost impossible, even the Catholic wife, see to it that the sacraments be not administered, that the body be interred in unconsecrated ground, that the soul go to hell. The impious wife sacrifices the salvation of her husband in order not to lose the life-insurance money.

But I erred; allow me to correct myself. The unfortunate man did not say to the lodge, "What will you give me?" but "what shall I give you?" for he gets not even a cent of all this price of blood. In many cases he had to save and scrape to have his assessments ready for the lodge, he had to put up with hard labor and privation to damn his soul. Now the widow reaps the benefit and already entertains the fond hope of a better chance of marriage. Judas, the traitor, was better off in one respect. He, at least, got his money. "What is that to us? Look you to it." Ah! how the devils in hell will, for all eternity, with grinning sneers, hiss these words at the damned soul, when it attempts to make them responsible for the sad lot into which they have plunged it.

The high-priests and pharisees were heartless; they were hypocritical at the same time. The treasury of the temple was not too sacred to furnish the price of the treason. The bargain with Judas appeared neither unprincipled nor disgraceful. But to have driven the poor disciple into despair, what was that to them? To restore the money to the temple, no, that would never do. The temple was too sacred. "It is not lawful to put it into the corbona," they said. That was a lie. Only the money by lechery was debarred![1] The greatest scoundrels swallow camels. Then they talk of conscience, play the hypocrites and strain at gnats.

[1] Deut., xxiii., 18.

Those hypocritical pharisees and priests find their exact counterparts in many free-masons of to-day. To lure Catholic men to perjury, to apostasy, to plunge them into the greatest of all misfortunes, causes them no pangs of conscience. But the appearance of religion must be preserved. Hence they carry the apron of "humanity" and "philanthropy"! From one end of the year to the other, they never appear in church; they never hear mass, but they open and close their meetings with sentimental prayers to the "Grand Architect of the Universe." And are there not Catholics who resemble the pharisees in that they are excessively strict in the observance of sundry devotions and customs, often of their own making, whilst they unhesitatingly neglect the commandments of God and especially the requirements of fraternal charity?

Let us now cast our eyes upon the last scene. It shows us the despair and the death of the disciple.

III.

Judas saw himself most shamefully abandoned by his alleged friends. It was his own fault. By his sin he had rendered himself despicable in their estimation. This was the last grace God gave him to bring him back to Christ. But instead of returning, he filled the measure of his sins by despairing of God's mercy.

In all this, we may recognize the infernal cunning of the wicked enemy. Before the deed, he obscures the understanding of the sinner, he seeks to deceive him by many sophistries; he benumbs conscience, he adds to the will fearlessness, courage and daring. But as soon as sin is committed, he opens the eyes of the unhappy sinner. With excessive exactitude he reproduces the malice of the crime; he now tortures conscience with the most excruciating pangs. He shows the sinner hell opened and the drawn sword of an avenging God. "Judas," said Satan, "what hast thou done? The voice of thy brother, thy master's blood crieth for vengeance to heaven from the earth."

Oh, if ever, on account of past sins and faults, the evil enemy should seek to arouse discouragement, distrust and despair in our hearts, we must crush such temptations in their very beginning. In such moments we should recall the consoling words which God spoke through His prophet Ezechiel, "I desire not the death of the wicked, but that the wicked turn from his way and live;"[1] and the words of the Saviour, "I came not to call the just, but sinners to penance."[2] We must then remember the love and mercy with which He pardoned Peter, Mary Magdalene, and the thief on the cross. We must pray to Him and follow the advice of St. Augustine, "If thou dreadest God, throw thyself into His arms."

Had Judas acted thus, had he given Christ a chance to glance at him, had he, at least, hastened

[1] Ezech., xxxiii., 11.
[2] St. Luke, v., 32.

to Mary, the refuge of sinners, he would have found solace, encouragement and pardon, and now he would belong to the choir of holy apostles. But the love of our blessed Mother was extinct in the heart of Judas; respect for her and confidence in her were wanting. One who truly reveres Mary, says St. Bernard, will never be lost. But Judas despaired. "O Judas," writes St. Leo,[1] "thou hast become more abominable and more unfortunate than all others, because penance hath not called thee back to the Lord, but despair hath drawn thee to the halter. Hadst thou only awaited the result of thy crime. Hadst thou postponed thy disgraceful suicide until the blood of Christ had been shed for all sins. . . . Why didst thou place distrust in the Goodness of Him who refused thee not the kiss of peace, when, with the band and cohort of armed men, thou didst approach Him?"

But Judas cast down the thirty pieces of silver in the temple,—he departed—he went away—he hanged himself with a halter. He burst asunder in the midst and all his bowels gushed out.[2] Such was the awful end of the traitor.

"The unhappy traitor," says Venerable Bede,[3] "found a worthy punishment in that the knot of a rope choked the throat whence issued the word of treason. He found a worthy place of demise. Having delivered to death the Lord of men and

1 Serm. 3 de Pass. c. 3.

2 Acts, i., 18.

3 S. Act. Ap. c. 1. Migne t. 92, col. 944.

angels, like to Achitopheles and Absolom who sought the life of David, their king, he perished, suspended in the air, an abomination in the sight of heaven and of earth, an associate of the evil spirits of the air. Death overtook him in a worthy manner in that his insides, where the venom of treachery had matured, burst and gushed out and from the air spread upon the earth." A few hours afterwards the Saviour was nailed to the cross which was high enough to look down upon the soulless corpse of the apostle at the bottom of the declivity.

To cover their misdeed with the cloak of piety and religion, the high-priests soon afterwards bought, with the blood-money, the field of a potter as a burial-place for heathens. They took the price of Him Who was prized and Who yet was priceless, Whom they had bought, not from the heathens, but, O disgrace! from a child of Israel, and they gave it for the field of a potter, of whom Jeremias, at the inspiration of God, had made mention.[1] Probably the field had become exhausted of its clay and was consequently useless and cheap. What hypocrites and fools the high-priests were! They had put their heads together and consulted how to dispose of the money, so that the declaration of Judas concerning the innocence of Christ, might be stifled in silence. But the wisdom of God foiled their prudence. The people soon began to taunt them about the money

[1] Note 8.

that had been paid for the potter's field. Already on the fiftieth day after the Lord's demise the field was called the field of blood.[1]

"This name," says St. Chrysostom, "proclaims their murder louder than any trumpet. Had they deposited the money in the treasury, the affair would not have become so public." But in this way the high-priests reared a monument to themselves to perpetuate their eternal disgrace. Besides, it is very noteworthy that the price of Christ's blood was used for the sepulchral repose of the heathens.

In this field the body of the traitor was buried. Judas was, then, the first Catholic who, to use a modern phrase, was buried in unconsecrated ground. According to ancient traditions,[2] this field had the wonderful and grewsome property of turning, within twenty-four hours, into dust and ashes all bodies buried therein. Untold dishonor burdens the name and the memory of the traitor throughout all ages. And his soul—and this is the saddest of all—burns in the deepest abyss of hell and shall continue to burn therein during all eternity. O crucified Lord Jesus Christ, through the intercession of Thy sorrowful mother, deliver us from such an end and grant us the grace of a happy death.

1 Acts, i., 19.

2 Adrichomius, Descr. Jesus, n. 216; cf. Corn. à Lapide Matth. 27, 8.

CHAPTER XI.

THE ACCUSATION BEFORE PILATE

> "They began to accuse him, saying: We have found this man perverting our nation, and forbidding to give tribute to Cæsar, and saying that he is Christ the king."
>
> (St. Luke, xxiii., 2.)

From the Garden of Olives Christ was led to Annas, from Annas to Caiphas, from Caiphas to Pilate. How many steps Our Divine Saviour had to take on this day before He finally was allowed to die for us! On the other hand, how many steps the sinner takes to offend his Saviour and to fall into the embrace of eternal death. On account of His increasing fatigue and of His continued maltreatment, the repeated marches of Christ became more tiring and, at the same time, more humiliating, it being now broad day-light and the number of curious and jeering people having increased. On the way, two circumstances especially must have offended, in the highest degree, the self-respect of the Redeemer. He was now bound, not with ropes, but with chains. It meant, that the accused, now bound over to the civil authority, had been found guilty and condemned by the spiritual authority. Then, the delivering of

Christ unto Pilate was not being done by a few subalterns, but by the entire grand council, by all the high-priests, the scribes, the ancients and the pharisees. Such an extraordinary cortege must naturally have produced among the onlookers the impression that the most abject criminal was being led to Pilate. Thus was accomplished what Christ foretold in the Gospel according to St. Matthew (xx., 19), namely, that He would be delivered to the Gentiles. Jesus thus became the real Joseph, delivered by his brethren unto strangers.

When the high-priests, the scribes and the ancients arrived before the house of Pilate, they made their servants and soldiers lead Jesus into the hall. They themselves did not enter, in order not to be defiled and thus prohibited from eating the pasch. Pilate, therefore, went out to them and said, "What accusation bring you against this man?" They answered and said to him, "If he were not a malefactor, we would not have delivered him up to thee." Pilate then said to them, "Take him you and judge him according to your law." But the Jews said, "It is not lawful for us to put any man to death." Then they began to accuse Him and said, "We have found this man perverting our nation and forbidding to give tribute to Cæsar, and saying that he is Christ the king."[1] Pilate, thereupon, retired into the courtroom to give Christ a hearing.

[1] St. John, xviii., 28–34; St. Luke, xxiii., 1, 2.

Let us consider:

I. The motives of the accusation,

II. The negotiations with Pilate concerning it and

III. The subject of the charge itself.

I.

First of all, the great council had no right to execute the sentence of death pronounced against Christ without the consent of Pilate. The very first Roman governor had received from the emperor the exclusive power of inflicting capital punishment. On its own authority, the great council could impose only subordinate punishments, such as the flagellation. When a criminal was condemned to any mode of execution provided for by the Mosaic law, such as stoning, decapitation, burning or hanging, the charge and the proceedings had to be submitted to the governor for approval. This held good also relating to blasphemy, sorcery or any other crime against religion.

In this case, however, a simple ratification of the sentence on the part of Pilate would not have served the purpose of the great council. As has already been mentioned, the council could not according to the Mosaic law, pronounce and, much less, execute a sentence of death on the day of the trial. This would relegate the execution to the following day. But the following day being the paschal Sabbath, it would have to be postponed until after the paschal holidays, or for fully eight days, as was afterwards done by Herod in the case of St. Peter. However, such a postponement might thwart all the plans of the high-priests. They still heard the hosannas ringing in their ears, and the fact that Christ had many secret adherents made them apprehend a change in public opinion which would render impossible any further proceedings. They therefore resolved to work the matter into the hands of Pilate in such a manner that he would cause his heathen soldiery to execute the sentence of death on that very day, before the advent of the Pasch.[1]

We shall now pass on to the negotiations with Pilate concerning the case.

II.

The Roman governors did not reside in Jerusalem, but in Cæsarea, beautifully located on the sea shore. There they had taken possession of the royal palace of the Herodians. When on the great festivals they came to Jerusalem to maintain order, they would dwell in the Herodian castle, called by the Romans Castle Antonia. It commanded a view of the court of the temple and had a garrison. There, near the temple and surrounded by their soldiers, the governors watched proceedings. As the Herodians could not well be deprived of all their holdings, they were left in possession of the royal palace on Sion, which was not a source of danger, because it was commanded by strong tow-

[1] See note 9.

ers in the neighborhood. Herod I., who built the castle, had lavished upon it all his love for splendor. It had the extent and the arrangement of a palace, and, as Flavius Josephus writes, "Its interior was so divided into compartments, halls, baths and gymnasiums that, owing to the universal conveniences of a city which it contained and to the splendor which it exhibited, it resembled a royal palace."[1]

When they arrived here, the high-priests and scribes caused the heathen menials to lead Jesus into the castle. They themselves did not enter, "that they might not be defiled, but that they might eat the pasch." The strict Jew, be it understood, considered the house of a heathen to be legally unclean.[2] To enter it, according to pharisaic tradition, entailed a defilement of seven days. Besides, old Herod had adorned the interior of the castle with many idolatrous and shameless statues, and the orthodox Jew looked upon it as a heathen temple and an abode of lepers. There were, then, two reasons on account of which the high-priests would not enter the castle. They would not be defiled. Legal defilement would hinder them from eating the paschal lamb.

Jesus, then, stood before Pilate, the representative of the Roman emperor. At the sight of the Saviour, so terribly mangled and maltreated, Pilate undoubtedly waxed very wroth at the high-priests. For his own sense of justice must have suggested

[1] B. J. V. 5, 8.
[2] Cf. Acts, x., 28.

to him that it was unfair and cruel to inflict on a sentenced criminal other punishments than those contained in the sentence, especially when the criminal stood before him in the quality of an accused only. Besides this, the remarkable calmness, dignity and majesty of Jesus Christ as opposed to the passionate clamor and ravings of the Jews, caused him to sympathize entirely with the Saviour. He was indignant, furthermore, at the insult offered him by the high-priest, who avoided entering his house as if he were an unclean dog. He therefore went out and gruffly and in a tone of indignation asked them, "What accusation bring you against this man?" They answered and said to him, "If he were not a malefactor, we would not have delivered him up to thee."

It appears singular, indeed, that against all custom the high-priests should suggest to Pilate that he approve and execute the sentence of death, merely upon their word and credit, without even looking into the facts of the case. They certainly had good reasons for such a maneuver. Had Pilate heard the contradictory testimony of the false witnesses, he would have branded them as barefaced calumniators. But the high-priests could not adduce any political grounds of action. To their crafty question about His earthly kingdom, the Redeemer had made no reply. The affirmation of the question put to Him at the midnight session, whether He was the Christ, was considered by the high-priests a blasphemy, on account of the added expression, "The Son of the living God." But they would not establish their accusation upon a blasphemy in the court of Pilate, the heathen. Thus, with legal documents and charges lacking and Pilate insisting on a definite charge, there remained nothing else to do for the members of the grand council but to play the role of the injured and, as it were in holy indignation, to cry out, "If he were not a malefactor, we would not have delivered him up to thee," *we* the guardians of the law, *we*, the judges in Israel, *we*, the priests of Jehovah. Pilate thereupon said, "Take him you and judge him according to your law." But the high-priests answered, "It is not lawful for us to put any man to death."

To determine with certainty the sense of these words of Pilate and of the high-priests, it would be necessary to have been present at the conversation and to have read the heart or, at least, the features of Pilate. Some interpreters deem it possible that by his language Pilate waived his right to hear and examine the charge, empowering the Jews, without any further ado, to inflict on Christ any mode of capital punishment allowed by their law. Perceiving their intention, he would thus shift all the odium on them, whilst remaining a stranger to the affair himself. But that explanation seems to be opposed to the sense of justice manifested by Pilate throughout the course of the trial until his private interest became involved. One does not readily grant a favor to an impertinent fellow against whom one is already prejudiced and who, besides, prefaces his demand with an insult.

Other interpreters are therefore of the opinion that Pilate, puzzled at the strange conduct of the high-priests in refusing him an insight into the documents, conceived the idea that there was question only of a small misdemeanor, the punishment of which lay within the competency of the great council. The good impression which Christ had made on him tended to confirm him in this opinion. Besides, the high-priests had not definitely charged any greater crime; they had merely called Him a malefactor. According to this explanation, the words, "It is not lawful for us to put any man to death" called the attention of Pilate to his error and gave him to understand that here there was no question of a misdemeanor but of a criminal case the adjudication of which belonged to the governor. But opposed to this view is the fact that Pilate, being acquainted with the customs of the Jews, knew full well that they would bring an accused to him only when there was question of meting out capital punishment.

The following is perhaps the best explanation: Pilate became highly incensed at the impudent suggestions of the proud Jews. To punish them, he reminded them, in a tone of derision and with cutting sarcasm, of their dependence on the Romans, which prevented them from executing their own laws without his permission, as if he said, "If you are not willing to bring a charge against Him, take Him and judge Him if you dare and if it be in your power.'' This made the high-priests comprehend that they could not play fast and loose with Pilate. Abashed, stifling their anger with an effort and acknowledging their helplessness, they then produced their charges.[1]

No matter from what point of view the conversation may be considered, one thing is certain. The high-priests learned that they would never attain their object unless they submitted definite charges. We are anxious to hear them.

III.

The accusation was as follows: ''We have found this man perverting our nation, and forbidding to give tribute to Cæsar by saying that he is Christ the king.'' Here we have an occasion to study in its most despicable form the infernal cunning, the deceit and the hypocrisy of the high-priests, the scribes and the ancients.

What *cunning!* To judge from the proceedings in the house of Caiphas, one would expect the subject of the charge to be blasphemy or the attack on the temple. But of all this not a word was mentioned before Pilate. Common sense forbade the accusers to mention the tearing down of the temple which was standing before them in all its grandeur. They would not appear ridiculous. And the charge of blasphemy would leave Pilate, the idolater, entirely indifferent. The high-priests,

1 See note 10.

therefore, dropped the former subject of accusation which had brought about the sentence of death, and they submitted to Pilate crimes of which he, the Roman governor and the representative of the emperor, would have to take cognizance. They brand the Redeemer as a person dangerous to the state, as a political criminal.

Furthermore, what *lying* and *deceit* there is in these accusations. "We have found him," they say, "perverting and disturbing our nation, and forbidding to give tribute to Cæsar." But which of the accusers had made even the remotest mention of these crimes before Caiphas? Now "they have found him." Christ had been asked nothing except whether or not He was Christ, that is, the Son of the living God. He had admitted nothing else. But they know how to help themselves. Using calumny as a means, they add the word "king," saying that he is "Christ the *king*." For, if He used the word "king," that is, if He proclaimed Himself a king, it follows naturally that He must have committed the other two political crimes.

Let us consider the three accusations in detail; they throw a clear light on the lying deceit of the high-priests. They call Christ a disturber. Christ, indeed, was a disturber above all others. He disturbed hundreds and thousands of men until they followed Him into the desert and listened for days to His instructions. He disturbed hundreds and thousands of sinners out of their sinful slumbers. But when did He ever excite the people against civil authority, against the governor, against the Roman emperor? Venerable sirs, we demand the proof of your statement, and we promise you that, when you will have furnished your proof, we shall join with you in your accusations against Christ. Furthermore, Christ was said to have forbidden the giving of tribute to Cæsar. But have you already forgotten? Have you not heard from His own mouth the words, "Render unto Cæsar the things that are Cæsar's and unto God the things that are God's?" Christ, you say finally, declared Himself a king. Are you not afraid that the people, on hearing your words, will publicly brand you before Pilate as contemptible calumniators? Are you not aware that the Redeemer hid Himself when the people wished to proclaim Him king?

And consider the *hypocrisy* of these men. They assume the appearance of loyalty. They pose as faithful and devoted subjects of Cæsar. They appear anxious for the welfare of the state. They therefore consider themselves bound in conscience to deliver over to Cæsar's representative for punishment, Christ, the most dangerous of rebels, perverters and enemies of the government. And certainly no more bitter enemies of Cæsar, no more dangerous rebels could be found than these very high-priests, scribes, ancients and Jews in general. The mere thought of Roman rule made them boil with anger. Unceasingly they planned to overthrow it, for which reason forty years afterwards, on account of continued revolts, their city was destroyed from the face of the earth. Even in latter years they had attempted a demonstration against the Roman rule, but it resulted to their disadvantage. In view of this incident, kings and emperors should at last learn to know where to look for those who are dangerous to the state and for enemies of their country. Then, instead of imprisoning and sending into exile bishops and priests and weak nuns, they would imprison and expatriate their accusers. But it is our consolation and our pride to know that God has permitted it in order to spread the holy Catholic church, to save many immortal souls and to make us, the unworthy servants of Jesus Christ, partakers of the glories of the holy Cross.

Then Pilate went back to the courtroom to give Christ a hearing.

How contemptible the vice of calumny and slander is! We ought to avoid even its shadow. The ignominy of it falls back upon Christ. For "as long as you did it to one of these my least brethren, you did it to me."[1] When we are unjustly attacked in our reputation, we shall not give vent to words of anger nor brood over feelings of revenge, but, in imitation of the Saviour, bear the wrong at least with patience.

Let us finally cast one more glance at the accused Lord. Silent He stands in the courtroom. He does not ask what they are saying against Him outside. He does not desire to face the accusers in order to defend Himself. He leaves to Al-

[1] St. Matthew, xxv., 40.

mighty God His defense and His justification. And truly He has reaped most abundant satisfaction. He had been accused as a perverter of the people, and He was silent. And behold! seized by an invisible power, all nations and peoples arise. One nation presses the other onward. They all hasten to embrace the doctrine of the Crucified. It had been said that He forbade to give tribute to Cæsar, and He was silent. And I see princes and kings and emperors who deem it an honor to pay to Christ the tribute of their fealty, princes and kings and emperors who spread before His feet their jewels and their golden crowns. He had been accused of aspiring to overthrow Cæsar, and He was silent. Wait but a few centuries and upon the ruins of the fallen Roman empire there arises a new kingdom, the kingdom of Christ, embracing the entire world. High upon the summit of the Capitol shines the Cross, the victorious symbol of the Hero of Golgotha. He had been accused of attempting to make Himself king, and He was silent—it cost Him His life. And now, for eighteen hundred years, with a mild sway, He has ruled heaven and earth. He is the king of glory, world without end.

CHAPTER XII.

THE FIRST HEARING OF CHRIST BEFORE PILATE

> "Pilate saith to him: What is truth? And when he said this he went out again to the Jews and saith to them: I find no cause in him."
> (St. John, xviii., 38.)

The accusation was high-treason. Pilate returned to the courtroom, took his seat on the judge's bench and cited Jesus before his tribunal. A remarkable trial, indeed! The judge is a pagan governor, the representative of the Roman emperor. The plaintiffs are the highest officials and dignitaries of the Jewish people. The accused is none other than Jesus Christ, the Son of God, the Lord of heaven and earth. The case was a novel one; none like it had ever been witnessed. This man who for three years by His inspired sermons had fairly carried away innumerable crowds of hearers; who, on account of His wonderful deeds, was looked upon as a superior being; a man of the people more than any other, who, some days before, had been led in festal triumph into Jerusalem--now, at the instigation of the same people, stood accused of high-treason before the tribunal of a pagan judge. Let us consider [1]

[1] St. John, xviii., 33–38; St. Matthew, xxvii., 11–14; St. Mark, xv., 2–5; St. Luke, xxiii., 3–7.

I. The hearing detailed and
II. The chief mistake of Pilate during the hearing.

I.

Pilate began the hearing with the words, "Art thou the king of the Jews?" This question reveals to us the keen and expert inquisitor. From among all the charges, he selects that representing the main issue. If Christ were a king, it would follow evidently that He would not allow His subjects to recognize a foreign king nor to pay tribute to him. Then Pilate gave to the charge of the Jews a different construction. He did not ask,, "Hast thou said that thou art a king?" but, "Art thou the king of the Jews?" The question was well put. Had Jesus asserted His claim only by way of boasting without any foundation in fact, there would have been in it no serious danger to the commonwealth. Again, he did not ask, after the indefinite and general manner in which the Jews presented the charge, "Art thou a king?" but, "Art thou the king of the Jews?" For had Christ really been a king, but of a foreign and independent realm, then proper honors were due to Him as an equal of the Roman emperor. The question at issue was whether He was the king of the Jews, of a nation subject and tributary to the Roman emperor. After all his dealings with the Jews, Pilate was certainly aware that they expected a king. He wanted to know whether or not the accused was this king.

Our Divine Lord desired particularly to hear from Pilate's own mouth, whether he had put this question as judge, as an official, or whether he wished, in his private capacity, to ascertain the truth. Certainly Christ had the right to presume that Pilate had a personal interest in learning who the accused really was. His innumerable miracles in proof of His Messianic dignity could surely not have remained unknown to Pilate, who had been in Judea during the entire public life of the Redeemer. Besides, the divine dignity and majesty of Christ, which shone even through His disfigured and sullied countenance, could not fail to make an impression on the pagan. Moreover, in that very moment the Saviour did not fail to supply the interior grace. He therefore asked Pilate: "Sayest thou this thing of thyself, or have others told it thee of me?" Pilate, provoked, answered roughly: "Am I a Jew? Thy own nation and the chief-priests have delivered thee up to me. What hast thou done?" In other words, "Personally, I am indifferent as to what thou art, for I am a pagan and no Jew. I ask thee as judge, because thou hast been accused before me. What then hast thou done? Mention the crime." In order not to provoke Pilate who, as Roman governor, had to shield the emperor, and to restrain him from undue haste and rashness, Christ answered evasively the question regarding His kingly power. He did not deny nor did He declare in express words that He was a king. He merely spoke of His kingdom, that it was not of this world and, therefore, that it bore no resemblance to other kingdoms. Pilate consequently need have no anxiety. No hostile movement would be set on foot against him or the emperor on the part of Christ, Who had neither armies, nor arms, nor strongholds.

This answer seemed to satisfy Pilate to some extent. But he desired more clearness and precision. A kingdom, he thought, without a king, is impossible. But he who has a kingdom must be a king. He therefore repeated his question, "Art thou a king?" With all the modesty becoming one arraigned Jesus answered, "Thou sayest, that I am a king." Then He answered the other question which Pilate had subsequently proposed: "What hast thou done?" But, O Pilate, should Jesus tell thee all that He has done, how, as God, He created heaven and earth, how, as man for three years, He wandered through Palestine dispensing benefits and working miracles, the evening would not see the end of the trial. However, Jesus said, "For this was I born and for this came I into the world; that I should give testimony to the truth." It is my calling and it was my business to teach the truth. Then in a delicate manner Christ gave him the well meant advice to join the ranks of those who were believers in His doctrine: "Every one that is of the truth," that is, who loves the truth, who is interested in learning to know the truth, "heareth my voice."

Now Pilate understood. The answers given convinced him perfectly that Christ was innocent and of no danger to the commonwealth. But how can this be explained? Had Pilate really understood, in its supernatural sense, the answer of Christ regarding His kingdom? No; by stating that personally He cared naught for Christ or for His doctrine, he showed that he had failed to grasp the true sense of Christ's answer, which would have proved so great a grace to him. He rather considered the Saviour Who had spoken to him about the truth and represented Himself as a teacher of the truth to be one of those men such as Pyrrho, Zeno, Thales and Epicurus, who from time to time endowed the world with a new philosophical system and who founded schools of philosophy named after themselves. And because, even at that time, people were wont to see in such founders extraordinary pride, limitless arrogance and excessive self-esteem, Pilate did not find it strange that this new teacher of wisdom vaunted himself as a king before his disciples. He might think it ridiculous, but not dangerous to the state. "To play at kings," he thought, "is done also by children."

But before going out to the Jews, Pilate could not help proposing casually the sarcastic question, "What is truth?" Does truth exist in fact? Is there a man who knows what truth is? Is not everything doubt and uncertainty? By this question Pilate also wished to show how little he, the pagan and statesman, cared for religious and philosophic questions and disputes. And to condemn any one to death because his scientific views differed from those of others, seemed to him entirely improper.

Pilate therefore went out and declared solemnly, "I find no cause in him." Then he caused Jesus to be led forth, whereupon the Jews again began their accusations. Pilate repeatedly urged Christ to defend Himself, but He answered nothing so that Pilate was greatly astonished. He had never met an accused person who was silent in his own defense, even though he knew that the judge favored him. Pilate also would have been extremely glad if Christ by a brilliant speech of defense had helped him out of the unfortunate dilemma in which he found himself. On the one hand, he did not wish to condemn Christ, whom he considered innocent, neither did he, on the other, wish to offend the prominent Jews. But Christ, Who had defended Magdalene and shielded the adulteress, was silent in His own case. Then the high-priests, in their renewed accusations, gave the judge a favorable chance to rid himself of the whole matter. With cries and much noise, the more easily to succeed, they repeated that Christ stirred up the people; that He did it by His teachings all over Judea; that He was not only a rebel Himself, but that He made it a point to preach insubordination and revolt all the way from Galilee to Jerusalem.

These last words the accusers were in hopes would be received as proof of their charge. For Galilee was notorious for its many seditions.

There Roman domination found its most stubborn and energetic opponents. Therefore, they meant to insinuate, Christ must necessarily be a rebel against the emperor, because He came from Galilee. Such methods prevail even to-day in the anti-religious camp: because some members of the Catholic church or of a religious society or order have been guilty of a fault, therefore they all amount to nothing.

Without, however, entering into the idea of the Jews, Pilate merely inquired whether this man was a Galilean, and, when he received an affirmative reply, a burden fell from his heart. He breathed easier. Jesus, then, was a Galilean, consequently from Herod's dominion, and just at that time Herod was in Jerusalem. Pilate immediately gave orders that the Saviour be led to Herod. By doing this, he hoped to rid himself of the case and, at the same time, by this act of politeness and of recognition of his judicial power, to reconcile to himself the good will of Herod, who was his bitter enemy. The high-priests were very well satisfied. By not acceding to their wishes, Pilate had caused them vexation enough. But from Herod, who aspired to the royal crown of Judea and to whom therefore every rival was odious, from Herod, the son of the child-murderer of Bethlehem, from Herod who had made short work of John the Baptist, presenting his head to a dancing-girl, they hoped to obtain better results. Thus closed the first trial of Our Lord and Saviour

Jesus Christ before the vicegerent of the Roman emperor.

Let us now consider the main fault committed by Pilate during its progress.

II.

Even at this first trial, Pilate showed several weak points; he gave evidence of irresolution and of human respect. He dared not liberate an accused whom he knew to be innocent. It was entirely unjust to expose an innocent person to the further ill treatment of the high-priests. But we shall now pass over these faults, which present themselves much more prominently at the second hearing, and consider only that fault which was the reason and source of all subsequent errors and which decided Pilate's eternal destiny. This main fault was indifference to the truth and contempt of it. "Am I a Jew?" he had asked, "What is it to me, a pagan, what thou art?" And when Christ presented Himself as the teacher of the truth, he exclaimed contemptuously, "What is truth?" and turned his back on Christ.

"What is truth?" was Pilate's question to the Saviour. "Does truth really exist?" By this question the pagan world, through the mouth of Pilate, declared itself insolvent and closed its accounts with truth. Through most curious philosophical systems, many pagan investigators and cavilers had arrived at the unanimous conclusion that there is no supreme truth, that everything ends in fallacy and uncertainty—a conclusion to which they more readily subscribed because it disturbed them not in the gratification of the most ignoble passions. Socrates, the wisest of them all, had ventured the statement that he had found the truth. In punishment, the poisoned cup was handed him. Plato, his disciple, died with the declaration that, should man ever arrive at the knowledge of the truth, a God must needs descend to convey it to him. Now, finally, that God had arrived. He stood before Pilate, the representative of paganism. And Pilate asked the happy question, "What is truth?" The Saviour was ready to teach him the truth. And He was all the more ready because Pilate had thus far treated Him justly. But the Roman, despairing of all truth, turns contemptuously from the teacher of eternal truth.

This moment in his life was the decisive one for time and for eternity. Had the pagan, entangled as he was by innumerable doubts, permitted himself to be taught by Christ, he certainly would have received from Him the grace to arrive at the knowledge of divine truth. He also would then have found courage to act and to give a decision according to the known truth. He would not have sentenced Christ to death, and he would have been saved. But he preferred to remain in his doubt; he was indifferent to truth, he despised truth, he resisted the Holy Spirit. That brought him into the "Credo" as a warning example to all despisers of truth; it put his name in that confession by which the Christian expresses his belief in the truth: "Christ, Who suffered under Pontius Pilate."

This indifference to and contempt of truth, this fear of truth and of the obligations it entails, are even nowadays the main reasons why so many are on the way to perdition and to eternal ruin. Indifference to truth and its contempt are the mother of free thought, of religious indifference, of current phrases such as this: that it matters not what or how much one may believe, nor to which religious denomination one may belong, provided one does what is right. This is a potent error. To accept or doubt or reject truth is not the same to Christ, the divine Teacher of truth. He demands the sacrifice of our understanding and of our will. Then again, there are many members of the religious sects, fallen away from the Church, who never get beyond their religious doubts, and many who are fully aware of being in error. What keeps them from taking the decisive step? Nothing but indifference to truth, often joined with a fear of truth and of its practical consequences.

Even among Catholics many follow in the footsteps of Pilate. They are those who feel no need of hearing the truths of our faith explained, although they lack even the most rudimentary knowledge of them. Although, every Sunday and holiday, in our churches, Christ announces the truth through the mouth of His ordained ministers, they allow months and years to pass by without listening to a single sermon. At most they are content with a low mass. Even in times of extraordinary grace, at missions and at jubilees, they turn their backs to Christ, the Teacher of truth.

But the saddest feature of all is that in many countries hundreds and thousands of Catholic children are systematically trained to be Pilates by impiously cruel parents. Without any legitimate cause, they are sent to schools from which religion and religious instruction are banished on principle. I do not wish to cast reproach upon all teachers who instruct in these irreligious schools, as if they purposely spread false doctrines or sought to lead the children into religious indifference. But because in these schools no favorable word may be spoken of religion, and least of all of the Catholic religion; because the text-books, although not always bad, are at the very least colorless and void of religious value; because prayer is an unknown quantity and positively religious education is entirely lacking; therefore, it is religious indifference and contempt of religion which, among all the branches, the poor children acquire the most readily and retain, as a rule, for their entire life. What, in the hour of their death, will such blind parents answer the eternal Judge when He asks them, "Father, mother, what hast thou done?"

There is no surer way to obtain in abundance the favors and grace of our divine Teacher than by being His willing disciples. We should therefore often pray to Him, "Lord, teach us the truth,

Thou hast the words of eternal life."[1] Let us seize joyfully upon all occasions which He presents to us in His church to learn the truths of faith and morals and to arrive at a better understanding of them. Finally, we must lead lives in accordance with the known truth. Then in death, when all outward show and deception vanish, truth will be our light, our solace and our strength, and in heaven it will be our felicity.

In conclusion, let us consider a word spoken by Christ in the hearing before Pilate; it deserves our attention. To the high-priest Caiphas the Saviour had presented Himself as the divinely anointed High-Priest of the New Law, as the promised Messiah, as the true Son of God. Before Pilate who represented the ruler of the Roman world-empire, He declared Himself to be a king as absolutely independent in His kingdom from all worldy power, as the emperor was in his own dominion. "My kingdom," He said, "is not of this world," its object is a supernatural one. But a kingdom which has a supernatural end, cannot possibly be subordinate to a kingdom pursuing merely natural ends. The Church of Christ, therefore, has the right of self-government in the fullest sense of the word. Thus the declaration of Christ before Pilate defined for all times to come the mutual relations of Church and state. Although both are not of the world, they are both in the world. They should use all the means which God has furnished them to attain their objects, which, although different, are not

[1] St. John, vi., 69.

therefore opposed to each other. And for a more perfect attainment of their respective objects, they ought, when occasion offers, to give each other a helpful and friendly hand. But, at the very first meeting in the court of the governor, we behold Church and state in conflict. It may, however, be mentioned to the honor of Pilate that he himself neither began nor fostered the conflict, as in later times was done by so many Christian kings and emperors to their everlasting disgrace and to their eternal woe. Against his will he was drawn into it. Until this moment, Pilate sincerely desired to give to the Church her proper freedom. The conflict between the Roman empire at the zenith of its power and the Church of Christ began later and ended in the downfall of the former. Thus shall crumble into ruin all governments which persecute the kingdom of Christ and in brazen temerity strive to destroy it from the face of the earth.

"My kingdom," my Church, says the Redeemer, "is not of this world." If we, then, would be true children of the Catholic Church, we must, like to our Holy Mother, strive for the supernatural. All other objects which we may legitimately strive for must be subordinate to our supreme, supernatural end. We must not busy ourselves about everything that is upon earth, but we must seek the things that are above, where Christ is sitting at the right hand of God [1] and where He rules as king for all eternity.

[1] Col., iii., 1.

CHAPTER XIII.

CHRIST BEFORE HEROD

"And Herod with his army set him at nought: and mocked him, putting on him a white garment, and sent him back to Pilate."

(St. Luke, xxiii., 11.)

For a long time a bitter enmity had secretly existed between Pilate and Herod. It had not escaped Pilate that Herod, the tetrarch of Galilee, maintained continual and direct negotiations with the imperial court for no other purpose than to bring about the removal of the governors and his own elevation to the throne of Judea. It seems that Herod enjoyed the especial favor of the emperor Tiberius after whom he named his capital city. This, it is said, was shown especially by the fact that Tiberius bestowed upon the tetrarch the dignity of king of Galilee. But it may be that Herod, relying on the favor of the emperor, placed the crown upon his own head as others undoubtedly did in centuries following. On the other hand, Herod was angry at Pilate because the latter had not assisted him in his war against the Arabians. The following incident, according to the narrative of the Jewish historian, Flavius Josephus, finally brought the enmity to an open rupture. For the construction of an expensive aqueduct, Pilate had extorted immense sums from the treasury of the Temple; the laborers he secured from Herod. His violent measures caused excitement and exasperation among the whole Jewish people. To increase the embittered feelings, wily Herod gave secret orders to the architects to provide for poor construction. They obeyed the order and, in consequence, the tower of Siloe collapsed, depriving eighteen artisans of their lives. In revenge for this perfidy of the Galilean ruler, Pilate, at the next paschal festivities, caused masked Romans to fall upon the Galileans while they were offering sacrifices in the Temple, and a great carnage ensued. The result was a rebellion during which several rebels, among others the notorious Barabbas and, probably, the two thieves were taken prisoners. And, to the great chagrin of Pilate, the emperor Tiberius entrusted to Herod the supreme care of the Temple's treasury. Partly on account of these ecclesiastical moneys, partly to protect his Galileans, partly to ingratiate himself with the Jews whose king he wished to be and partly "to satisfy his devotion," Herod wended his way toward Jerusalem to the paschal festivities. As behooved a good father, he took his family with him. By taking part in the paschal supper, they would give a good example to their subjects, repair any possible scandal they might have given and testify publicly to their own orthodoxy.

To this man Herod Pilate ordered the soldiers

to lead Jesus. Again the high-priests, scribes and ancients accompanied Him. Divine Providence so willed it. Had Pilate liberated the Saviour, the high-priests would say, "No wonder! Who knows what lies Christ told Pilate in His own defense when they were alone." Before Herod they could be convinced of His silence. Besides, they could not charge Herod, as they could Pilate, with ignorance and contempt of their law. Their confusion was so much the greater, when Herod did not condemn Him. "And Herod seeing Jesus was very glad, for he was desirous of a long time to see him, because he had heard many things of him; and he hoped to see some sign wrought by him. And he questioned him in many words. But he answered him nothing. And the chief-priests and scribes stood by, earnestly accusing him. And Herod with his army set him at naught; and mocked him, putting on him a white garment, and sent him back to Pilate. And Herod and Pilate were made friends that same day, for before they were enemies one to another."[1]

Let us consider

I. The joy of Herod,
II. The disappointment of Herod,
III. The revenge of Herod.

I.

"And Herod seeing Jesus was very glad." This was not the first time a man was glad to see

[1] St. Luke, xxiii., 8–12.

the Saviour. How glad were the pious shepherds, when following the admonition of the angels, they hastened to the stable and found the Child with Joseph and Its Blessed Mother! How, at the sight of the new-born Saviour, were the wise men of the East recompensed for all the trouble and discomfort of their long journey! "Now thou dost dismiss thy servant, O Lord, in peace," joyfully exclaimed Simeon, the holy old man, when Mary placed the Divine Infant Jesus in his arms. Zacheus also desired greatly to see the Lord and for this purpose he climbed up into a tree. It was the happiest day in his life. If, then, Herod was glad on beholding the Saviour the first time, if, to express his joy, he prepared a splendid reception, if he surrounded himself with his entire court and spoke to Christ with condescending favor, we find nothing strange in it; on the contrary, it appears to us quite natural.

Meanwhile the chief-priests, scribes and ancients were standing there in speechless surprise and ready to burst with anger because Herod, while scarcely noticing them, devoted all his attention to the Redeemer and treated Him, not as a criminal, but as a most welcome guest. All the hopes they had placed in Herod, seemed to evanesce in a moment. Then they began to accuse Christ and could hardly make an end. They charged Him with having aspired to the throne of Judea which belonged to Herod; with having blasphemed God; with intending to destroy the temple; with being a relative of that John who had meddled in such an uncalled for manner in the king's domestic affairs and thereby caused the latter so much annoyance. They charged that Christ had afterwards praised John for the stand he had taken against the king; that Christ, in fact, was the soul of the whole affair; that He had incited John against the king; that in a public sermon He had called the king a fox, saying, "Go and tell that fox, Behold, I cast out devils."[1] When, later, they saw that Herod began to look upon Christ as a fool, they cleverly shifted their position and cried, louder than before, that Christ was a cunning rascal and an infamous hypocrite, and that He was merely shamming in order to obtain His liberty.

But to come back to the joy of Herod, what casts some suspicion upon it are the words of the Gospel telling us that *of a long time* he was desirous to see Christ because he had heard many things of Him. If he had been desirous for a long time to see Christ, why did he not make use before this of the innumerable opportunities he had had of seeing Him? For three years, the Redeemer had passed through the cities and villages of Palestine. He had made Galilee especially the scene of His activity; Capharnaum, where Herod often resided, was the sojourn of predilection, the second home of Christ. There He would preach in the synagogue, on the streets, in the houses; and Herod had never seen Him. This is the way of many prominent people. They prefer not to mingle with the com-

[1] St. Luke, xiii., 32.

mon people at religious services. It would be beneath their dignity. Again, the air in the church is usually too sultry. Besides — and this is the main point—they fear to be told unpalatable truths in the sermons. Therefore they remain away. The Scriptures mention as the chief reason of Herod's joy the hope of seeing Christ work a miracle. But why did he not with the other thousands follow the Saviour into the desert? He surely would have received his share of the miraculously multiplied bread.

The Redeemer was now to have the honor of appearing as a skilled magician before his majesty, king Herod, the members of the royal household and the officials of the court. Like a clown in a play-house, He must entertain the brazen-faced crowd for a few enjoyable hours. Such was the suggestion of Herod to a man who stood before him in the deepest humiliation, a disfigured picture of misery and woe. O God, were He merely a man! But He was the One of Whom the Psalmist chants, "O Lord God of hosts, who is like to thee? The world and the fulness thereof thou hast founded: the north and the sea thou hast created. Thabor and Hermon shall rejoice in thy name."[1] He was the One of Whom Job said: "Who hath removed mountains, and they whom he overthrew in his wrath, knew it not. Who shaketh the earth out of her place, and the pillars thereof tremble. Who maketh Arcturus, and Orion, and Hyades, and the

[1] Psalms, lxxxviii., 9, 12, 13.

inner parts of the south. Who doth things great and incomprehensible and wonderful, of which there is no number."[1] All that, O Herod, does not suffice thee. Thou demandest new miracles. Thou demandest charlatan tricks and magic craft of God Almighty. And ye, unruly waves of the Galilean sea, on whom the Lord once enjoined repose, ye do not break through your dams to engulf the impudent blasphemer? Ye awful chasms in the earth, whom He robbed of the dead, ye do not open? Ye Powers and Thrones, ye Cherubim and Seraphim, ye legions of angels, all ye who sang the Gloria, do ye not rise to avenge the sacrilege against your Creator? But the Redeemer stood in silence, without complaint, full of dignity and majesty. Indeed He proved the truth of His word, "I am meek and humble of heart."[2]

Then Herod began to use all means at his command to attain his object. He began with flattery. For a long time, he assured Christ, he had deemed himself happy to harbor in his kingdom such an excellent man, whose renown as an enlightened teacher and as a great miracle-worker had spread far beyond the bounds of Galilee. It afforded him exceeding satisfaction finally to have the opportunity of making His acquaintance. Then Herod added promises of favor and reward. Christ would not be required to do it for nothing. Money, liberty and life were assured Him, provided the performance were satisfactory. Then he begged

1 Job., ix., 5–10.
2 St. Matthew, xi., 29.

and insisted that Christ produce at least a few specimens of His art. Should He not have with Him the material and instruments necessary, something less difficult would be sufficient. Then he perhaps caused water to be brought, which He might change into wine. We can readily understand the anxiety and agony of the chief-priests lest Christ save Himself by a miracle and why they kept on accusing Him all the while. Finally Herod reminded the Redeemer that His life was in his power and that it would be imprudent to provoke the ire of a well-meaning judge.

This was wonderful eloquence. We shall not deny it proper recognition. But the greater the gladness and hope of Herod had been, so much the greater was also his disappointment.

II.

The Redeemer had often worked miracles of His own accord and without being asked. He beheld Himself surrounded by a hungry multitude and He satisfied them with a few loaves. He met a sorrowing widow, walking behind the bier of her only son, and he commanded the bearers to stand. He saw tears in the eyes of two sisters, and He began to weep and exclaimed, "Lazarus, come forth!" But Herod wasted time and trouble striving to induce Christ to perform a miracle. The Lord did not even deign to address a single word to him. Herod, says Holy Writ, questioned Him in many words, but He answered him nothing. It was very strange, indeed. At other times, Christ was silent only under injury, calumny, maltreatment or when asked to defend Himself. He was wont to answer questions put by a legitimate judge. Thus He declared before Pilate that He was a king, and before Caiphas, that He was the Son of God. Why, then, did Herod not receive an answer to his questions? He was the ruler of Galilee and consequently the legitimate judge of the accused; besides, the governor had entrusted to him the conduct of the trial. Let us inquire into the reasons of this mysterious silence before Herod.

Some recent commentators designate the impure life of Herod as the chief cause. Although united in lawful wedlock with the daughter of the Arabian king Aretos, he was living with Herodias, the wife of his step-brother, whom he had abducted during a sojourn in Rome. He probably thought that a point might be stretched in this regard in favor of kings and princes who enjoyed special privileges on account of their rank. Three years had passed since John the Baptist upbraided him for his crime. It cost John his head, and the public scandal continued. If he expected an answer from the Saviour, Herod ought certainly to have removed the shameless woman from his house. Certainly his sinful life made him entirely unworthy of an answer. For it almost seems that nowadays the Lord will not address a word of grace to those Christians who sin against purity. I do not mean those who fall occasionally through weakness, but those who abandon themselves entirely to this vice, who make of it a business and a source of revenue, and especially those who for years live in sinful relations. How could they otherwise live on seemingly so happy and apparently without remorse? How seldom does it happen that such unfortunate people break the interior and external fetters which bind them; how seldom do they truly turn to God! To work such miracles of grace seems to be reserved by Divine Providence to the Immaculate Virgin. But, on the other hand, when I behold the Saviour in conversation with the Samaritan woman, who surely was a great sinner, when I consider that He himself caused this conversation, I cannot imagine that the impure life of Herod, considered in itself, was the main cause of the silence of Jesus Christ. More ancient commentators, indeed, merely touch upon this reason in a cursory manner.

There is more weight in the reason that Herod, who had been brought up in the Jewish religion, although not a descendant of Abraham, had well nigh entirely lost his faith. To ingratiate himself with the Jews, he was led by political prudence and craft to observe certain precepts of the Mosaic Law, which he ridiculed in his heart. Thus he lived continually in sins against the Holy Ghost, and it is these sins above all which stifle the voice of Christ's grace. For this reason hundreds of Protestants who grow up in good faith, will be converted more easily than one apostate Catholic. Faith teaches that a Catholic abandons and denies his religion not from inner conviction, but through contempt of innumerable pangs of conscience, through mortal sin. Such a one lives in continued antagonism to the Holy Ghost and in continued defiance of Him. Then Christ is silent. He finally addresses no more reproaches, so that such apostates apparently enjoy the most unruffled peace of soul. It is truly enough the peace of the graveyard. There can be a hope of conversion only when they begin, by cries of fervent and humble prayer, to induce the silent Saviour to speak, when with confidence they turn to His Divine Heart that they may obtain the necessary strength to return and courage to overcome impending difficulties.

We may adduce as a further and more important reason of the mysterious silence of Christ the fact that Herod had deprived Him of His voice by beheading His forerunner, the voice of one crying in the wilderness. How then could Christ speak? Woe, therefore, a threefold woe upon all rulers who, when Christ would speak to their peoples, deprive Him of His voice either by making it impossible, through diabolical laws, for the servants of Christ to exercise their teaching power in school and church, or by banishing them from the country. And still, if Herod had done even more than that against Christ and His followers, had he only asked with Saul, "Lord, what wilt thou have me to do?"[1] he undoubtedly would have received an answer.

We must then look for the chief reason of the

[1] Acts, ix., 6.

silence of Christ, on the one hand, in the impious and frivolous suggestion of the impure and infidel persecutor of Christ that the Saviour use His Divine Power for the venal purposes of a juggler and, on the other hand, in the equally frivolous and curious questions which he proposed. First, he is likely to have asked Him whether He it was at whose birth the kings of the East had arrived, causing so much disquiet to his father and so much excitement in Jerusalem. Then he wished to know how His parents had accomplished their flight. "Or," continued he, "is it true, as so many claim, that Thou art John the Baptist, whom I had beheaded but who, it is alleged, is risen again to work miracles?"[1] Then he asked for sundry information about miracles and it is not improbable that he requested the Redeemer to initiate him into the secrets of His art. All these reasons take away the mystery from the silence of Christ.

The silence of Christ, is for the rest, the most dreadful punishment which God can inflict upon the sinner. It is the almost infallible presage of eternal damnation. Even the Saints dreaded nothing more than that the Saviour, to punish their smaller faults and infidelities, might no longer speak to them in inward impulses and inspirations or through the voice of conscience. "O my God," they therefore prayed, "be not Thou silent to me: lest if Thou be silent to me, I become like them that go down into the pit."[2] We should pray in

[1] St. Luke, ix., 7, 8.
[2] Psalms, xxvii., 1.

like manner, but we should also order our lives in accordance with the words addressed to us directly by God Himself or indirectly through the voice of His representatives.

Herod, therefore, found himself thoroughly foiled in his expectations. He felt his mortification so much more because it took place before such a distinguished assembly, before his court, even before the chief-priests and scribes. But he would not issue a decree of death in a strange city, outside of his realm. It might increase the ill will of many well disposed Jews who had not yet forgiven him the execution of the Baptist and thus entirely destroy his prospects for the Jewish throne. But he planned revenge. In what did it consist?

III.

We cannot suppose that Herod will treat Christ as did the common Jews; that, like to the chief-priests and scribes, he will belabor Him with two fists, drag Him by the hair, or give Him kicks and blows. Oh no, for that he was too much of a courtier, he belonged to the aristocratic and educated class. Such conduct would be beneath his dignity. The threefold vengeance which he took on the Redeemer is narrated in the Holy Scriptures in the following words: "Herod with his army set him at naught: and mocked him, putting on him a white garment, and sent him back to Pilate."

First, he and his courtiers set Him at naught and mocked Him. Herod thought, and so expressed himself before those present, that an accused who acted as did this man, who would say nothing in his own defense, who would do nothing for his own liberation, who would not answer by a single word the questions of a ruler in whose hands his life lay, could not possibly have his wits about him. He ought to be in an asylum for the insane rather than in a prison. We may imagine that peals of laughter and applause from the royal family and others present, testified to the wisdom of the king's words. But we hear the thundering voice of Isaias, "Woe to you that are wise in your own eyes, and prudent in your own conceits."[1] On the day of judgment He Whom you now mock as a fool, shall put to shame all your wisdom. "He it is," you shall cry, "whom we had some time in derision and for a parable of reproach. We fools esteemed his life madness and his end without honor."[2] "The Lord shall then laugh you to scorn. And you shall fall after this without honor, and be a reproach among the dead forever."[3] Herod, on account of his witty remarks, deserved to be looked up to as a patron by lustful Voltaire and his associates, who derided all that is holy and divine with their fine sarcasm and their acrimonious scorn.

Then he had Christ clothed in a white garment. Among the Jews, madmen were clad in white, so that passers-by could see that they were mentally

[1] Isaias, v., 21.
[2] Wisd., v., 3–5.
[3] Ibid., iv., 18, 19.

weak. Among the Romans white garments were worn by those who aspired to some office. Indeed, to aspire to office also borders on madness, at least when, as often happens in some localities, months are spent in purchasing votes with money and by dispensing intoxicating drinks. It is certainly not a proof of overmuch sense nor of qualification for the office. But Christ, as the charge went, aspired to the crown of Judea. For several reasons, then, Herod had the garment of a fool put on Christ—and the Redeemer did not resist. O ye heavens! The Son of God in the white robe of a visionary, of an ambitious office seeker, the thrice Holy One in the robe of a hungry politician, Infinite Wisdom in the garment of a fool! It is indeed a scene that defies all description. Holy Church conceived that she could offer no better atonement for this disgrace than by sharing its ignominy and making her servants appear at the altar in long white robes.

Lastly, Herod sent Him back to Pilate, clad, as He was, in the robe of a fool. He sent Him back when the day was already far advanced and when thousands were upon the streets and filled the air with cries of irony and shouts of diabolical rejoicing. What a cruel revenge! What a terrible humiliation! What a sad Corpus Christi procession! It is indeed meet and just that the same Christ, veiled under the appearance of bread, be borne annually in festive march, as in triumph, through the streets of cities and villages. It is indeed meet and just that He be greeted with enthusiastic songs of praise and hymns of thanksgiving to make Him forget, as it were, the wrong done Him in that ignominious procession. It was ordered by a king. Ye kings and emperors, redeem the honor of your station and accompany with your entire court, humbly and devoutly, the Most Blessed Sacrament.

When the chief-priests came back with Christ to Pilate, they delivered to the latter the thanks and best wishes and polite compliments of Herod together with the assurance of his distinguished consideration and entire devotedness. For the Gospel says that "Herod and Pilate were made friends that same day, for before they were enemies one to another." Similar occurrences take place nowadays. In the halls of legislatures, godless parties may antagonize each other in continued strife, the dark powers of this world may attack each other with bloody weapons; in the hatred of Christ they are a unit. When the alarm is sounded for an attack on the Catholic Church, they shake hands and form a brotherly pact.

Herod, then, had a desire to see Our Divine Saviour and to speak with Him. In itself, this desire was praiseworthy. Who of us would not nourish the same desire? If so, our desire can be satisfied. But we must use the right means. "The Lord's communication is with the simple," says Holy Writ.[1] Let us be simple, humble, of a believing heart, and Christ will speak to us. The

[1] Prov., iii., 32.

simple, those of child-like faith, can hold converse with Him in prayer for hours and never grow weary. For they need not carry on all the conversation themselves. Christ speaks to them and answers all their questions. If furthermore we wish to see Christ, we know that "blessed are the pure of heart, for they shall see God."[1] We should, therefore, avoid even the shadow of impurity. We must preserve our hearts pure and stainless, and we shall see God. Yea, even more. We shall then see miracles of the Saviour, wonders of His Power, wonders of His Mercy, wonders of His Love, both here and in the next world.

[1] St. Matthew, v., 8.

CHAPTER XIV.

CHRIST AND BARABBAS

"But the whole multitude together cried out, saying: Away with this man and release unto us Barabbas."
(St. Luke, xxiii., 18.)

The effort of Pilate to rid himself of the unpleasant trial and to hand the case over to others had proven a failure. Herod had sent Christ back to him, and thus Pilate had to reassume the case by virtue of his office. Standing in the vestibule of the palace, he first called together not only the chief-priests and ancients, but the entire people, of whose attachment to Jesus he was well aware. Then he again declared in a solemn tone, "You have presented unto me this man, as one that perverteth the people, and behold, I have examined him before you."[1] Pilate could truthfully say these last words, inasmuch as he personally did not wish to have a secret hearing. That the high-priests, during the trial, remained outside, was their own doing. Pilate then continued: "I find no cause in this man touching those things wherein you accuse him. No, nor Herod neither. For I sent you to him, and be-

[1] St. Luke, xxiii., 14–16.

hold, nothing worthy of death is done to him.'' Thus far, his address was excellent. But Pilate noticed how the chief-priests and, at their instigation, the scribes also, were working themselves into a gradually increasing excitement and frenzy of which they gave evidence by threatening gestures and clenching of fists. For it angered and provoked them to be reminded by Pilate, in presence of the whole people, of their disgraceful fiasco before Herod and to perceive that he had the word of liberation on the tip of his tongue. Then Pilate lost his cue. If the popular excitement increased and developed into a general revolt, something readily to be feared among the Jews, it might prove very embarrassing to the governor, especially now during the festival of the Passover. In order, therefore, to appease the prominent people and to calm the lower classes, he conceived the sudden idea of making some concessions, wherefore he added the singular conclusion: ''I will chastise him therefore, and release him.'' But, before he could give more minute directions regarding the chastisement, the people, to his great satisfaction, reminded him of another expedient which he immediately made use of.

We shall therefore consider [1]

I. The effort of Pilate to release Christ and

II. Its result.

[1] St. Matthew, xxvii., 15–23; St. Mark, xv., 6–14; St. Luke, xxiii., 17–22; St. John, xviii., 39, 40.

I.

"Now upon the solemn day," narrates St. Matthew, "the governor was accustomed to release to the people one prisoner, whom they would." The origin of this custom cannot be stated with certainty. According to some commentators it was a very ancient custom to select, on the eve of the paschal feast, some criminal or other, and, in commemoration of the deliverance from Egyptian thraldom, to open unto him, at the beginning of the feast day, the doors of the prison. The remaining criminals were then executed in warning example, as were the two thieves this year. It is said that later on the Roman governors very willingly accommodated themselves to this custom, partly not to offend the people and partly because they had observed the same custom in Rome, where the emperors, when in good humor, would grant pardons and amnesties on the feasts of the gods. However, other commentators are of the opinion that the governors themselves granted the people this privilege in order to indemnify them somewhat for the loss of their judiciary power and to nullify the bad feelings resulting from this loss. The proper understanding between the Jews and the governor was arrived at on the eve of the feast.

The people were reminded of this custom by the words of Pilate, "I will release him." Then they began to shout and to beg that he do as he always had done. Some of the crowd undoubtedly begged thus in favor of the Redeemer, whose liberation they desired and began to hope for. But most of them thought of no such a thing. Of the entire address of Pilate, which contained a twofold declaration of Christ's innocence, they had caught only the word "release." Without, therefore, giving a thought to the main question and with a view only to their privilege, they reminded Pilate of the old custom.

Pilate readily accepted their proposition. But, in order to be more sure of his object, he proposed to the choice of the people, besides Christ only *one* other, and a most notorious criminal at that, Barabbas by name. The Gospel does not mention whether or not he was brought from prison and placed opposite to Christ. The evangelists delineate the character of Barabbas in the darkest colors and in the most forbidding manner. St. Mark and St. Luke testify that in a sedition he had committed a murder, according to St. John he was a murderer, and St. Matthew calls him a notorious murderer. He was a pest to the country, a scourge of Judea, an abomination to all Jews. Now, thought Pilate, it cannot go amiss. The people, who for the most part were attached to Christ, would certainly not give the preference to an arch-fiend. Under this impression he said to them, "You have a custom that I should release one unto you at the pasch: will you, therefore, that I release unto you the king of the Jews?"

The question was well put. Pilate, as yet, made no mention of Barabbas. He merely proposed Christ and, to stimulate the sense of honor of the Jews, he honored Him with the title of King of the Jews. Their national pride, he hoped, would cause them to demand without delay the release of their king. But no answer followed. Pilate therefore had to ask further, "Whom will you that I release to you, Barabbas, or Jesus that is called Christ?" Now the fall of Pilate is rapid. The means he employed to liberate Christ were entirely unworthy as far as moral value was concerned. He proposed Jesus and Barabbas for the choice, and therefore for the comparison, of the people. But every comparison presupposes a certain similarity. It was as if he had said: I have here two criminals; which of the two shall I release? This means deserved to be rejected because, even if favorable to Christ, it would not redeem His honor. On account of the comparison there would always remain attached to His name the stain that He had obtained His freedom, not because of His innocence, but because of popular favor or because of being the lesser of two criminals. His whole career as a popular preacher would, humanly speaking, have thereby been ruined.

Before it came to a choice, Almighty God granted Pilate a great grace. Whilst he was sitting on the judge's bench, that is, on an elevated seat in the vestibule, a messenger suddenly entered who said to him in the name of his wife, "Have thou nothing to do with that just man. For I have suffered many things this day in a dream because of him." Probably God had shown this woman the misery in which her husband would involve himself, should he not release the Saviour. Had Pilate himself received this revelation from God, the Jews might claim that it was an excuse invented by him. And perhaps he himself would have considered it an idle dream and have said nothing about it.

The message of Pilate's wife was well considered. Claudia Procula, such was her name, first addressed Pilate in his capacity as judge, who durst not condemn an innocent man. Then she addressed him as her husband. She urged him to be courageous enough to liberate Christ out of love for her, to spare her new sufferings. And Christ amply rewarded the good will of this noble-minded, although pagan woman. After the unfortunate death of her husband, who committed suicide, Claudia embraced Christianity and, it is said, died in the odor of sanctity.[1] But Pilate set aside the warning of his wife and let the people proceed to a choice. Probably he entertained confident hopes of a favorable result. What was the result?

II.

The result would probably have been favorable if the high-priests and ancients had not moved about among the people, urging them on and persuading them to demand the release of Barabbas. They found the desirable time and occasion for

[1] See note 11.

this purpose whilst Pilate was busy with the messenger sent by his wife. Do you not perceive, said some, the trap which Pilate has slyly set for us? Whom shall I release unto you, he has asked, Jesus, King of the Jews, or Barabbas? If we give our suffrage to Jesus, we declare thereby that he is our King and that we acknowledge Him as such. Then woe to us and our city. A murderer, said others, is, at any rate, better than a blasphemer or a false prophet. For if He were really the Son of God, He would before this have released Himself. Besides, His own disciples must consider Him an impostor or they would not have abandoned Him. Vote, said others again, for the death of Christ in order that His deceit be brought to light, if He arise not on the third day. If He is to rise again, He must first be put to death. Then, if He arises, we shall believe in Him. Barabbas, they continued, is indeed a bad man, but sad experience has probably reformed him, and he will always be grateful to us. But Christ, even if you release Him, will always harbor ill feelings against you and charge you with the insults heaped upon Him. You have destroyed the possibility of being in favor with Him in any event.

Whilst the messenger of his wife was departing, Pilate, as an answer to his message, again asked the people, "Whether will you of the two to be released unto you? The whole multitude together cried out, saying: Not this man, but Barabbas." Away with this man and release unto us Barabbas. They feared, it appears, that Pilate would release both. The chief-priests could now be well satisfied with the result of their agitation. But they forfeited the right to charge the Redeemer with being a disturber of the people.

Some of the people shouted because they, in good faith, believed Christ to be a great criminal. "Our priests," thought others, "undoubtedly propose what is right; they understand the matter better than Pilate, the pagan, or than we understand it." Others shouted out of fear. They feared the emperor; they feared the chief-priests, they feared a sedition, they feared Christ Himself and His rebukes and warning look which they would avoid for all time. Others again wished to furnish Christ with the opportunity to perform His crowning miracle, the resurrection. Finally, many shouted because they heard the others shout.

O ungrateful, faithless, shameless synagogue! Thus dost thou repel thy Divine Bridegroom, the Chosen of millions, and thou choosest for a bridegroom a murderer, dragged from the scum and dregs of the slums. Truly it is thine own fault, for which thou art responsible, that forty years later thy adherents shall fall victims to murderers in an awful massacre.

How fickle and inconstant are the masses! How little in harmony with the solemn Hosannas and Benedictus is the cry, "Not this man, but Barabbas release unto us." And thus it happens. No matter how well meaning the people may be, a few disturbers and agitators suffice, by revolutionary speeches, by threats and promises, to make them vote and act against their consciences, so much so that they allow themselves to be drawn to the meanest acts of violence against Holy Church and her ordained ministers. Therefore he is a fool who builds on popular favor or who relies on it.

The choice of the Jewish people, preferring Barabbas to the Redeemer, can be viewed from three standpoints. If we, before all, cast our glance on the mysterious workings of Divine Providence, the choice appears to us as the expression of Divine Justice. To Almighty God, at this moment, His only begotten Son was responsible for greater guilt and therefore subject to greater punishment than the great criminal Barabbas. Certainly, Christ, the innocent Lamb of God, the Holiest of holy ones, was free from all personal sin. But God had laid upon Him the sins of the whole world. In comparison with this mountain of sins upon the shoulders of Christ, rising up through the clouds of heaven, the dreadful crimes of Barabbas were as small as a grain of sand. The latter had on his conscience only his personal sins, whilst Christ carried the sins of the entire world.

The choice of the people was, in the second place, the expression of Divine Love for us. What, indeed, would it have availed us had Barabbas died and Christ been released? "Let my Son die," said the heavenly Father, "but all sinners, represented by Barabbas, shall be saved." Therefore Holy Church sings in exultant gratitude, "To redeem the servant, Thou hast delivered to death Thy Son. O admirable condescension of Thy Divine Goodness! O inestimable proof of Thy Love."

But if we consider the choice in as far as it concerns those who made it and Him Whom it affected, it is for the choosers a perpetual stain of dishonor, and for the Redeemer, rejected and voted down by them, a nameless ignominy. It was indeed an awful offense against the Son of God when the rebel angels preferred Lucifer, their leader, to Him. The offense was so great that Divine Justice immediately relegated them to the eternal tortures of hell. But, at least, it was an angel who was preferred to Christ; it was the highest, the most perfect of all angels, endowed with the grandest gifts of nature and of grace. But in this case, Christ had to yield to a robber and murderer. The ignominy wounded the Heart of Christ so much the more because, among those who rejected Him, many had partaken of His abundant benefits and had experienced in their own persons His miraculous powers. But the humble heart of Jesus was glad to be able again to offer a sacrifice to God.

The result of the choice came upon Pilate like a clap of thunder. He beheld all his hopes destroyed and the case more difficult than ever before. As if in agony, he cried out to the Jews, "What shall I do then with Jesus that is called the Christ?" It is strange, Pilate, that, being a judge, thou shouldst not know what to do with an accused person who has been found innocent. Art thou indeed so blinded? There remains nothing for thee to do but to release both Him and Barabbas: the latter as a paschal gift to the Jews, and the Redeemer, because of His innocence. Thou shouldst be ashamed of thy words, "What shall I do with Jesus?" Is Jesus, then, such a trifling, unimportant, contemptible and useless person that one knows not what to do with Him? Declare Him innocent. Then crave His pardon and ask Him again, but this time with holy earnestness, "What is truth?" Pay attention, then, and listen seriously to every word that proceeds from His mouth. Keep it in thy heart and arrange thy life according to it. Behold what thou shouldst do with Jesus.

But Pilate knew not what to do with Jesus. Had he but asked his conscience! Instead, he asked the people, the enemies of Jesus Christ. Then the high-priests began to shout, "Crucify Him." And, as out of one mouth, the cry resounded in a loud chorus, "Crucify Him! crucify Him!" In vain were now all the declarations of the Saviour's innocence on the part of Pilate, in vain all the attempts to release Him, in vain even the promise to chastise Him. Again and again, amid ever increasing tumult, the cry resounded, "Let Him be crucified! crucify Him!"

In this dilemma, Pilate resumed his former idea of calming the excited people by a concession at the expense of the Redeemer. But he realized that a trivial chastisement would no longer be sufficient to pacify the Jews. He therefore resolved to subject Him to the terrible punishment of flagellation. Thereby, he hoped, the chief-priests and the people would be satisfied and would refrain from insisting on further punishment. It is indeed a rather uncommon manner of administering justice and a rather curious system of logic which permits one to humor the accusers by administering bloody stripes to the accused with a view to releasing him afterwards. And Pilate delivered Him to the soldiers that He be scourged. On account of this command the excitement of the people was somewhat calmed and, for the nonce, the storm was quieted.

We wax wroth at Pilate for having compared Christ with a murderer, we are indignant with the Jews for having preferred Barabbas to the Son of God. And it is right that we do so. But does the soul not inflict a similar outrage on the Saviour, when she places alongside of Him the lustful pleasures of life, earthly treasures, human praise and favor, and then remains undecided as to where to give the preference. And when the scales then sink to the Lord's disadvantage, and when man chooses the slavery of passion instead of the sweet yoke of Christ, hell instead of heaven, Satan instead of the All-holy God, is this not, in fact, even a greater outrage? "Be astonished, O ye heavens," exclaims the prophet Jeremias (ii., 12, 13), "at this, and ye gates thereof, be very desolate. For my people have done two evils. They have forsaken me, the fountain of living water, and have digged to themselves cisterns, broken cisterns, that can hold no water."

May such an ingratitude be far removed from us. Out from among millions of human beings, the Saviour has chosen us to be members of His Holy Church and to partake of His abundant benefits. He has sanctified us in baptism, He has nourished us with His Sacred Flesh and Most Precious Blood. To our souls has He said:

What then, in heaven and upon earth, shall we choose outside of God? May the Lord be our inheritance — may God be the God of our hearts and our portion forever.

CHAPTER XV.

THE SCOURGING OF CHRIST

"Then therefore Pilate took Jesus, and scourged him."
(St. John, xix., 1.)

As soon as Pilate had communicated to the people his intention of having Christ scourged and had given a command to this effect, he retired as quickly as possible from the raging multitude and went to the inner part of the court-building. The scourging took place in an enclosed courtyard in the rear of the building. The evangelists do not describe the flagellation. They merely say, "Then Pilate took Jesus and scourged him." Everybody knew full well what that meant. Mayhap the description of details was too painful for them. But for the solace of Our Saviour and for the benefit of our souls, we shall consider more minutely this incident and its various circumstances. Let us consider, then,

I. The scourging in itself; and

II. The special reasons why Christ wished to endure it.

I.

The flagellation was to the Saviour very *humiliating* and, at the same time, very painful. That it was humiliating, may be deduced from three circumstances. In the first place, the scourging was done by the Roman soldiers, and therefore according to Roman, not Jewish, usage. But scourging, when applied not only with rods but with whips or still more cruel instruments, was usually administered only to slaves, that is, to persons who at that time were no longer considered as human beings; to creatures who were ranked below the brute; to creatures who were accustomed to all manner of disdain and contempt; whose feelings were, by bad treatment, rendered so coarse and stunted that only the most cruel and degrading punishments could make any impression upon them. When scourging was applied to free-born men, they were culprits who had committed such extraordinary and fearful crimes that they forfeited all right to consideration and humane treatment. It is self-evident that they were to be found guilty before this punishment was administered. It was especially a Roman custom to scourge those who were condemned to be crucified.

This punishment which degraded its victim to the level of a slave or of the most abject criminal, was now imposed, not upon the son of an ordinary Roman citizen, but upon Jesus, the son of David, the scion of a royal family, in whose veins coursed royal blood; upon Jesus, the Son of the purest Virgin Mary, the Son of the future Queen of heaven and of earth; upon Jesus, the only begotten Son of the King of kings; upon Jesus, the Son of God, in Whom was hidden all the fullness of the Godhead, all the dignity and majesty of the Divine Being. And all this, notwithstanding the fact that the judge had himself testified to the innocence of Christ.

The fact that the scourging was done in public, made the humiliation of the Redeemer so much more poignant. To understand this better, we must remember that in the Heart of Jesus all human feelings existed in their utmost perfection. This Heart was in no wise insensible to injury; It felt most keenly every insult; Its sense of honor was extremely delicate. And if there be no greater mortification for a high-spirited child than to be punished before others; if it would rather take a double amount of chastisement provided it be spared the public humiliation; what must have been the feelings of the noblest of all hearts? It need hardly be mentioned that during the public flagellation, the Redeemer was the butt of the lowest jests and of the most vulgar wit. "That was a good stroke," we may imagine that one cried. "Hit harder," shouted another. "This will bring him to time," roared a third, and thus it continued.

The greatest humiliation of Christ, however, arose from the fact that, according to Roman usage, He was stripped of all clothing with the exception of the loin covering. Once upon a time, after a similar humiliation, David had exclaimed, as if carried away by sorrow, "They have looked and stared upon me."[1] "The confusion of my face hath covered me."[2] "And they opened their mouth wide against me; they said: Well done, well done, our eyes have seen it."[3] When, in later centuries, chaste Virgins, a St. Agnes and a St. Barbara, had to endure the same mortification, heaven enveloped them in such a wonderful light that they became, as it were, invisible. When others were about to be disrobed, they fell dead on the ground from terror and fright. But the purest Son of the purest Virgin had to drain this cup to the very dregs. He had to submit to be stared at by a low, impudent crowd, by lustful eyes, just as a shameless person in a museum. This torture of being ignominiously disrobed was without doubt one of the greatest in all His passion. What trembling, what convulsions in His entire Body from shame and confusion! How He longed for the fool's garment with which Herod had clothed Him! There was only one relieving feature in this suffering: the innumerable lashes which cut His flesh, soon disfigured His Body to such an extent that it lost all appearance of being human.

The scourging, then, was humiliating, but besides, it was very painful. Considered by itself, the Roman flagellation was something dreadful and terrible. After the unfortunate victim's

[1] Psalms, xxi., 18.
[2] Ibid., xliii., 16.
[3] Ibid., xxxiv., 21.

hands, feet and neck were bound to the pillar so tightly that a move was hardly possible, six strong and muscular soldiers approached and, in pairs, they beat the culprit with thorny clubs, with lashes interwoven with wire, and with thin, iron chains. The number of lashes was not fixed. It lasted until the voluptuous cruelty of the spectators, used to such bloody exhibitions, was satiated. Not infrequently it happened that slaves expired under this torture. However, for various reasons the flagellation was more painful to Jesus than to others. In the first place, the Sacred Body of Christ, born of the purest Virgin through a miracle of the Holy Ghost, was undoubtedly more refined and more delicate, and therefore more sensitive than the bodies of sinners. Then, to better attain his object Pilate had probably recommended a more strenuous scourging. The torturers, therefore, used all their strength. Furthermore, the other soldiers continually spurred them on. And in proportion as the patience and meekness of the Divine Lamb of Sacrifice manifested themselves, the cruelty of the torturers increasd. As often happens with low-bred villains, the meekness of the victim infuriated them to complete madness. They would ascertain whether or not they could draw from Him a cry of anguish. Finally, the flagellation of Christ—and this was the main reason—was so cruel because the anger of God was incensed against Him. For God saw Him covered with the sins of the whole world. Many opinions regarding the number of the strokes and of the drops of blood shed have been advanced and supported by visions of holy persons. To form a decision on that point is by no means necessary. I say with St. Augustine: "If, according to Holy Writ, every sinner deserves many strokes of the scourge, how many did not the innocent Saviour deserve, Who had taken upon Himself the thousands of millions of sins and Who now was to render complete satisfaction to Divine Justice."

At last a halt was ordered, and the cords were cut. Weak and fainting, exhausted by the loss of blood, the Redeemer fell to the ground, into His own Precious Blood. Had He been the Jew who had fallen among the robbers, perhaps some tender-hearted Samaritan might have come by and poured oil and wine upon His wounds. Had He been poor Lazarus, covered with bloody ulcers, perhaps some dog would have had pity on Him. But He was the Son of God. And therefore, according to some holy fathers, the torturers continued to beat Him as He weltered in His Blood, and they mutilated those parts of His Sacred Body which the pillar had protected.

But why is He divested of His garments Who dressed the firmament with stars and the earth with flowers? Why are those hands so cruelly bound which never were extended except to offer benefits? Why those feet which were never tired in hastening after the lost sheep? Why is that immaculate Body so terribly beaten which Christ, in His Love, had destined to be the nourishment of our souls? Why was it that no help came to

Him from any quarter; neither from the earth, which almost ravenously drank His Precious Blood; neither from the angels, who in apparent indifference, looked down upon the scene; neither from His heavenly Father, Who rather appeared to increase the strength which the menials applied to His Son. Let us together examine the special reason, why Christ wished to endure the lashes of the scourge.

II.

In the first place, Christ wished, by submitting to the flagellation, to atone for all sins of impurity: for the sins of pagans, for the sins of Christians, for the sins of children, for the sins of growing youth, for the sins of married persons, for the sins of old people, for the sins of thought, of desire, in look, word and deed, for the sins of all times and of all classes of men. By His ignominious disrobing, He wished to atone especially for those sins which are committed and provoked by shameless clothing. Christ thought then not only of such persons who, as slaves of lust and open libertines, walk barefacedly the way of vice; not only of those frivolous women who, according to the custom of some places, walk about publicly, in open daylight, in such scanty costume that every one who loves his soul, is forced to cast down his eyes in fear. But He thought also of those Catholic women and girls who, in our country, notably among the wealthier and more prominent classes, appear on certain occasions, at least, in attire which readily provokes and begets sin. Of course, it is then claimed, that fashion and the custom of the wealthy excuse and justify such a scandal. But, even if it were the fashion of the most prominent in the country, it is a fashion which comes from the devil and leads to the devil. These are sins and customs on account of which Christ suffered Himself to be disrobed and scourged.

Secondly, He would give us an idea of the hatred God entertains for the vice of impurity. Almighty God had done a great many things since the creation to bring home this conviction to mankind. He repented of having created mankind and He engulfed it in the waters of the deluge. He destroyed the inhabitants of Sodom by fire from heaven. He caused 24,000 men to be put to the sword for having sinned with the daughters of the Moabites. Almost the entire tribe of Benjamin was violently rooted out, in punishment of lustful abominations. Almighty God announced through Moses [1] that every adulterer and every adulteress should be stoned by the people and that the incestuous should be burnt. Great God! If these penalties, incomprehensible to modern legislation which flirts with sensual lust, were still in force, how often would we not be called upon to go out the gates of the city to stone an adulteress? But how the vice of impurity appears to the eyes of God is shown more clearly

[1] Levit., xx., 10–15.

and definitely by Christ, scourged for us, than by all the Divine judgments and the Mosaic Law itself.

Thirdly, the Saviour wished to portray vividly before our eyes the terrors of the punishments to be inflicted in hell, after the resurrection, on the bodies of those who shall be condemned for this vice. Certainly faith teaches us that the bodies of the damned, monsters of hideousness, shall burn in eternal flames. In vain will they cry out for a garment to cover their nakedness, to hide from their terrified gaze forever the rottenness, corruption and horror of bodies pampered heretofore in shameless attire. But I recognize more easily the greatness of these pains when I contemplate the innocent Body of Christ, which was scourged for our sake. Truly, if this happens in the green wood, what shall happen in the dry?

Fourthly, the Redeemer would be the solace and the strength of the holy martyrs. Ah! it need no longer be a matter of astonishment that the apostles were joyful and exultant when leaving the courtroom. What then had happened? What was the cause of their joy? They had with the Divine Master been lashed with the scourge. And when, later on, the holy martyrs were devoured by wild beasts, when with iron hooks and tongs the flesh was torn from their bodies, when weak virgins, like to heroes, ascended the awaiting pyres, who consoled and strengthened them but Christ Who was scourged for us?

Finally, Christ wished to be the model of confessors and of all penitents; and who of us does not rightly belong to this class? At the head of this long and immense procession of penitents we behold Paul, the apostle of the Gentiles. With a loud voice he cries out to all coming generations, "I chastise my body: lest, perhaps, when I have preached to others, I myself should become a castaway."[1] He is followed by the untold number of all those saints who retired into solitudes and hideous caverns and within quiet monastic walls and there chastised their bodies by continued fasts and by the most exquisite and painful works of penance. What sought they there? What did they strive for? To become similar to Christ who was scourged for us.

If we find ourselves too weak for such extraordinary works of mortification, if we are not called by God to perform them, we, at least, should never abuse our bodies in works of impurity, and we ought to clothe them as Christian modesty and decency suggest. Furthermore, we ought at least to perform those acts of penance which God and Holy Church demand of us by observing conscientiously the law of abstinence, and, when in duty bound, the law of fasting. And that we may keep such resolutions, let us draw the needed strength and courage from the fountains of the Saviour, from the bleeding wounds of the Redeemer Who was scourged for us.

[1] I. Cor., ix., 27.

CHAPTER XVI.

THE CROWNING WITH THORNS

"And the soldiers platting a crown of thorns, put it upon his head." (St. John, xix., 2.)

By the bloody scourging the Sacred Body of Christ was undoubtedly torn and disfigured in the most frightful manner. But His Sacred Head was still untouched. At this point, Holy Writ narrates the following incident: "The soldiers of the governor gathered together the whole band and put a scarlet cloak about Jesus, and platting a crown of thorns, they put it upon his head and a reed in his right hand. And they came to him and bowing the knee before him, they mocked him and began to salute him, saying: Hail, King of the Jews. And they gave him blows. Spitting upon him, they took the reed and struck his head. And bowing their knees, they adored him."[1]

Listening to this narrative, one is filled not only with aversion and horror, but also with astonishment. One naturally asks how such a thing was possible. How did the torturers happen to think of doing such a thing? Who had given orders

[1] St. Matthew, xxvii., 27-30; St. Mark, xv., 16-19; St. John, xix., 2, 3.

that the Sacred Head be thus tortured? And how dared they, without being told and without higher orders, venture upon such an outrage? How did they escape punishment for this deed? But thus it is when evil proceeds from above, from those who are in high stations or who are in the lead in any way. Then evil not only finds approval among those in lower stations of life, but these last add evil to evil of their own accord.

These pagan soldiers were, without knowing it, the instruments of a mysterious Divine decree. The Jews had before wished to proclaim Christ their King and to crown Him. But He fled from them. They were not worthy of the honor. He was to be crowned by the heathen, by those who, after the rejection of the synagogue, were to gather in thousands around the glorious banner of Christ. Besides this, Christ was not pleased with the program of coronation ceremonies as proposed by the Jews. This ceremony, according to the Saviour's intention, was to be conducted in a manner befitting a king Whose kingdom was not of this world, a king Who in a few hours was to die the death of a criminal. Therefore the crowning could not be any longer delayed. It was necessary to make haste; it was high time.

Let us consider

I. The legitimate title of Christ to a crown,

II. The insignia presented to Him and

III. The homage offered Him.

I.

First, Christ, *as God,* had the right to a crown. The heathens, whose representatives were to place a crown on His head, understood that the gods deserved a crown. Therefore they adorned the images of their divinities with gold and jewels, with crowns and wreaths of flowers. They wreathed the head of Apollo with laurels; they adorned the heads of Bacchus and Juno with the leaves of the vine; upon the head of Hercules they placed olive branches, and golden crowns upon the heads of Jupiter and Saturn. Now Christ had declared before Caiphas that He was the Son of God, and He confirmed His declaration with an oath. Therefore He ought to be crowned.

Christ, furthermore, as *King,* had the right to a crown. "Art thou a King?" Pilate had asked. And Christ had given the answer, "Thou sayest, that I am a King." It was therefore proper that a crown should adorn His head, and this with greater reason, because His kingdom must excel all others in greatness, power and glory.

Then Christ as *High-Priest* of the New Law had the right to a crown. When the high-priest of the Old Law offered sacrifice, his head was adorned with the tiara. But Christ was about to offer the infinitely meritorious sacrifice of the New Law. Hence at this sublime sacrificial feast the crown should not be missing.

Christ, as a *glorious conqueror,* had the right to a crown. "I have overcome the world," He had declared the evening before, to all His apostles, in His address of leave-taking.[1] Now if Roman generals, who had conquered a small speck on the earth's surface, were granted the honor of a triumph and of a crown of victory, how much more worthy of a crown was Christ, the Conqueror of the whole world, the Victor over even sin and hell.

Finally, according to Jewish custom, the *bridegroom* wore a sort of diadem on the day of his espousals. "Go forth," says the Canticle (iii., 11), "ye daughters of Sion, and see king Solomon in the diadem, wherewith his mother crowned him in the day of his espousals." Now Christ, the true Solomon, the true Prince of peace, was about to redeem, with His Blood, His Bride, the Holy Church, and to celebrate His espousals with her.

The Redeemer, therefore, had the most incontestable titles to a crown. Only two of these titles were known to the pagan soldiery. They had been present when Christ declared Himself a king before Pilate. Besides, they had heard what He had testified under oath, regarding His Divinity. It was these two titles, especially the former, which prompted the soldiers to proceed to the coronation. They quickly called together the whole band so that all could take part in it. Let us now consider the insignia which they presented to Christ.

[1] St. John, xvi., 33.

II.

The insignia of a king consisted of a royal mantle, of a crown and a scepter. Following the custom, the soldiers first presented to the Saviour the kingly mantle. It should have been a purple one. But lacking a mantle of purple, richly interwoven with gold, they made use of the best they could procure. To begin with, they tore off His garments, causing cruel pains, because they were incrusted in the many wounds. They then wrapped about Him an old, worn-out, scarlet rag. "Lord," they probably said, "the emperor of Rome sends you this purple, it will become You when You are on your royal throne." It was correctly put, for no other mantle was befitting for the Redeemer of the world. He was the picture of the world's sins, which were red as scarlet, but, through Christ, were to become white as snow. The mantle should be red as a sign that His kingdom, founded in blood, was to be spread only by means of blood, that is, by the blood of the apostles and of the martyrs. It was ragged and torn in token that, in imitation of Christ, His ministers would redeem the souls of men and subject them to Christ, not by means of gold and silver, but through the hardships of poverty. As for the rest, words are wanting in which to qualify properly the wretchedness of this ignominious scene. I shall therefore neither be indignant at the torturers, nor unfold the shame of the Divine Heart. One suggestion, however, forces itself upon me. If a king allows himself to be clad in poor and miserable rags, how can we justify in His subjects a luxury in matters of dress which exceeds by far all reasonable, even all extreme demands of one's station in life; a luxury such that one can no longer distinguish the daughter of an ordinary citizen's family from the high-born princess, nor the maid from her mistress. There is many a poor little church in missionary countries where the Body of Christ is hardly better clad than at His crowning. Hundreds and thousands of members of the same Sacred Body, in these same countries, lack even the most necessary garments. In whole droves, they die from sheer poverty and misery. Instead, then, of using the excess of your money in a sinful way, use it to clothe Jesus Christ in one of the manners suggested. Then He will not address to you the reproach, "I was naked and you covered me not. Depart from me into everlasting fire."[1]

Then they put the crown upon the head of Christ. Undoubtedly, it was a crown of most beautiful roses or of most precious gems, or of the purest gold, adorned with pearls and the most exquisite jewels! But the Almighty in His anger had cursed the earth. "Thorns and thistles shall it bring forth to thee." To remove from the earth this curse, this king must carry on His head upon the cross the signs of this curse. The ram, also, which was to be immolated instead of Isaac, stuck fast by the horns amongst thorns and briars. The

[1] St. Matthew, xxv., 43.

soldiers then, from mighty thorns with strong and sharp points, platted a crown in the form of a wreath or of a helmet and put it upon the head of Christ in such a violent manner that the blood poured forth from the forehead, the eyes and the cheeks. "Now keep your head straight and still," a soldier would remark, "and we'll give you what you have desired for such a long time." That, indeed, was correct. For Christ had earnestly longed for the crown of thorns and its sufferings in order that He might atone for the sins of crowned heads. To preserve a crown or to increase its splendor or to add new jewels to it, how many bloody wars have they not carried on, of how many acts of infernal cruelty or of enormous injustice have they not been guilty? Christ also wished to atone for the many sins of thought whereby we have so often offended Him, for thoughts of pride and vanity, for thoughts of worldliness, for uncharitable thoughts, and finally for the impure thoughts and imaginations of unchaste people.

When the head suffers, necessarily all the members suffer, because they are joined to the head in the unity of the body. Whoever, therefore, does not or will not suffer, whoever leads a sumptuous life, whoever pursues all sorts of pleasures or complacently wallows in sinful lusts cannot possibly belong to a body whose head is pierced with thorns.

Finally, there was presented to Christ a reed, as a scepter, to remind Him of all the misery, emptiness and evanescence of His kingly sway. But there ye are in error, ye soldiers! Do ye not know that the windstorm may indeed uproot mighty oaks and cedars, but that it cannot harm the reed which bends and turns? Have ye never heard how rushing floods wash away palaces, but pass without harm over the deep-rooted and yielding reed! Where are now the proud thrones of the ancient world? Where the golden scepters of the Cæsars? What is there left of so many once powerful kingdoms and empires? Nothing but ruins and heaps of rubbish, nothing but remnants in a thousand scattered fragments. But the King Whom ye have crowned, still wields His mild scepter and He shall reign to the end of time.

The coronation is over. Christ is clad in the emblems of His royal dignity. Sitting upon the pillar of flagellation as upon a throne, or leaning against it, He now receives the homage of the soldiers. It corresponds perfectly with the insignia they have offered Him.

III.

The evangelists have carefully described to us the whole ceremony. First the soldiers went up to Christ, bowed their knees before Him and began to salute Him, saying, "Hail, king of the Jews." It is again a scene from hell, mock reverence, grinning faces, scornful looks, laughter now partly suppressed, now louder and then ringing through the air, salutes and addresses with tongues stretched out toward Him. One seeks to outdo the other in mean vulgarity. Every new coarseness, every successful jest is greeted with general applause.

But they did not stop at words and gestures. They advanced to deeds. They gave Him blows. They spat upon Him. They took the reed and beat His head with it. When dry, the nether part of the sea-reed, although hollow, is as hard and tough as wood. The Saviour had been accustomed to the blows and the spittle by His experience in the house of Caiphas. But then His eyes were bound. Now, however, He receives the homage of His future people with open eyes. Through the violent beating upon the crown, one of the thorns is said to have pierced an eye, so that its point appeared on the surface of the eye-ball. The worst feature of the homage was its last scene. They bent their knees and acted as if they worshipped Him as their God. Thus the ceremony of coronation reached its climax in the most awful blasphemy. "My people, what have I done to thee? Or wherein have I saddened thee? To thee I gave a kingly scepter, and thou gavest my head a crown of thorns! For thee I slew the kings of Canaan, and thou hast beaten my head with a reed!" A mean reward!

The thorny crown of Jesus Christ has since become, for all pious Christians, an object of veneration. "What!" exclaimed Godfrey of Bouillon, after capturing Jerusalem, "shall I carry the crown of a king where my Lord and Saviour hath carried a crown of thorns?" "Not the crown of roses, but the crown of thorns," exclaimed St.

Catherine of Siena, after Our Lord, in a heavenly vision, had offered her the choice of the one or the other. But no one was ever happier than St. Louis, the holy king of France, when the occasion was presented to him of possessing himself of the Saviour's crown of thorns. For miles, he and his court went to meet it. His eyes were streaming with tears, when, bare-footed and with uncovered head, carrying the precious relic in his hands, he entered his capital city as if in triumph. In these latter years, the Church has even established a special feast in honor of the crown of thorns, and, in Catholic countries, the priest of Jesus Christ, in holy pride, carries its semblance on the crown of his head.

As to Our Saviour Himself, the ignominy and torture of the scene of coronation was changed, even on the third day thereafter, to glory and immeasurable felicity. Surrounded by light and splendor as once upon Thabor's heights, clad with heavenly beauty as with a garment, the purple of glory upon His shoulders, upon His anointed Head the kingly diadem, He stands with the banner of victory in His hand. Eternal Love is spread upon His Divine countenance, Divine majesty rests upon His brow, a holy victorious joy beams from His transfigured eyes. It is no longer the menials nor blood-stained soldiers who accompany Him, ah, no! Now the patriarchs and the prophets and all the just of the Old Law meet Him in joy and exultation, pay their homage to the glorious Hero and adore their Divine King. Even the angels circle joyfully about the triumphant Conqueror and sing to Him heavenly lays. Let us also take part in the homage of heaven and earth! Glory and praise and adoration to Thee, O Lord Jesus Christ, Who for us hast been crowned with thorns. Praise to Thee, Thou Conqueror over sin and hell! Praise and glory to Thee, O glorious King! We worship Thee, Thou God and King of our hearts for time and for eternity.

CHAPTER XVII.

ECCE HOMO!

> "Jesus therefore came forth bearing the crown of thorns, and the purple garment. And Pilate said to them: Behold the man. When the chief-priests therefore and the servants had seen him, they cried out, saying: Crucify him, crucify him."
>
> (St. John, xix., 5, 6.)

After the soldiers had scourged Christ and crowned Him with thorns, they brought Him back into the court-room of Pilate. We cannot imagine otherwise than that Pilate was somewhat abashed at the sight of the mangled and thorn-crowned Saviour. And, considering his sense of justice, his blood must have boiled in anger and indignation. Undoubtedly he had commanded that the scourging be more severe than usual. But the soldiers had gone far beyond his intention. Besides, without his orders, even without his knowledge, they had, of their own accord, driven the thorns into the Lord's head. But he soon recovered, he ordered no punishment for the subordinates, he did not even reprove them. He overlooked the matter, for the hope arose within him that now he could more easily carry out his plan, that is, to obtain the consent of the Jews to the release of Christ. Let us consider [1]

I. Another effort of Pilate to release Christ and

II. Its result.

I.

The new effort to release Christ consisted in this, that Pilate led the Redeemer out of the court-room into the vestibule, presented Him in His pitiable condition to the Jews, and, in a few words, recommended Him to their sympathy. "Behold," said he to them, "I bring him forth unto you, that you may know that I find no cause in him." But, Pilate, what would you yourself think of a father, who after beating his son to the shedding of blood, would say to the other children, "Behold, I show him to you that you may know that I find no fault in him?" Is it not most natural to measure the enormity of a crime by the severity of the punishment determined for it by the judge? However, it is the property of sin to entangle him who commits it in the most glaring contradictions so that he is at variance not only with God, but also with good sense and sound reason. Or, do you perhaps mean that the mere circumstance of leading him out to the Jews should prove His innocence, because, if you had found Him guilty, you would immediately have sent Him to prison or to the place of execu-

[1] St. John, xix., 4–8.

tion? But what has happened at this particular moment to convince you again of His innocence? During the long scourging and crowning with thorns, you could not possibly have questioned Him. But if you previously considered Him innocent and if you still so consider Him, why do you postpone His liberation? The sense of Pilate's words, therefore, amounts to this: "I have ordered this innocent man here before you to be punished severely as a favor to you. Now, on your part, make a concession to me and make no further demands." But these words of Pilate contain a fearful self-condemnation. How could he as a just judge be swayed by human motives against his own better knowledge and allow such an excessive wrong to be done to an innocent man?

The Gospel continues, "Jesus therefore came forth bearing the crown of thorns and the purple garment. And he (Pilate) saith to them: Behold the man." Note the prudence of Pilate. He calls Him no more a king of the Jews, in order not to offend or exasperate them. He says, "Behold the man." This is the man whom you have accused as an aspirant to the throne. Whatever He may have done, He is now, without a doubt, sufficiently punished. If you intended to humiliate Him, was ever a greater shame inflicted? If you demanded blood, who ever shed more than He? If He ever had a desire for the throne, it undoubtedly has left Him by this time. Nor could He now find any adherents. Be you therefore contented and demand no more punishment. Have pity on Him.

He is neither a stone nor a dog. He is a human being like to yourselves. Why, it would be against human nature not to pity a man in such a miserable condition. And, while thus expatiating on the "Ecce Homo," Pilate pointed his finger at Christ, the soldiers held back the scarlet mantle so that all could see the terrible wounds, and for this purpose, they turned Him around in a circle.

"Behold the man!" These words certainly demonstrate the merciful heart of Pilate. But his great error was that, through his own fault, he recognized in Christ only a man. Thus it is even to-day. Whoever overlooks the divine element in Christ and in His Holy Church, will always be unfair in judgment and impious in conduct. What result did Pilate achieve?

II.

It appears that the sight of the Redeemer produced a sad impression on the multitude. For there were many among the crowd who joined in the cry "Crucify Him!" impelled more by ignorance and fear than by malice. The chief-priests noticed this. Lest their plans be frustrated, they therefore shouted as loud as they could, "Crucify Him! Crucify Him!" What an indecorous sight! Howling high-priests! How ye have forgotten the dignity of your priestly station and of your white hairs! What fanatical hatred in these men! What adorns the priest more than mercy for the unfortunate? Has he not, by virtue of his office, both the privilege and the duty to invoke grace and pity upon sinners? But like wild beasts after tasting blood, the chief-priests fall upon their victim to dismember it and to tear it to pieces. Holy Writ declares that, because they so cruelly scourged and crowned the Saviour, therefore they demand the crucifixion. They could indeed no longer turn back without bringing upon themselves the greatest embarrassment. Were Christ now released, His very maltreatment would regain for Him the hearts of the people so much sooner, and their entire fury would turn against the chief-priests. Their infernal prudence, therefore, urged them to demand the crucifixion.

Then Pilate, indignant and disgusted, said: "Take him you, and crucify him: for I find no cause in him." As if he said, "If according to your law, it be allowable to kill an innocent man, do it yourselves. I shall not commit such an outrageous injustice; our laws do not permit it." But the chief-priests would not allow this reproach and the slur cast upon the Mosaic Law to go unnoticed. "We have," they said, "a law; and according to the law he ought to die, because he made himself the Son of God."

Words cannot adequately characterize this conduct of the chief-priests. Nothing ever equaled it in meanness, malice and low cunning. Having found that with their charge of high-treason they would not attain their object, they drop it then and there, and by charging blasphemy, which heretofore they dared not mention to the pagan judge, they, by one stroke, give the trial a new direction. Now, finally, the section of the Mosaic Law according to which Christ ought to be put to death was found. Only it is strange that the high-priests did not propose the penalty of stoning as the Mosaic Law required, but the illegal crucifixion. In later centuries the enemies of Christ and of the Church were not always fortunate enough to find in their constitutional laws and other codes such provisions as would empower them to proceed against the Church. Nothing then remained to preserve legal appearances, but for legislative majorities hurriedly to fabricate new sections. Then they could, with a calm conscience, appear before the astonished world and say, "We have a law, and according to section so and so,—he must die."

Contrary to all expectation, the charge of the chief-priests that Christ had proclaimed Himself to be the Son of God, made a deep impression on Pilate. "When Pilate therefore," says the Gospel, "had heard this saying, he feared the more." Pilate then had feared before this. He feared, first of all, the chief-priests, whom he would not offend. He feared the emperor to whom all the official documents of the trial must be sent. The unjust treatment of an accused and his unjust condemnation, would certainly entail removal from office. And undoubtedly his conduct toward Christ also caused him the most poignant pangs of conscience. Why then should he fear the more? It need not seem singular to us that Pilate was strangely affected at the thought that perhaps

Christ, Whom he had so cruelly and unjustly scourged, was after all the son of a god. According to the ancient Greek and Roman mythologies, with which Pilate was undoubtedly acquainted, there were many gods, with families and numerous sons and daughters. Many of these were said to have repeatedly appeared upon earth and to have held intercourse with mortal men. In his surmise that Christ was such a scion of divinity, Pilate was confirmed by Christ's truly Divine dignity, calmness and majesty, by His inexplicable patience and meekness amid such inexpressible sufferings. He thought of the extraordinary deeds of the man, and of what He had told him of His kingdom: that it was not of this world. Finally, the warning of his wife came to his mind: "Have nothing to do with this just man; there is something extraordinary about him." Now, according to heathen ideas, it was a dangerous matter to excite the anger of the gods. Jupiter threw thunderbolts upon his enemies, Apollo cast poisoned arrows that caused pestilential ulcers, Mars devastated the territory of an enemy with bloody war, Neptune caused the sea to overflow its limits, Vulcan opened the earth and exhaled fire. Pilate then, if he assaulted the son of a god, would not escape the ire and revenge of the older divinity.

This frivolous man of the world, then, this doubter and scoffer, this prudent official, who, a short time ago, had superciliously asked, "What is truth?" was not free from religious presentiments. But because he was too proud to submit to faith, he had become a slave to superstition. Thus even to-day infidelity and superstition are very close neighbors.

Pilate, then, feared the more and resolved to be more careful and to again examine the case thoroughly before proceeding any further against Christ. He therefore took the Redeemer back with him into the court-room to give him a second hearing. The thought that *perhaps* he was in the presence of the son of a god whom he had wronged and whom he was about to wrong even more, filled the heathen with fear and anxiety. The Christian, on the other hand, knows and believes with all certainty that he is close to God, that God is omnipresent and all-knowing, that in God we live, and move, and are. Still there are many who are not disquieted at the thought of their many offenses against the omnipresent God; many who do not fear to provoke His anger by new offenses.

Ecce Homo! Behold the Man! Such was the proclamation of Pilate to the Jews. The chief-priests, however, would not look upon the picture, Ecce Homo; it pleased them not. They shouted, "Crucify Him! Crucify Him!" Almighty God will again present this sight to them and to all impenitent sinners, against their will, on the day of judgment. They will see Whom they have crucified, Whom they have offended by their sins. We, however, shall attentively gaze upon the Ecce Homo and impress it deeply upon our hearts. Yea, may the Lord be ever before our eyes, as He, bleeding from a thousand wounds, with the crown of thorns on His head and the scarlet mantle about His shoulders, stands publicly, as it were, in a pillory. Let us continually thank Him for His incomprehensible love and repay the same with our love. Let us thank Him especially for having given us in the Ecce Homo a shield against which all the arrows of hell shall be of no avail. How, let us say when Satan tempts us to sensuality, to avarice or to pride, how can I offend Him Who has suffered so much for me? Yes, who would think it possible, the Ecce Homo disarms even the anger of Divine Justice. "Regard, O Lord"—let this be our prayer when the thought of our sins fills us with fear and trembling—"Regard, O Lord the picture of Thine only begotten Son; and, for the sake of His Blood, pardon Thou our misdeeds." May the Ecce Homo, finally, in the hour of death be our strength and hope, so that we may happily withstand the last attack of Satan and, through the merits of the crowned Redeemer, obtain the grace to behold Him in His glory, world without end. Amen.

CHAPTER XVIII.

THE SECOND HEARING OF CHRIST BEFORE PILATE

> "And from thenceforth Pilate sought to release him. But the Jews cried out, saying: If thou release this man, thou art not Cæsar's friend." (St. John, xix., 12.)

The new effort of Pilate to liberate Christ, was a complete failure. The Ecce Homo was followed by the cry, "Crucify Him," and, owing to the fresh accusations of the high-priests, Pilate found himself in the awkward position of having to begin the trial anew. For such is the effect and the penalty of irresolution and unfinished effort that the man who once yields to them is plunged into ever new and more elaborate entanglements, until it becomes impossible for him to extricate himself.

Let us consider[1]

I. The hearing in detail and

II. The mistakes of Pilate during its progress.

I.

Pilate began the trial with the question, "Whence art thou?" He did not inquire about

[1] St. John, xix., 9–12.

the country or town in which Christ was born, for that he already knew. The meaning of his question was rather, "Who is thy father? Who is thy mother?" For he wished to know whether, as the charge had it, He was indeed the son of some deity. Pilate received no reply. "Jesus gave him no answer." This may seem strange to us. The Saviour had replied to several questions put to Him by Pilate, His legitimate judge. Whence the silence now? We may mention as a first reason that, in the meantime, Pilate had rendered himself unworthy of a reply. At the end of the first hearing, he had contemptuously asked, "What is truth?" and turned his back upon Christ. Besides, Pilate had, to some extent, yielded to the Jews, and, against his better knowledge, permitted the Redeemer to be scourged. Then the fear which elicited his question was merely a servile fear. He feared not so much to offend the gods by mistakes as to draw down upon himself their revenge. Now whoever fears only the punishment and not the sin; whoever submits through the fear of temporal misfortune only, does not deserve an answer from the Redeemer.

As, furthermore, Pilate had asked his question from a pagan point of view, that is, from the standpoint of polytheism, an answer from Christ either would have confirmed him in his erroneous opinions, or would have been entirely unintelligible to him. Besides, further information concerning the person of Christ was altogether superfluous as, owing to previous answers, Pilate must have attained to a perfect conviction of His innocence and, in fact, he had expressed himself repeatedly to that effect. It was sufficient for him to know that Christ was a king in a supernatural sense. And even this he had not rightly understood.

Finally, the main reason why the Saviour did not answer the question of the judge was that Pilate deemed he had a right to know truths which cannot be accepted without due humility of heart and of intellect. Caiphas had adjured the Redeemer in the name of Almighty God to tell whether or not He was the Son of God. He was, besides, as high-priest, the legitimate custodian of the pure doctrine in Israel. But it was arrogance and curiosity which prompted Pilate's question, "Whence art thou?" Ah, Pilate! To fathom the origin of Jesus Christ, how, in His Divinity, He is begotten from all eternity by the Father, how in His Humanity, through the overshadowing power of the Holy Ghost, He was born of Mary, His virginal Mother, means to penetrate into the inmost depths of the Godhead; it means to be introduced into the inscrutable secrets of the Most Holy Trinity and of the Incarnation. If thou wouldst know more about these truths, thou shouldst not ask in a domineering tone nor with pompous self-esteem, but rather thou shouldst fall upon thy knees and humbly ask the Saviour for enlightenment, or, in the privacy of thy home, betake thyself to prayer and remain therein until it please God to reveal Himself to thee.

The silence of the Redeemer hurt the pride of

the Roman, the otherwise well-disposed judge. Offended and indignant, he said to Christ, "Speakest thou not to me? Knowest thou not that I have power to crucify thee, and I have power to release thee?" What, Pilate! thou hast power to crucify Christ and power to release Him? Certainly not. Thou art in error. Since thou hast so often declared the Saviour's innocence, thou art no longer free to crucify Him or to release Him. There is nothing left for thee but to liberate Him without delay. Thou confoundest the idea of external power with that of right, of authority to act. The mere possession of crude, material power does not convey a right. Listen to what St. Ambrose [1] says of thee: "By thine own words, O Pilate, dost thou judge and condemn thyself. For not according to principles of right, but only because thou hadst in hand the power, thou hast liberated the robber and put to death the Giver of life." A good judge does not render decisions according to caprice but according to justice and equity.

In face of the erroneous, destructive and blasphemous view of Pilate on the origin of power, Christ was obliged to break His silence. To honor His heavenly Father and to instruct mankind, He definitely and solemnly declared that there is no power except from God. He more particularly gave Pilate to understand, that His passion and death did not depend upon Pilate's will and pleasure but upon a free dispensation of God; that,

[1] Serm. 20 in Ps. 118. n. 38 (in vers. 4.)

notwithstanding the power conferred upon him by Cæsar, Pilate could not possibly put Him to death, if it had not pleased God at this time to give free scope to the powers of darkness. He therefore said to Pilate, "Thou shouldst not have any power against me, unless it were given thee from above."

To this instruction Christ added a last, impressive warning that Pilate should not, by an unjust sentence, use the power of which he boasted to his own destruction. Therefore, Christ continued, "he that hath delivered me to thee, hath the greater sin." Which means, the sin of Caiphas is *such a great* one, just because he delivered me to a man to whom God really gave power over me; this sin is *greater than it otherwise would be,* if thou, like other people, hadst no power over me. Reflect well what responsibility thou art loading upon thyself, if, against thine own conscience, thou abusest the power given thee.[1] Pilate understood both the instruction and the admonition. In order not to offend the gods and not to draw upon himself the enmity of a superior being, he now wished to free Christ, in whom, notwithstanding all enquiries, nothing punishable could be discovered. "From thenceforth," says the Gospel, "Pilate sought to release him." Indeed, he had repeatedly willed the same before, but he had never ventured to show it as plainly as now. He therefore left the court-room, and in concise words declared to the people his intention of giving Christ

[1] See note 12.

His liberty on account of His innocence. The words he used are not mentioned in the Gospel.

It acted like a clap of thunder upon the chief-priests. Their accusation of blasphemy had, then, proven abortive. But, while Pilate was giving the Redeemer a hearing within the palace, they had to some extent prepared themselves and the people for this move by powerfully inciting and embittering the latter against Christ. And thus it happened that, according to agreement, they now all cried out together, "If thou release this man, thou art not Cæsar's friend. For whoever maketh himself a king, speaketh against Cæsar."

One would really believe that, at this moment, hell had opened its jaws and that all the demons together had come up to put these words into the mouths of the Jews. What infinite cunning and malice they denote. The charges of treason and of blasphemy had failed. They knew of naught else. They therefore dragged into the trial the personal interests of the judge by clearly giving him to understand that they would accuse him to the emperor in Rome and insist on his removal for having released a man convicted by the high-priests of the Jewish people as a pretender to the crown and a rebel against Cæsar. "Cæsar's friend" was an honorary title of imperial legates and governors.[1] Wherefore, "thou art not Cæsar's friend" meant the same as "thou canst no longer remain governor." What a base mixture of

[1] Sepp. Das Leben Jesu Christi, vi. (ch. 66), 264.

lying and calumny! Formerly the statement was that He said He was a King. Now it is said that He made Himself a King against all legitimate right, probably through rapine and bloodshed. Finally, what hypocrisy! The Jews again pretend to be the devoted servants of Cæsar and the props of Roman dominion.

Now Pilate was outmaneuvered. The certain prospect of being accused in Rome as was Herod the Elder, and of being accused to Tiberius Cæsar whose suspicious cruelty would be roused to fury at the mere shadow of a lese-majesty or of revolt; the well-founded fear of even provoking a bloody insurrection by the release of Christ and of eventually being responsible for it to Cæsar, all this was too much for Pilate. He yielded; he caused Christ, Whom he had left in the court-room, to be led forth; he seated himself upon the judge's bench, and in a few minutes the sentence of death was pronounced upon Christ.

Let us now try to discover the faults of Pilate during this hearing.

II.

As we have repeatedly seen, Pilate had many good qualities. Especially did his sense of justice contrast favorably with the craft of the chief-priests. But, alas, these good qualities were dimmed by great faults and weaknesses. The latter are indicated by an expression of Holy Writ which in appearance praises Pilate. The words of the sacred writer are, "From thenceforth Pilate sought to release Him." "From thenceforth," it says. That is well. But why only from thenceforth? Why not sooner? Before that, Pilate had often declared the innocence of Christ. Why does he only now show signs of really meaning it? Why has he, time and time again, put off the fulfilment of his most sacred duty? This was the first of Pilate's faults. It had led him into many mistakes and unfair dealings before. It began his progress towards ruin, because, by continually postponing, he became so accustomed to infringements of duty that he finally persevered in this state of neglect.

This contains an important lesson for the sinner who desires conversion. Do not procrastinate, otherwise naught will come of these good desires. It contains an important lesson for those upon whom rests the duty of restitution in matters of honor or of property, the duty of forgiveness or the duty of breaking with occasions of sin. Do not procrastinate or everything will remain as it has been. It contains an important lesson for the lukewarm Christian whose conscience admonishes him to greater zeal. Do not procrastinate or you will wear away and become putrid in your sloth.

But even now—and this is the second fault—Pilate is only half in earnest. He wishes but wills not. For if he indeed seriously means to release Christ, why does he look around as if for means to accomplish it? He has told the Redeemer to His face that he had the power to release Him. And since the release will cost him only a word, why does he hesitate so long? For none other than human motives, for nothing else but pitiable, miserable human respect. He wishes to release the Saviour, but at the same time he does not want to offend the chief-priests. He therefore tries to find a way of satisfying both parties. He is attempting the impossible, because the claims of the two parties are diametrically opposed to each other. Owing to this condition of things and to the embarrassment resulting therefrom, his mind became obscured and his will paralyzed. After that, frightening him with the phantom of removal was sufficient to bring Pilate to the end of his resources.

Therein, again, is contained an important lesson for us. He who, in his dealings with others and in his daily routine, does not confine himself to consulting God and conscience alone, he who is continually fretting about what other people will say to what he does, stands directly on the brink of sin's abyss. To bring on the fall, a threat of removal from office or of greater evils is not at all necessary. A word, a look, the smile of a ribald scoffer, of a miserable profligate is sufficient. Like to Pilate, however, all slaves of human respect shall be most poignantly deceived.

The source of all these aberrations of Pilate, as we have pointed out in considering the first hearing, was his indifference to truth, his contempt of truth. He had turned his back upon Christ. For whoever is indifferent to the truths of religion, or despises and opposes them, or spurns them, whoever, to be brief, does not and will not fulfill his duties towards God, the Origin and Teacher of truth, will also be unfaithful in the performance of his duties towards his neighbor.

The history of Pilate is therefore the clearest and most patent refutation of so-called religious indifference. It is the refutation, the moral annihilation even of free-thinkers, who maintain that one can be a just man without God or Christ or religion or faith. Whoever is not just towards God, will not long be just towards his fellow-man. In one way or another he will be unjust to him. Even the honesty of which free-thinkers boast, that honesty which is about the sum and substance of all their faith and morals, stands on tottering foundations. Not all of them may be detected as swindlers and thieves; not all of them abscond to foreign parts with other people's money; not all of them bring about fraudulent bankruptcies to enliven the business world from time to time; but their justice is certainly more fragile than a house of blocks put together by a child. At most, it is but a natural virtue, without any value for eternity.

As for us, however, who do not and will not belong to the number of these unhappy men, but who are proud of being faithful children of the Catholic Church, Pilate's sad history ought to confirm us in a threefold resolution. First, we ought to renew our resolve always to have an open, willing and grateful heart at the service of Christ, the Divine Teacher of truth, and to do all in our power to know and to love more and more the truths revealed by Him. Then we ought never to postpone the execution of our good resolutions, but should put our hands to the work immediately. Finally, all kinds of human respect and attention to the criticism and ridicule of men ought to be far removed from us when there is question of the performance of our duties. Then, and only then, shall we be able confidently to exclaim with the Apostle, "Who shall separate us from the love of Christ? shall tribulation? or distress? or famine? or nakedness? or danger? or persecution? or the sword?"[1] No, none of all these, no power of hell will be able to make us act against our conscience, as Pilate did. We shall remain true to Christ in life and in death. Then, indeed, we shall hear from His lips the consoling words, "Well done, good and faithful servant, because thou hast been faithful over a few things, I will place thee over many things: enter thou into the joy of thy Lord."[2]

[1] Rom., viii., 35.
[2] St. Matthew, xxv., 23.

CHAPTER XIX.

THE CLOSE OF THE TRIAL

"Then therefore he delivered him to them to be crucified."
(St. John, xix., 16.)

Let us to-day in spirit go to Jerusalem, into the vestibule of Pilate's palace, to hear the sentence which, in answer to the charges and demands of the Jewish people, Pontius Pilate, governor of Judea, in the name of the Roman emperor Tiberius, is to pronounce upon Jesus Christ, the Son of God and of the purest Virgin Mary. It is not without reason that St. John, the Evangelist (xix., 13, 14) narrates so minutely all the circumstances of time and place regarding this sentence. He wishes to use every means to render credible and to place beyond a doubt this incident so incredible in itself. Thus we are informed that Pilate's judgment seat in front of the building stood on the place called Gabbatha, meaning elevation. We learn that this elevation was upon the Lithostrotos, that is, a surface inlaid with small, colored pebbles. Then again, it was a Friday, the day of preparation for the paschal feast,[1] on which the paschal lambs

[1] See note 9.

must be slain, at about eleven o'clock in the morning according to our time. Thus even the shadow of suspicion that St. John had narrated an imaginary tale would disappear.

After Pilate had led Jesus out and placed himself upon the judge's seat, he made another desperate, but equally unsuccessful attempt to obtain the consent of the Jews to the release of Christ. Then he washed his hands in token of his own innocence and finally pronounced upon Christ the sentence of death.

Let us, then, consider[1]

I. The last attempt of Pilate to release Christ;
II. His solemn declaration of his own innocence, and
III. The sentencing to death of the Redeemer.

I.

Pilate, indeed, did not fail to make attempts to liberate Christ, but they were without result. Neither his eloquence in repeatedly defending the innocence of Christ, nor the shrewd scheme of opposing Jesus to Barabbas, nor the resort to scourging, nor the Ecce Homo had availed anything. Now he took a last refuge in sneers and ridicule. The Jews had said, "If thou release this man, thou art not Cæsar's friend. For whosoever maketh himself a king, speaketh against Cæsar." Pilate had somewhat recovered from the terror which these words had injected into

[1] St. John, xix., 14–16; St. Matthew, xxvii., 24, 25; St. Mark, xv., 15; St. Luke, xxiii., 24–25.

him and slyly pretended not to have understood anything of their threats. He now railed at the foolishness of the Jews in considering as their king such a piteously mangled being. "Behold your king," said he, "He, indeed, looks like a king!" Carried away by anger at this insult, not the high-priests alone, but all present cried together, "Away with him, away with him, crucify him." The whole world indeed was shouting for Jesus, the Redeemer. The whole world forced into His grasp the emblem of Salvation, the Holy Cross. The Saviour could not resist, He must needs carry it.

Then Pilate said to the Jews in a more serious tone, "Shall I crucify your king? Are ye not ashamed to demand of me the crucifixion of your king? Is it not an unnatural and monstrous demand? Is it not the mark of a degraded and unprincipled people?" But the chief-priests answered, "We have no king, but Cæsar." Now, ye chief-priests and scribes, if ye have no more a king, if the scepter hath in truth departed from Juda, then He Who stands before you is truly the Messias. From the crown of His head to the sole of His foot, He appears exactly as the prophets have described the Messias. But they say, "Cæsar is our king." These words imply the formal rejection of the Old Covenant. For the old testamentary pact between God and the Israelites was that He would be their king and they should be His people. He had confirmed and consecrated this pact with innumerable, astounding miracles for the welfare of His people; He had blessed it with torrents of benefits. He had, indeed, often had reason to complain of infidelity and breach of the solemn covenant on the part of His people, as we find recorded in the touching elegies of the prophets.[1] And therefore He even had, for some time previous to this, retired from the direct government of His people as He had exercised it through Moses and through the almost uninterrupted succession of the prophets, the custodians of the Divine compact. But until now the *legal status* of His Kingly Power had never been denied. Now, however, the degenerate priesthood called upon God to depart, declared theocracy abolished, betrayed the hallowed constitution into the hands of the civil power, allowed an imperial official to sit in judgment over the King-Messias and violently demanded His death. "Crucify Him! We have no king but Cæsar." Thus spoke the same Jews who a short time before, when the Redeemer promised them that the acceptance of His doctrine would give them freedom, had answered Him by saying, "We have never been slaves to any man: How sayest thou: You shall be free."[2] The effects of their change of government became apparent after forty years. The last effort, then, of Pilate to save Christ had collapsed. The proclamation of the synagogue declaring the Roman emperor king of the Jews, imposed silence on him and deprived him of all argument. Pru-

[1] v.g. Is. 1 sq.; Jer. ii., 5; Mich. vi., 3.
[2] St. John., viii., 33.

dence forbade him to raise a protest. He would remain a "friend of Cæsar," and thus the trial ended. There was no thought of calling witnesses in rebuttal, nor of presenting a defense by an able attorney. The only remaining feature was that the governor prepared to justify himself before the assembled multitude concerning the sentence to be pronounced, and to solemnly aver his innocence in the judicial murder about to be committed.

II.

The Gospel continues, "And Pilate seeing that he prevailed nothing: but that rather a tumult was made: taking water washed his hands before the people, saying: I am innocent of the blood of this just man; look you to it." It is remarkable that Pilate is continually seized with a dread of the crime he is about to commit, and that its fearful responsibility is clearly before his eyes. So indelibly has God engraved His Law upon the hearts of men that the conscience of even the pagan trembles in presence of guilt and of its penalty. He is, therefore, impelled to remove the crime from himself by the washing of hands and the protestation of his innocence and to load upon others the responsibility and the penalty. However, let us examine more closely the conduct of this man.

He washed his hands. When a murder had occurred, it was customary among the Jews to testify by the washing of hands that one had no part in the crime. In Deuteronomy (xxi., 1, 6–8) we read: "When there shall be found in the land the corpse of a man slain, and it is not known who is guilty of the murder, the ancients of that city shall come to the person slain and shall wash their hands . . . and say: Our hands did not shed this blood. And the guilt of blood shall be taken from them." Pilate, who, on account of his official position as judge and of his continual relations with the Jews, was undoubtedly aware of this custom, made use of it now to manifest his innocence in the crucifixion of Christ, soon to take place. But why all this vain acting which in no wise could denote innocence of the heart? "Though thou wash thyself with nitre," O Pilate, "thou art stained in thy iniquity."[1] And though thou shouldst lead all the waters of the Jordan and all the waves of the Red Sea over thy hands, they will not wash away the stain of blood. By this wretched mummery, the fool would deceive himself and save the appearance of his innocence before the public. There is scarcely anything so ridiculous, disgusting and demoralizing as hypocrisy.

After washing his hands, Pilate, in accordance with the Mosaic Law, declares his innocence by spoken words. But how contradictory they were! He calls Jesus a just man and, in the same breath, he speaks of the blood which this just man is to shed. He seems to have forgotten the fearful injustice this just man has already suffered at his

[1] Jer., ii., 22.

hands, or perhaps he thinks that it was justified by a good and noble purpose. Now, when he has on the tip of his tongue the sentence of death which, according to his own utterances, is unjust to the last degree, he affirms the innocence of Christ.

Finally, he relegates the entire responsibility to others. "Look you to it." I shall not answer for the consequences; they will be upon your consciences and upon your shoulders. The people were satisfied. They declared themselves to be of the same mind. But what a dreadful deed! Even future generations were to carry the weight of guilt. Even unborn children are now pawned for the price of this Blood. For the people exclaimed as with one voice, "His blood be upon us and upon *our children.*" A fearful curse they invoked upon themselves, a dreadful curse upon their children. How, after that, could anybody be found to curse himself and others? And how terribly has this curse been realized! It followed the Jews like a ghastly shadow, making them shudder at the thought of it even before the time for its fulfilment had arrived. Seized with dread when the apostles preached about the Risen Saviour, they exclaimed, "You have a mind to bring the blood of this man upon us."[1] And when later the powerful armies of their chosen king, the Roman emperor, swept over the country, the woeful effects of the curse showed themselves in their

[1] Acts, v., 28.

most fearful colors. Blood flowed in streams, the deicides and their children were slaughtered by the thousands, until finally that clamor of the Jews for blood was silenced by the ruined walls of the holy City, the burning temple, the roads filled with crucified people, the hills of heaped-up corpses. And even now the curse has not departed from this people. Even now they wander about in foreign lands, like exiles far from the paternal domains, without sacrifice, without altar, without a king, an object of the anger of God and of the scorn of nations; a living monument of their ancestors' disgrace.

But this judgment of God should not prevent us from crying with our whole soul and with a most yearning desire, "His Blood be upon us!" And you, Christian parents, add the prayer, "His Blood be upon our children!" Most Sacred Blood of Jesus Christ, come upon us and purify us. The destroying angel beheld the blood of the paschal lamb on the door-posts of the houses, and the Israelites were saved from bodily death. Protect us then, O Jesus, through Thy precious Blood, against the onslaughts of the evil enemy, protect us against the death of the soul. O Blood of Our God, flow in all Thy plenitude into our hearts! Sanctify us! And may not a single drop be lost to us.

Finally the moment had arrived when the trial was to close with the death-sentence.

III.

"His blood be upon us and upon our children." This declaration seemed to quiet Pilate. It encouraged him to order the release of Barabbas for the paschal feast and to pronounce the sentence of death upon Christ. Clad in the official robe of a Roman prætor and surrounded by soldiers and servants who bore the insignia of civil power and of the penal court, Pilate arose with affected calm, dignity and majesty. As if by magic, the tumult and clamors of the raving multitude ceased. A dead silence reigned in the entire assemblage. Every one listened, every one was intent upon the sentence of the judge. Every one hung on his lips. Even the angels descended from heaven to be witnesses of the unheard-of tragedy and to ascertain for what cause the Immortal One deserved death. But what a disappointment! What an astounding procedure! There was no trace of a regular judicial sentence, no indication of a definite crime, without which even a purposely unfair judge would not venture a sentence. There was no reference to the statute according to which the accused had forfeited his life. There was happening something impossible, such as the world had never before witnessed. Indeed, many an innocent man had already been condemned, but no one had ever been condemned for being innocent. "And Pilate," says Holy Writ, "gave sentence that it should be *as they required.* Jesus he delivered up to *their will* to be crucified." It was, then, not to punish a crime, but to please the people and to gratify their wishes that Pilate delivered the Redeemer to death. Be ye amazed, O ye heavens! May the crimson of shame cover thy face, O earth! The Son of God is sentenced as a criminal. Innocence is betrayed to sinners, the Lamb to ravenous wolves. Now the prophecy is fulfilled: "The Son of Man shall be delivered to the Gentiles, and shall be mocked and scourged, and they will put Him to death."

The sentence was pronounced. In the case of a murderer or robber the trial might have lasted days or weeks. In the case of Christ everything was done in a few hours. At other times, O Pilate, thou couldst subdue the seditious crowds with soldiers and swords and lances; why not now? Where is thy courage, thy strength of will? Why didst thou not, at least, postpone the sentence till the storm had quieted down? Wholly astonished at the quick and favorable ending of the trial, the crowd burst forth into wild rejoicing. It roared with pleasure. It gave vent to satanic shouts of derision. The chief-priests meanwhile crowded around Pilate. They complimented him, and, in token of friendship and gratitude, they shook his hand. But the most happy of all was that consummate scoundrel, Caiphas, the high-priest. He sent messengers throughout the whole of Jerusalem to announce the joyful news and he invited the whole people, men and women, old folks and children, to take part in the execution of Jesus Christ, the Son of the living God.

Mute and speechless, the Redeemer stood before the bar of the tribunal. Mute and speechless He heard the cruel sentence. Mute and speechless He heard the blasphemies and the jests of His enemies. His answer was a silence full of heavenly majesty. But the sorrows of His humbled Heart He offered up to God and declared Himself now ready to suffer death for the infinite glory of His heavenly Father, for the redemption of the souls in Limbo and for the salvation of the whole world. It is certain, infallibly certain, that at this moment Christ thought of each one of us. We shall thank Our Redeemer for this memento. Indeed, we need it, we need His grace. For in paradise, the sentence of death had been pronounced against us. We all must die. But alas! we shall not die innocently as Christ died. Vouchsafe then unto us, O innocent Saviour, condemned to death as Thou art, vouchsafe unto us the grace, at least, not to die the death of the sinner, but rather the death of the just.

CHAPTER XX.

THE CARRYING OF THE CROSS

"They took off the cloak from him and put on him his own garments, and led him away to crucify him." (St. Matthew, xxvii., 31.)

Pilate had delivered the Redeemer to the will of His accusers that they might crucify Him, and they set to work without delay. Since the advent of Tiberius to the imperial throne, criminals sentenced by the Roman senate were reprieved for ten days, and when the emperor had pronounced the sentence, even for thirty days. Usually, at least one day of grace was granted. Very rarely did the execution take place on the day of the sentencing. The chief-priests would not grant Christ such a reprieve for reasons already mentioned and for fear lest Pilate come to his senses and regret and change the sentence of death already pronounced. Therefore, they were very anxious to get Christ out of the way as soon as possible. Let us consider [1]

I. The preparations for the last journey;
II. The journey to the gate of the city.

[1] St. John, xix., 16–22; St. Matthew, xxvii., 31; St. Mark, xv., 20; St. Luke, xxiii., 32.

I.

The preparation for the last journey consisted in the following four things. First the cross was procured. Either it was now hurriedly constructed, or it had been made during the final trial, or perhaps the Romans kept on hand a supply of crosses for purposes similar to the present one. The cross of Christ was at least fifteen feet long including the part in the ground. For the feet of the Saviour suspended on the cross were quite distant from the ground, since Scripture says that He was exalted. Then there was a rod needed to apply to His mouth the sponge saturated with vinegar. The cross-piece either at right angles with the main piece, or, in two parts, turned upwards at either side, may have been six feet long. Thickness and width were suited to the purpose of the cross, and we may truthfully say to Jesus in our prayers, "Who hast carried the *heavy* cross for us."

Then they prepared the title of guilt which was to be attached to the cross above the head of the Redeemer. Wooden tablets coated with plaster were used for this purpose, and for official notices there were always some on hand. The tablet had on it the name of the crime. In the case of Christ, Pilate caused the title to be written in the Latin, Greek and Hebrew languages, the first being the language of the emperor, and the other two the popular tongues. For many Jews, living in foreign parts and present for the paschal feast, understood the Greek better than the Hebrew tongue. Moreover, the use of three languages in the title had a deeper meaning. The confusion of languages at Babylon was the expression of God's anger. The holy cross, the sign of reconciliation, was to restore the unity of tongues. In the unity of faith and of love the peoples of all tongues should be united in the worship of the Crucified One. The title read, "Jesus of Nazareth, King of the Jews." Now we have it in clear terms from the judge himself that Christ was not executed on account of a crime, but because He was Jesus, that is, the Redeemer, and because He was *King* in the realm of truth.

Whether Pilate, in framing this title, purposely desired to vex the chief-priests, cannot be stated with certainty. It suffices to remark that they felt and showed themselves offended and aggrieved. Therefore, according to the opinion of several commentators, they entered a protest at once in front of the court building, against the wording of the title, although St. John narrates it as happening later on. They said to Pilate, "Write not, the king of the Jews; but that he said: I am the king of the Jews." But Pilate, who towards the end had been so yielding, answered, "What I have written, I have written"; from which words they could draw the conclusion, "and thus shall it remain." For an official document cannot well be changed; it might diminish the respect due to authority. Thus Pilate, unwittingly gave testimony unto the truth. Thus, unwittingly, at an early date, did he produce a short gospel. Not to lose time and not to anger Pilate, the chief-priests relinquished their wish.

Meanwhile, the soldiers prepared the Saviour for His last journey. They tore from Him the scarlet mantle and put on Him His own garment. This was done, as St. Ambrose says, in order that, clothed in His own garment, He might, when led forth, be more easily recognized by the populace as the now unmasked deceiver Who had been acclaimed by their hosannas a few days before. This change of garments was again most painful to the Redeemer. The scarlet mantle tightly adhered to His wounded body, whence the blood began to flow anew. Just as painful to His Sacred head was the putting on of the outer garment. It was not in parts and had but a small opening at the top and therefore had to be drawn over the head to the shoulders. They then violently and amid jests pushed against the crown of thorns, if indeed they were not constrained to remove it and press it on again, owing to its long and branching thorns.

Finally they led Christ to the place where the cross was. We cannot help but think that at the first sight of it, undoubtedly of His own free will, the Saviour was filled with fear and dismay and that He trembled even to the very marrow of His bones. How a child will tremble at the sight of the rod, a criminal at the sight of instruments of torture, a condemned man at the sight of the sword or of the gallows! Thus and even more did the Saviour tremble, for, sin excepted, He had taken upon Himself all the infirmities and weaknesses of our nature. But at the same time His soul raised itself from purely human sensations to loftier, divine thoughts and sentiments. He had so often yearned for the cross. How He had longed to see the sacrifice consummated! Now the desired hour had finally arrived. The Redeemer had, therefore, hardly beheld the cross, when he saluted it as the instrument of the salvation of the world. He embraced it as a most intimate friend, long expected and finally found. His Divine lips imprinted upon it a tender kiss. He pressed it most joyfully to His Most Sacred Heart, and, with His own hands, He laid it upon His hallowed shoulder.

Then a trumpet gives the signal and the triumphal procession of the King of kings is set in motion. Thus, in the future, the Redeemer will appear with the cross in the clouds of heaven to sit in judgment upon the good and the bad. Let us follow Our Saviour in His journey to the gate of the city.

II.

Although we know with certainty who took part in this procession, the order in which they moved is not given. We may imagine in the lead the centurion (who was at the head of one hundred soldiers), to whom, according to Holy Writ, had been entrusted the work of escorting the Saviour to the place of execution and carrying out the sentence. The commander of the thousand soldiers remained to guard the palace. Without doubt a strong convoy of troops accompanied the procession and surrounded the prisoners, to effectually hinder all attempts at rescue. The chief-priests, scribes and ancients formed an escort of honor to the centurion. Then followed a soldier, who carried attached to his lance, as a herald, the title of Christ's guilt. Then came the Redeemer. After Him followed the two thieves with their titles around their necks, under proper military guard. According to custom, they also had to carry their own crosses, which however, was not very difficult for them as they were men of strong constitution and accustomed to bodily exertion. Nor had they sweat blood or passed an entire night in agony and suffering. Lastly followed an immense throng of people who were impelled from different motives to witness the execution, some from curiosity, some from bloodthirsty morbidness, others from diabolical malice and a few from sympathy and pity.

Now, the various figures of the Old Law were rapidly being realized. The Redeemer, dragging his cross to the city gate, is innocent Abel, who was led forth by his envious brother to be slain with a club of wood. He is the true Isaac, Who carries on His shoulders the wood of His sacrifice; in fact, He takes His cross upon Himself in the very place where Isaac of old had deposited the wood laid on him by his father.[1] He is the

[1] See note 13.

true Moses, Who holds the rod in His hands to divide the Red Sea and to liberate His people from Egyptian thraldom. He is David, Who, with a staff in His hand, goes forth to meet Goliath.

The procession, starting from Pilate's mansion, moved in a westerly direction over twelve hundred paces through the middle of the city. The most frequented streets were carefully chosen for the march. "Whenever we crucify a criminal," writes Quintilian,[1] "the most populous streets are selected so that the multiude may look on and be seized with fear."

What the Redeemer suffered on this way of the cross goes beyond all we can conceive. At every step on the uneven, hilly street, the wounds of His scourged shoulder become deeper and more yawning. Often the heavy cross-beam fell against the thorn-crowned Head. The Saviour, tired unto death and without strength, drags Himself wearily along under the mighty load. Suddenly the procession halts. What has happened? The Almighty, the infinitely Powerful has sunk exhausted, and upon Him has fallen the wood of martyrdom. He writhes in pain in the dust like to a worm trodden upon. But the soldiers know a remedy. With scourges and sharp thorns applied according to Roman usage, they help Him to His feet, and again Christ staggers along. But behold, after a few hundred steps, He falls a second time and, near the gate of the city, a third

[1] Sepp., vi., 303.

time.[1] Our relapses into sin are the cause of this.

If the sufferings of His body were great, the sufferings of His Divine Heart were still greater. I shall not speak of the scorn of His avowed enemies, who gave vent to their satanic joy by blaspheming Him and spitting upon Him, by blows and kicks, and by throwing dirt and stones upon Him. It caused Christ more sadness that the official sentence of death had not failed to make an impression upon those who, during the trial, had been partly in sympathy with Him. "He must then," they said one to another, "have been an impostor, a magician, a blasphemer and a rebel, or matters would not have taken such a bad turn."

But the greatest grief of the Saviour, a grief which pierced His Heart, was the sight of His sorrowful Mother. When formerly He worked His miracles before the astonished multitudes, when He celebrated His triumphs, when amid the rejoicings of the whole people, He entered Jerusalem, His Blessed Mother never met Him. But now, after the death-sentence had been finally pronounced against Him, the Queen of Martyrs goes to take part in the ignominy and in the cross of her Son, and to assist Him in the hour of death. She, therefore, accompanied by St. John, hurried after the procession by a circuitous route, and, at the crossing of two streets, suddenly stood face to face with Him. Oh! what a sad meeting! What

[1] See note 14.

a heart-rending scene! Floods of tears stream from the eyes of the sorrowful Mother, floods of tears from the eyes of the Divine suffering Son. As burning fire, the sufferings of the Son tortured the heart of the Mother, as burning fire, the sufferings of the Mother tortured the Heart of the Son. To address each other consoling words was not allowed them. But their pitiful looks were more eloquent than any words. Truly the Saviour, carrying His cross and meeting His Blessed Mother, is a scene which ought to soften a stone to pity.

Finally, the column arrived at the "Garden Gate," so called from the wonderfully beautiful garden which lay just outside of it and stretched round about the foot of Calvary, the hill about to bear aloft the tree of life. The Redeemer slowly passed through the gate. The dignity of a king was upon His shoulder. Now one step, then another, then a third and a last step and His back was turned upon Jerusalem, without recall, for all times, for ever. A few days before He had complained, "How often would I have gathered together thy children, as the hen doth gather her chickens under her wings."[1] But Jerusalem would not. It banished Him out of its walls. Now the time of grace was lost, now the days of visitation were past. Now Jerusalem was rejected and abandoned to destruction and ruin.

As Christ turned His back upon Jerusalem and

[1] St. Matthew, xxiii., 37.

the Jewish people, He has also, in the course of the centuries, turned away from many a Christian nation, from many a Christian family and from many a Christian soul, without recall, for always; however, and let us mark it well, only when they, like the obstinate Jews, had first violently driven Him out. If many lands in Asia, Africa and eastern Europe where once Christian faith and morality held majestic sway, lands which exhaled the aroma of consecrated virginity and which were saturated with the blood of martyrs, are now become dreadful deserts, dreary and dying under the yoke of the effeminate slaves of the Crescent; if the imposing patriarchal churches in which general Councils were held and Catholic doctrine defined, are now a heap of ruins still smoking from the thunderbolts hurled at them by the Almighty,—all this has its reason in the fact that the people, by rebelling against the supreme teaching authority of the Church or by continuing the practice of horrible impurity and of other vices, dragged Christ the Lord violently out of their cities and out of their countries. If, in later times, many parts of Germany and of other countries of Europe, by a fearful judgment of God, were cut off from the maternal trunk of the Catholic Church and are now decaying in their false beliefs, the crime is upon the conscience of those princes and governments, who to satisfy their pride and their greed, clung to a runaway, immoral monk as to a divinity, and, by violently driving Christ in His priests over the frontiers, also most cruelly banished Christ from the hearts of their subjects. If, furthermore, we behold in this country many families descended from Catholic ancestors, but now in the clutches of infidelity, of heresy, of free-thinking or of secret societies, the reason of it is to be found in the fact that the parents either by an unchristian education, by irreligious schooling given the children, or by admitting the spirit of the world into the sanctuary of the family, showed Christ the door against His will, or closed the door on Him from the very start by beginning their married life with sacrilegious confessions and marriages outside the Church. If finally there are Catholics, who, notwithstanding their Christian education, live like pagans and apparently enjoy it, we may be sure that it cost them more difficulty and more efforts to drive Christ forever from their souls, than it cost the chief-priests to lead Christ out of Jerusalem.

But there is nothing more terrible than to reject Christ. Should there be among us an unfortunate soul who has rejected Him by mortal sin, let him use the time of visitation and of grace and, by prayer, contrition and works of penance, force the Redeemer speedily to return. But we should all renew our resolutions to keep Christ with us and in us at any cost. Let us ask Him for this grace in the words of the disciples who went to Emmaus: "Stay with us because it is towards evening." Yea, may Christ remain with us, may He remain in our country, may He remain in our families, may He remain in our hearts and unite us with Himself for all eternity.

CHAPTER XXI.

THE MARCH TO THE PLACE OF EXECUTION

"And as they led him away, they laid hold of one Simon of Cyrene, coming from the country: and they laid the cross on him to carry after Jesus. And there followed him a great multitude of people, and of women who bewailed and lamented him." (St. Luke, xxiii., 26–27.)

After the Redeemer, carrying His cross, had passed through the "Garden Gate," the procession, in the order already described, slowly wended its way towards Mount Calvary. At some distance from the ribald mob, followed the sorrowful mother and St. John. They were joined, probably at the gate of the city, by those pious women whom we shall meet later on with Mary at the foot of the Cross. There is only one circumstance which makes this second part of the way of the Cross remarkable: the circumstance that, for the first time since the beginning of His Passion, Christ receives sympathy from the Jews and, therefore, relief and consolation. In the first place, the chief-priests show sympathy, albeit a cruel sympathy. They prevail on the soldiers to take the cross from Christ and to make a stranger carry it. Then He received pity from the women who were among the throng; they lamented and bewailed Him, and one of their number even offered Him her kerchief to wipe off the drops of blood. Let us therefore consider [1]

I. The sympathy of the chief-priests;

II. The sympathy of the women of Jerusalem.

I.

The farther the procession advanced, the greater became the anxiety of Christ's enemies lest He should not reach Mount Calvary. While still within the city walls He had thrice broken down under the cross. But now, when the ascent of the hill began, His exhaustion reached its climax. There was danger, then, that Christ would succumb to weakness and not die the ignominous death of the Cross. This must be prevented. The enemies therefore pondered over how to afford Him some relief. But who was to help the Redeemer carry the cross? Even the Roman soldiers would have been ashamed to do it. For the cross was the wood of ignominy and a curse. Just at this juncture they were met by a stranger, whose name was Simon of Cyrene. From his Jewish name some commentators draw the conclusion that he was of Hebrew origin. But others opine with St. Hilary, St. Ambrose, St. Leo and Venerable Bede, that he was a heathen. For, after the rejection of the deicidal synagogue, the pagan world

[1] St. Matthew, xxvii., 32; St. Mark, xv., 21; St. Luke, xxiii., 26–31.

was called to the imitation of Christ. A pagan, then, should have the honor of carrying the cross after Christ. Perhaps Simon was a convert to Judaism. He was returning from his field outside of Jerusalem to the city, as it was almost noontime. As soon as the chief-priests saw him, they advised the soldiers to lay the cross on the shoulders of the stranger.

This proposition greatly pleased the soldiers. Presumably they had been active since midnight and were therefore very tired. And as events had followed each other in rapid succession, they had probably had no opportunity of taking any nourishment. For this reason they had for some time been impatient to see the end of the whole affair and had forcibly cursed every delay occasioned by the repeated falls of the Saviour. They therefore made use of the privilege of Roman soldiers in the provinces of pressing into service any one not a Roman, in a case of necessity. They seized Simon and put the cross on him. Although he inwardly rebelled, he preserved a cheerful face, because to the one who declined to serve the Romans applied severe punishments. "When pressed into service," says the pagan writer Arrian,[1] "and driven by the soldiers, let it happen, resist not, grumble not, or thou shalt receive blows and lose thy mule besides." Whether Simon carried the cross alone or whether he merely helped the Saviour carry it, cannot be definitely stated. The

1 Sepp., vi., 306.

former opinion is the more probable. It is more in accord with the words of St. Luke that Simon carried the cross after Jesus, and again, it is in harmony with the object of the chief-priests, which was to prevent, at any price, the untimely death of Christ.

Here the question presents itself: why did Christ, Who on other occasions hailed with delight new sufferings and never accepted relief, now make an exception to His usual custom? Undoubtedly His exhaustion had reached the extreme limit and, humanly speaking, He could no longer drag His cross along without help. But had He not already suffered to an extent far beyond the limit of natural laws? Was there not required a continued miracle, even before this, to enable Him to sustain such great sufferings? Why, then, this notable exception during the way of the cross? First, the Redeemer wished to remind us that sinners, represented by Simon, should in justice carry the cross and suffer death, and that His death was due to sinners and not to Himself. Therefore, after first bearing the cross as a sign of His victory over Satan, Christ relinquished it to Simon. Then He would again impress on our hearts the important truth so often taught by Himself, that to obtain eternal salvation, it was not sufficient that He should carry the cross for us, but it was necessary that we, also, should carry it after Him. He inculcates, finally, that we must patiently bear not only the cross sent to us directly by God, but also the cross imposed on us by the malice of men, as it was imposed on Simon of Cyrene. The latter cross is certainly no rarity and, it is withal, very burdensome. There are parents who drag along a heavy cross. Who loaded it upon them? Unruly children, children who are disobedient and given to worldly pleasures. Many a Christian husband has a heavy cross to bear. Who has burdened him with it? A wife forgetful of duty, negligent in household affairs and in the training of children, and carrying on flirtations with suspicious characters. Many a wife has a heavy cross to carry. Who has placed it upon her? A husband given to drink, whose tongue continually defiles his home with curses and blasphemies. There are many other Christians who wearily drag along their cross. Who has put it upon them? Calumniating tongues that have robbed them of their good name.

Indeed, in itself, it is difficult and humiliating to carry the cross patiently and with resignation to God's Holy will. But it becomes easy, when, like Simon of Cyrene, we continually have Christ before our eyes and look more upon Him than at the cross dragging behind us. And if, at the first moment, Simon stood abashed at the shameful burden of the cross, this burden, through the grace of the Redeemer, became lighter and sweeter at every step, aye so sweet that at the end he gave up the cross with as much reluctance as when he at first received it upon his shoulders. Then let us look at the fruits and the usefulness of carrying the cross. In consequence of it, Simon, as well as his entire family, afterwards believed in Christ. His sons Rufus and Alexander became bishops; he and his sons became saints of the Catholic Church, saints of heaven. Happy then is he whom God has destined to carry the cross.

Let us now consider the sympathy of the women of Jerusalem.

II.

They manifested their sympathy by wailing and lamenting. This probably [1] happened outside the city where the road was considerably wider, which made it possible for the women to gather around the Saviour in great numbers. This they could more easily do as He was no longer forced to carry the cross. It is and will always be to the immortal glory of the female sex that, whilst not one of the men of Jerusalem in the long column did the least to alleviate the burden of the Saviour, these women shed bitter tears and showed their compassion by loud lamentations. As a general rule, we find in the history of the Passion more pity among the women than among the men. Procula, the wife of Pilate, had taken the lead. It is just so even now. The attendance at sermons on the Passion and at the devotions of the way of the Cross show that when there is question of meditating on the suffering Redeemer and of thereby showing Him sympathy, it is as a rule women and girls who flock around Christ. For this reason it is so much the more inspiring and edifying to see in some places

[1] See note 15.

so many men and youths affording a laudable exception to the general rule. They thereby give honorable testimony to their own pious sentiments and their manly character. They are worthy imitators of St. John, of Nicodemus, of Joseph of Arimathea.

The public manifestation of sympathy on the part of the women of Jerusalem who, oblivious of the soldiers and the chief-priests, loudly raised their laments, borders on the heroic. For, according to the report of the Jewish writers,[1] it was strictly forbidden to bewail loudly any one who was executed with the consent of the grand council. The nearest relatives were even compelled to salute the judges and the witnesses as a sign that they harbored no grudge against them and that they were satisfied with the sentence. This ceremony could, of course, not take place in the case of Christ, because the execution followed the sentence so quickly. The Romans—and Christ was condemned and executed by the Romans—overstepped in this regard all the bounds of human decency. It was nothing unusual for the Roman tyrants to force parents stolidly to assist at the execution of their children without shedding a tear. The emperor Caligula sent a litter to a father who excused himself on account of indisposition. The same emperor invited another to a festive banquet immediately after the execution of his son. It is all the more surprising that on

[1] Sepp., vi., 310.

the one hand, notwithstanding all prohibitions, the women loudly bewailed the Divine Sufferer and thereby, as it were, publicly accused the judge of unfairness, and that, on the other hand, the soldiers did not for that reason molest the women. The women were indifferent to the noise and uproar and curses of the chief-priests. They paid no attention to them.

The Saviour recognized the heroism of these women. Forgetting His own sorrows, He spoke kindly to them and rewarded their sympathy with words of zeal and admonitions to be contrite and repentant. For among all these women in the large crowd there were but few who were real followers of the Lord. The latter accompanied the sorrowful mother at some distance in the rear. The tears shed by most of the weeping women were not the result of supernatural causes nor of sorrow over the injuries done to Christ as the Son of God. They arose from natural human pity. Undoubtedly some of them did not even believe in His divinity. They saw in Christ either an innocent man condemned to death, or a criminal who, though guilty, was punished beyond all reasonable measure. The contemplation of His sufferings was, therefore, for most of these women without any spiritual value or merit. For this reason the Saviour demands of them that they cease to bewail Him, but that instead they weep for themselves, for their sins, and for the sins of their children. But to help them to a supernatural sorrow, He pointed out to them the divine judgment which would overtake Jerusalem on account of the deicide, foretelling the complete destruction of the holy city from which they might learn the dreadfulness and malice of sin. "For if in the green wood they do these things, what shall be done in the dry?" The Redeemer meant to say, if I, the Innocent One, resembling the green wood, must suffer so much for the sins of others with which I am burdened, what will happen to the dry wood, to the impenitent sinner himself? Thus in gratitude for their sympathy, natural as it was, the Redeemer offered these women cogent motives for sorrow and penance; in other words, He taught them the right manner of contemplating His bitter Passion.

This lesson of the Saviour deserves every attention on our part also. For it may happen that we also, especially those of the female sex who are naturally more tender-hearted and consequently more prone to pity and to tears, contemplate the sufferings of Christ in a manner too natural and therefore barren of result. Of course, we all believe that the Crucified is the Son of God. But we forget this too readily in meditating upon His Passion, and we see in Him only a suffering man. If meditation on His Passion and death is to be really pleasing to Christ and salutary for our souls, we must recognize in Him the suffering God-man. Such a meditation must be joined with contrition for our sins or at least it must lead us to a spirit of contrition and of penance.

There was, however, among these weeping

women one who, according to tradition, brought relief to Christ in His sufferings not merely by cries and tears, but also by her deed. The name of this woman was Seraphia, or, according to some, Berenice. She is said to have belonged to the family of Herod and to have been the same woman whom the Saviour had relieved of a bloody flux of long years' standing. The memory of this benefit had never left her. Now she beholds the benefactor in such misery, in such pain, and His countenance so covered with blood that in her love she puts aside all fear and all human considerations; she forces her way through the crowd; she heeds neither soldiers nor Jews; she falls prostrate before her Saviour; she holds up to Him her kerchief and begs Him to wipe away with it the drops of blood. The soldiers stand aghast but do not interfere. Christ does as she desires. But what was her astonishment, when the Redeemer handed back the cloth to her, to behold imprinted on it the image of Christ's Holy Face. No one had ever received such a gift, the portrait of the Son of God. She preserved it carefully, and daily honored and contemplated it. She would not have parted with it for all the world's treasures. It was only to preserve it to Christendom that she afterwards gave the priceless treasure to St. Clement, the third successor of the Prince of the apostles, St. Peter. From that time she was no longer called Seraphia, but Veronica, which means, the true image.

Nowadays, alas! the image of the suffering

Saviour is not held in such esteem or at such value by many Christians. Their dwellings are adorned with various pictures, but you will look in vain for the image of the Crucified One. And indeed, the images of the suffering Saviour and of His Blessed Mother would be out of place among all the ridiculous, even indecorous and obscene pictures which are found, not only in art galleries and in the palaces of a neo-pagan world, but also in Christian houses, in the houses of such as still make pretensions to religion and Catholicism. "What concord hath Christ with Belial?"[1]

In conclusion, let us make a short application flowing from the incidents just considered. It is true that Jesus Christ is no longer in a passible state. He has entered into His glory, into the splendor of heaven. We cannot therefore relieve Him personally of His cross as did Simon of Cyrene, nor present Him the towel as did Veronica. But the suffering Redeemer still lives in His suffering, cross-laden brethren, and the sick and the dying need our ministrations. Now if we consider that Christ has said, "As long as you did it to one of these, my least brethren, you did it to me,"[2] it follows that we should firmly resolve to lighten, as much as we can, the cross of our fellow-men by works of mercy, especially the cross of poverty, and to assist the sick and the dying in all charity and patience, to wipe from their brows the feverish sweat, to encourage and to console them. Christ,

[1] II. Cor., vi., 15.
[2] St. Matthew, xxv., 40.

in His reward, will be extremely generous to us. He may not impress His image upon the sweat-cloth, as He did for St. Veronica, but—and that is more precious—He will impress it upon our hearts. The cross, however, which we carry patiently and joyfully after Christ, the cross which we strive to lighten for our fellow-men, shall lead us, as it did Simon of Cyrene, to holiness and to the joys of paradise.

CHAPTER XXII.

THE EXECUTION

"And when they were come to the place which is called Calvary, they crucified him there."

(St. Luke, xxiii., 33.)

Very often, in the thirty-three years of His life, the Saviour had been extremely weary. He was weary on the return from Egypt. He was weary when, at the age of twelve years, He went up to Jerusalem. Hard labor in the house of Nazareth and, later on, during His apostolic travels had often tired Him. He was fatigued when the Samaritan woman met Him at the well of Jacob and when he sought the lost sheep of the house of Israel. But He had never been so weary as on this day when He had to ascend Mount Calvary. But lo! now they had arrived at the summit of the hill, and all His tiring wanderings were to have an end for evermore. Only a few hours more and He would enter upon His eternal rest.

Mount Calvary, also called Golgotha or the Skull, was, in itself, not a very high hill. What made it look imposing was the depressed level of the lower part of the city. It had its name from its resemblance to a human skull.[1] Here, then, the Redeemer was to die. The execution of a criminal was never permitted to take place inside the walls of the city. St. Paul calls our special attention to the fact that Christ had to die outside the gate of the city, just as the scape-goat laden with the sins of the people, had to be led outside the camp. "Christ," says St. Leo,[2] "was slain as our paschal lamb. But because He offered Himself to the Father as the new and real sacrifice of propitiation, He was to be crucified, not in the temple whose privilege of sacredness was at an end, nor inside the walls of the city which was awaiting its destruction on account of its crime, but 'outside the camp,' in order that, after the mysteries of the ancient sacrifice had ceased, the new sacrifice might be offered on a new altar, and that the cross of Christ be an altar not for the temple, but for the entire world."

When they arrived at the top of the hill, the two thieves were probably first scourged according to the Roman law. Flagellation always preceded crucifixion. Meanwhile the Saviour, Who had already been scourged, is said to have been brought into a rocky cavern and His feet put in the stocks to prevent His escape. This probably gave rise to the legend of the Saviour's prison, although

1 Wetzer und Welte, edit. 2, Article — Calvarienberg. *Lohmann,* S. J. Das Leben und Leiden U. H. J. Chr. Edit. 2, p. 269.

2 Serm. 8 de Pass. c. 5.

this legend may also have reference to the cell in which He was confined during the night.

When the scourging of the thieves was at an end, they proceeded to the execution of the Redeemer. Let us consider [1]

I. The final preparations for the crucifixion;
II. The crucifixion itself.

I.

The last preparations for the crucifixion consisted in offering the Saviour wine with myrrh and in stripping Him of His garments. The first incident is narrated by St. Mark in the following terms: "They gave him to drink wine mingled with myrrh; but he took it not." The evangelist St. Matthew describes it thus: "They gave him wine to drink mingled with gall. And when he had tasted, he would not drink." Apparently these two narratives are contradictory in two particulars. St. Mark says that the wine was mixed with myrrh, whilst St. Matthew says that it was mixed with gall. Again, the former states that the Saviour did not drink, while the latter asserts that He tasted and then refused the potion. But, as stated, the contradiction is only an apparent one. The Greek word, which we translate as meaning "gall," has a broader signification. It means not only gall proper, but in general every bitter, aromatic herb, such as aloes, cassia, saffron

[1] St. Matthew, xxvii, 33, 34; St. Mark, xv., 22-28; St. Luke, xxiii., 33; St. John, xix., 18.

and myrrh, and even every liquid in which such herbs have been steeped. Furthermore, the second difficulty arising from the fact that St. Mark does not mention that Christ tasted the myrrh and wine is removed by the consideration that St. Matthew, in narrating this incident, had in mind the prophetic passage, "And they gave me gall for my food,"[1] which denotes that Christ would actually take some of this bitter aliment.[2] St. Matthew therefore describes the same incident which St. Mark records, only more fully and more definitely.

In order to lessen the pains of the execution, it was customary with the Jews to offer to those who were condemned to death a generous drink of wine to which had been added benumbing opiates and sleeping potions. The myrrh also had, to a high degree, the power of deadening the sensory nerves. Usually it was compassionate women, and sometimes noble matrons who deemed it an honor to tender this service of charity to the condemned. In other cases the myrrh and wine was furnished at public expense. This custom was continued under the Roman prætors.

The drink of criminals was therefore presented to the Redeemer. He tasted it, but did not empty the cup. He would not die in a condition of stupor as did the pagan philosopher, Socrates, but in the full possession of His senses. For, notwithstanding all His sufferings, the Redeemer had

1 Psalms, lxviii., 22.

2 See note 16.

not yet suffered any particular pain in His tongue and in His palate. This however had to happen to Him as well in reparation for all sins of the tongue, for all sins of blasphemy, of uncharitable words, of calumny and of obscene language, as in reparation for all sins of intemperance, and for all transgressions of the law of fast and abstinence. For this reason the Saviour sipped the wine which, owing to the myrrh with which it was mingled, had a very bitter and sickening taste.

Then Christ was despoiled of His garments. It was a custom of the Romans to strip to the loincloth those who were to die on the cross.[1] As we have witnessed a similar scene at the scourging, we may pass briefly over this one. I wish to remark merely that this last disrobing was much more painful than the first, especially to the sacred shoulder on which Christ had carried the cross. The wounds torn open anew, burned like fire. Moreover, it was much more humiliating because it took place not only in presence of the soldiers as before, but in presence of the whole people and of persons of both sexes. But the Redeemer desired to offer a complete and superabundant satisfaction for the shameless crimes of mankind, and as He had pledged Himself to poverty upon His advent into this world, He would remain true to this pledge until death and die in the embrace of direst poverty. Let us now pass on to the consideration of the crucifixion.

[1] See note 17.

II.

To begin with, let us consider the reasons for which the Saviour wished to undergo this very manner of death and no other.

We are already acquainted with the principal reason which induced the chief-priests, scribes and pharisees to insist on the crucifixion. They wished to vent on the Redeemer all their anger and hatred, therefore they chose the most cruel manner of death. Their purpose was to cover the name of Christ with ignominy and disperse His following, therefore they chose for Him the most dishonorable death. "It is a misdemeanor," exclaims a Roman writer, "to bind a free citizen; a crime, to beat him; but it is almost parricide to condemn him to the cross." St. Paul also represents the death on the cross as the greatest of humiliations. Another reason may be taken from the circumstance that the cry, "Crucify Him!" was heard for the first time immediately after the choice between Christ and Barabbas had resulted in favor of the latter. The Jews transferred to Christ the punishment of the cross deserved by Barabbas.

The Romans themselves, furthermore, significantly elevated on the cross those who had rebelled against the emperor and who had striven by strategy or force, to be elevated to the throne. Besides, as they had placed on the Redeemer's head the crown of a king, they ought also to provide for Him a royal throne, such a throne, in fact, as would be in keeping with the coronation ceremonies.

Then, the Heavenly Father desired to be glorified in the death of His Son. The more painful, therefore, and disgraceful this death was, the more would it redound to His glory and the more brilliantly would He reveal the Power of the Son, Who overcame the world and made men partakers of the honors and wealth of heaven, not with the sword nor by means of gold and silver, but through the folly of the cross.

Again, the Redeemer had come into the world to overthrow the dominion of Satan, who had overcome our first parents through the fruit of the tree, and to destroy the tyranny of sin and of death. He had come into the world to reconcile heaven and earth, to embrace all men with outstretched arms and to press them to His heart. He could hardly accomplish all this better than by hanging between heaven and earth on the tree of the cross. The Church therefore sings in joy and exultation, "Through the wood we became slaves, and through the wood of the cross we again found freedom. Where death took its beginning, there should life arise from the grave."

Moreover, it was the Redeemer's desire to firmly convince us of the greatness of His love, of the malice and destroying power of sin, of the fearfulness of hell's punishment, of the value of the soul and of the splendors of heaven. He teaches all these truths in the most intelligible and impressive manner from the wood of the cross. The cross has become His pulpit. Again, Christ demands of us that we imitate His virtues, His humility, His patience and His obedience. We must strive to become like to Him. For this reason it is useful, necessary even, that our Divine Model hang high upon the cross so that we may easily perceive Him. We might otherwise, in the turmoil of the world, completely lose sight of the Saviour. "Look," said He once through Moses, "and make it according to the pattern, that was shown thee in the Mount."[1]

Finally, the Redeemer would give us the instrument and sign of redemption as a shield to repel the three sinful concupiscences. Now the sign of a pyre, or of a hungry lion, or of a glowing rack would not be easy to employ. On the other hand, there is nothing easier than to form the sign of the cross in the hour of temptation; it can be done everywhere and at all times. The image of the Crucified One, the crucifix, should therefore be our constant weapon. May every Christian carry it on his breast as a most precious ornament.

Such were the reasons which actuated the Redeemer to chose the crucifixion from among all other modes of death. Let us see how it was accomplished.

Crucifixion was performed by the Romans in two different ways. Usually the cross was first raised, then the criminal was bound to it, arms

[1] Exodus, xxv., 40.

and feet, after which the hands and feet were pierced with nails. In some cases the criminal was nailed fast to the cross upon the ground and then the cross was raised. It is not certain which of the two methods was followed as regards the Saviour; for which reason we shall adapt our meditation to that method which is employed, according to ancient usage, in the representations of our stations of the cross.

The cross, then, lay upon the ground, and, first of all, they had to bore the holes wherein to drive the nails. For this purpose they took the measurements of the Redeemer; the length of the extended arms and the distance from feet to hands. Thereupon Christ laid Himself willingly upon the altar of sacrifice. The first nail was put to His right hand and pierced it under heavy blows so that the sacred Blood leaped to the face of the executioners. There resulted a spasmodic contraction of the muscles and the members had to be violently stretched to bring the left hand to the hole bored in the cross. Then this left hand was pierced with a nail. Whose mind does not here revert to all the sins committed by the abuse of the hands? Some extend them to take the property of others; some abuse them in assault and murder; others—and there are so many of these—in unchaste works; others, finally, in flooding the world with impious and immoral books and pictures.

Then the sacred feet were nailed and for this purpose two nails were used. History tells us that, when the crosses were found, four holes and four nails were found in each of them. This is also in accord with what St. Bonaventure tells us of the stigmata of St. Francis. Had the right foot of Christ been placed on the left one and both pierced with one nail running to a point, the wounds of the left foot would evidently have been smaller than those of the right foot. Now, on the feet of St. Francis, the two wounds on the upper surface of both feet were of equal size as the two wounds on the nether surface. Besides, were the executioners likely to have used only one nail, when it would have been more difficult and have required more time? Here we may well think of all the sins which are committed through the abuse of the feet. What are the paths trodden by so many people, by so many Christians? Whither do they wend their way, by day and by night? One cannot even mention it. Neither is it necessary to mention it, because the broad road leading to perdition is sufficiently known to all.

Our Divine Saviour is now nailed, hands and feet, to the cross so tightly that He can no longer move a member. Thus the type, the Jewish paschal lamb, which, in the form of a cross, was roasted on a spit, found its realization. Now no one can wrest from the hands of Christ, the cross, the instrument of His victory. Oh! that we also, by love, might be nailed to the cross so fast that nothing could make us leave it and abuse our liberty.

The moment had now arrived when the great

sign of the covenant and of reconciliation between God and man was to appear upon earth and be visible to all; the moment had arrived when the throne of the King of kings was to be erected. But what untold tortures, what indescribable pains! Have you ever beheld what labor it is to erect on high and wedge into the earth a great, heavy beam? What swaying! what shocks and jolts! But a man is nailed to the beam of the cross. Rough soldiers raised it up with vehemence and let it slide into the ground, where it struck the bottom with such force that hell felt the concussion, and the old serpent writhed in torture. Oh, how cruelly the wounds of hands and feet were torn! What a torment for the Sacred Head when the crown of thorns violently struck the beam! What pains in all parts of the Sacred Body! After the cross had been made fast in the ground, a soldier attached the title of guilt above the Head of the crucified. This title was to publish to the whole world why the Redeemer had been nailed to the cross. More brilliantly than the sun's rays did it illumine the majesty of Jesus Christ's Kingdom. Thus was the execution finished.

Meanwhile, the two thieves had been nailed to their crosses by other executioners. According to our time, it was exactly twelve o'clock. The appalling sight of the Crucified One caused a momentary lull of astonishment and horror. Just then the sound of trumpets from the hill of the temple announced the sixth hour.

Christ, then, was exalted on the cross. His most

ardent desire was realized. For the cross was the object for which He strove during His whole life. It was the object of His ambition. He would be lifted up from the earth, exalted on the cross. We should now remind Him of the promise He has made us, that after being lifted up He would draw all things unto Himself. May He, therefore, in His bounty draw our hearts to Himself and unite them to His own Heart in the bonds of the most fervent love. If only we resist Him not, the Redeemer will keep His word. For on the cross He not only thought of us, but He also looked toward us. Even on the cross, He had His face turned away from Jerusalem. His regard was cast towards the occident, towards holy Rome, and from there, over the ocean, to the furthermost west, upon each one of us. With greater confidence, therefore, than that of the Israelites looking up to the brazen serpent, let us look up to the Crucified One and go with confidence to the throne of grace, that we may obtain mercy, find grace in seasonable aid [1] and die a happy death on the cross.

[1] Hebr., iv., 16.

CHAPTER XXIII.

THE FIRST WORD OF CHRIST ON THE CROSS

"Father, forgive them, for they know not what they do."
(St. Luke, xxiii., 34.)

Our Divine Saviour had most ardently desired to be exalted from the earth. Suspended on the cross, He would draw all things to Himself and, as from a sovereign throne, subject all hearts to the royal scepter of His Love. A few hours later, this cross would serve as His altar of sacrifice; upon it, in a bloody death, the High-Priest of the New Law would offer himself as a victim to the Heavenly Father. Meanwhile, He used it as a pulpit. All external circumstances, indeed, were very conducive to preaching. During all His public life, Christ had never faced such a numerous and such a choice audience. There were thousands of Jews from the whole of Palestine, among them the most distinguished of the people; there were, besides, Greeks and Romans, who represented the civilized world of that time. The place, also, was very well situated for an address; it was a hill with a gradual decline. The pulpit or the cross stood on the summit or, very probably, a little lower so that the hilltop formed a rear wall.

It was the proper height and location from which to be understood at great distance. From this pulpit, therefore, Christ wished not only to preach by His example but also to give expression by words to His sentiments, feelings and desires. However, His sermon was very short; it consisted of only seven words or sentences. To be sure, His sufferings did not permit Him to say more; and moreover, their brevity caused them to be more readily impressed on the memory of His hearers and, like darts of love, to penetrate into their hearts. Christ pronounced the first three words just after the cross was raised. Then there was an eclipse of the sun and an awful silence during three hours. Immediately before His death, He spoke the four other words.

Every child is intent upon the last words of its dying father. Even the pagan considers them sacred and revers them as being oracular. With how much greater attention and reverence should we not then hear and take to heart the last words of Our dying Redeemer.

Let us now meditate on the first of the seven words, "Father, forgive them, for they know not what they do." This word contains a petition. Let us consider

I. The object of this petition and

II. The reasons adduced by Christ why it should be granted.

I.

The object of the petition contained in the first word was forgiveness, grace and mercy.

In the Old Law, the Lord God manifested particularly His justice, wherefore the Psalmist even calls Him the "God of Vengeance." As soon as our first parents had committed their sin, they were driven out of paradise into a valley of tears. Cain, the fratricide, roamed about the earth without rest or peace, in fear and trembling and in constant dread of the avenging arm of God. The indignant Judge submerged an impure world in immense floods of water. He destroyed Sodom and Gomorrha with fire and brimstone, and He drowned Pharaoh and his armies in the sea. And, as if divine judgments were not frequent enough, king David calls upon the Almighty to enter into judgment with His enemies: "Lift up thyself, thou that judgest the earth: render a reward to the proud. How long shall sinners, O Lord: how long shall sinners glory? Shall they utter and speak iniquity: shall all speak who work injustice?"[1]

But as soon as the Son of God was extended on the cross, there resounded from its summit the words, "forgiveness, grace, mercy." This message flew over the hills, it flew over the seas, it found its echo at the extreme ends of the earth, it continued to resound throughout all Christian centuries and shall continue to resound to the last of days. Forgiveness, grace, mercy; behold the

[1] Psalms, xciii., 2–4.

watchword of the New Law. Heaven was astounded, hell trembled and gnashed its teeth, the pharisees and scribes scoffed, "Behold the hardened criminal! How he feigns innocence and denounces us as sinners. Miserable man, pray for thyself." But at this very moment, the first ray of hope beams on the thief to the right. This incident appeared so remarkable to the prophet Isaias that he foretold it centuries before: "He hath borne the sins of many and hath prayed for the transgressors."[1]

Occasionally, the crucified were driven by their cruel and constantly increasing pains to a despair which brought on outbursts of frenzy of one sort or another. They blasphemed the gods, they cursed heaven and earth, they cursed themselves and the hour of their birth, they spat upon the lookers-on, they avenged themselves on their enemies by revealing their misdeeds or by falsely imputing crimes to them. Opposed to this, what a touching scene on Golgotha! Christ is suspended between heaven and earth in the most fearful torments; round about the cross are His murderers, resembling serpents with pointed tongues, roaring lions with open jaws, wolves thirsting for blood. His suffering has reached its extreme point and commands Him to be silent; His tongue cleaves to His palate, and still the Divine lips open to utter words of forgiveness.

Let no one say henceforth that he cannot for-

[1] Is., liii., 12.

give his enemies; that it is too difficult. Thou hast not fared as did the crucified Saviour. Thou wert perhaps offended by spoken words, but not beaten with scourges. Thou wert perhaps hurt in thy sense of honor, but thou wert not crowned with thorns. Thou wert perhaps despoiled of thy property, but they left thee thy blood. I see not on thy face the defilement of thine enemies. I see thy hands, but I find thereon no wounds. Thy head is uninjured, thy hair is not torn from it, nor is thy brow bleeding. And even hadst thou been scourged and had thy flesh been torn, thy sins have merited it all a thousand times. But Christ is innocent, He is the Holy of Holies. How then, I repeat, how canst thou say: I cannot forgive, it is impossible?

However, we have not yet considered the object of the petition of Our Divine Saviour in all its bearings. Christ on the cross was not only ready Himself to forgive, but He did more; He asked God to forgive His offenders. There are Christians who have words of forgiveness on their tongues and who even in their outward demeanor show no aversion to their enemies, but in their hearts they desire that God be their avenger and that He withhold not from their enemies the punishment which they deserve. How differently did the Divine Redeemer act! He desires not that His torturers be punished, He wills that both guilt and penalty be condoned, and this at a time when they have not even, as yet, repented of their crime. He ardently desires their repentance, He wishes for them the joys of heaven, and He longs for it definitely and unconditionally, not, as He prayed for Himself in the Garden of Olives, "if it be possible." He therefore places Himself between Divine Justice and His enemies as an impenetrable wall, He protects them with His prayer as with a shield from which the darts of an irate heaven are dashed back.

It is indeed true that the commandment to love our enemies does not demand of us the greatest heroism or super-human virtue, that is, it does not oblige us under sin to suffer in silence all injuries and injustices. There are even cases in which one has not only the right but even the duty to defend himself by using all legitimate means at his command. But while doing this, we must love the person of our enemy and, according to the example of Our Lord, wish him from our heart all temporal and eternal happiness.

The object, then, of the Redeemer's petition was forgiveness, grace and mercy. Let us now consider the motives adduced by Christ why His prayer should be granted.

II.

There were two reasons which Christ brought to bear on Almighty God in order to have His petition granted. He represented to God that He was the Father, and that, on the other hand, the torturers knew not what they were doing.

Christ did not say, "*Lord,* forgive them," but, "*Father,* forgive them." Thereby He placed

Himself before the irate God as His Son. Now when a son asks his father for anything, the prayer has naturally an entirely different power and efficacy from that of a servant to his master. This Son, moreover, strengthened His petition by proffering at the same time a most valuable gift. At the moment in which Christ appealed to the Love of His Father, the latter beheld in the hands of His Son a gift, a sacrifice of infinite value. And this Son was suffering in the throes of death. Now, if at other times a father may not feel disposed to grant the petition of his son, he will surely attempt the impossible to fulfil the wishes of a child on his death-bed. Finally, the generosity of the Son Who, forgetting Himself and His sufferings, was anxious only for the welfare of His tormentors, must have touched the paternal heart of God and inclined it to reconciliation.

Nor did Christ pray, "*My* Father, forgive them," but "Father, forgive them." Thereby He represented to God that He was not only His Father, but that He desired to be the Father of all men. He pointed out to Him how He, the Father, desired to have many sons and to recognize Him, the Son, as the First-Born among many brethren, and how that would be impossible were He, the Father, to punish with severe justice these enemies and all others who offend the Son, were He to refuse them the grace of repentance and of the adoption of sonship.

Christ therefore prayed, "Father, forgive them," which means: Thou art My Father and their Father, and they are My brethren. Thou wouldst, once upon a time, have spared Sodom for the sake of a few. Have mercy, then, for the sake of Thy First-Born, on these My brethren. Whatever wrong they do, Father, is amply outweighed by My death. In fact, it is they who make it possible for me to give Thee such infinite honor. Certainly, their acts are not to be justified. But the greater their guilt is, the more glorious will be the splendor of Thy paternal Love. The more unworthy they now are of Thy favor and of Thy adoption, the more grateful will they be as Thy children later on. Hearken, therefore, to the voice of My Blood, crying for reconciliation and not to their voice, demanding that My Blood be upon them. Rather grant, O Father! that this Blood of Mine be shed for their salvation, especially as they know not what they do.

That these last words of the Redeemer applied in a strict sense to many of those present, goes without saying. The heathen soldiers, in particular, and, it may be, many others considered Christ a very culpable criminal, deserving of no mercy. But how could Christ invoke ignorance as an excuse for the chief-priests, scribes and pharisees, who had knowledge of the innumerable miracles which He had wrought to prove His Divinity? It is certain, however, that they were included in His prayer. For the words of St.

Paul, "If they had known it, they would never have crucified the Lord of glory," [1] refer undoubtedly also to the chief-priests and pharisees.

In the first place, the enemies of Christ were in ignorance, inasmuch as they knew not how to appreciate the value of the sacrifice of the cross, in the offering of which they were instrumental. Furthermore, it is peculiar to the sinner that he generally does not do evil because it is evil, but because it presents to him some desirable feature or other, that is, it appears to him as something pleasing or profitable. The ignorance, however, which Christ pleaded to excuse His enemies, is rather to be considered in a different sense. To understand this well, we must remember that the proofs of Christ's Divinity, no matter how cogent or how exclusive of any reasonable doubt, do not, nevertheless, command the assent of reason with such intrinsic necessity as, for instance, the truth that two and two are four, that there is a sun, a moon or a visible world. The possibility of a doubt, unreasonable, of course, still remains. It is now the duty of the free will—and this explains exactly the merit of an act of faith—to command reason to despise all unreasonable doubts, resolutely to accept the truth, more than sufficiently substantiated, and to submit itself to it. If this is not done and if the will permits the reason to dally with such unreasonable doubts, then the reason embraces what is false and is, in fact, immersed in ignorance.

[1] I. Cor., ii., 8.

Moreover, the words of Christ contain a truth which concerns us also, who are children of the Catholic Church. It is in truth an awful truth that the sinner can bring himself into a condition in which he boldly commits the gravest sins without knowing what he is doing. For, after the will has become accustomed to sin and has learned to love it, it brings such a pressure to bear on reason that the latter looks upon as allowable or, at least, as less evil what, in itself, is sinful in the highest degree. This ignorance, freely willed and freely produced, either in regard to faith or to the works of faith, does, of course, not absolve man from mortal guilt, for it had its origin and its rise in mortal sins. However, it is true that this ignorance, when once in fact existing, does, to some extent, diminish the deliberateness and, in consequence, the sinfulness of a particular act. Now, as the Divine Redeemer could not deny the facts themselves, viz., the hatred and envy of the chief-priests, the perjury of the false witnesses, the cowardice of Pilate and the cruelty of the soldiers, He did what, in a similar case, a prudent and careful attorney would do. He anxiously clung to even the most insignificant grounds of excuse to recommend His clients to the mercy of the Court.

Naturally the heavenly Father could not withstand the ingenious love of His Son. The earth did not open her yawning abysses, fire fell not from heaven neither did hell devour the culprits, but, owing to the prayer of Christ, Almighty God gave the sinful people a respite of forty years in which to do penance. Even more: the thief, who was converted; the heathen captain who professed belief in the Divinity of Christ; the people who struck their breasts in contrition; the thousands who on Whitsunday and thereafter embraced Christianity, all these show the effects of Christ's prayer on the cross. Ay, and as for us who perhaps have sinned mortally, that we still live and are not burning in hell, that time has been given us for repentance and penance, is owing to Our Divine High-Priest, Who, before offering the Most Holy Sacrifice on the cross, included us in His memento.

We should, then, no longer be astonished that, in view of such great love on the part of the Redeemer, St. Stephen cried out, "Lord, lay not this sin to their charge,"[1] nor that St. Paul said, "We are reviled, and we bless: we are persecuted, and we suffer it. We are blasphemed, and we entreat;"[2] nor that, afterwards, so many martyrs and confessors prayed for their enemies, as Christ prayed, "Father, forgive them, for they know not what they do." We should rather be astonished at the perversity of our own hearts, we who are so much inclined not only not to excuse our enemies but to magnify the evil they do us, to minimize their good deeds and to impute to them bad or ignoble motives. If we have ever acted thus, we should now repent of it; according to Our Saviour's

[1] Acts., vii., 59.
[2] I. Cor., iv., 12.

example, we should not only be always ready to excuse our enemies and offenders, but also look upon them as what they really are, as our brethren in Christ and children of the heavenly Father. Then the duty of forgiving will no longer be difficult to us.

We ought, however, not to close this meditation without again praising the love and mercy of Our Saviour and assuring Him of our unwavering confidence in His bounty. And, indeed, if Christ asks pardon for people who in satanic malice have brought upon Him the most dreadful tortures, if He craves grace for them even at a moment when they do not show the least sign of repentance; what sinner ought to despair, were his sins as red as blood and as innumerable as the grains of sand upon the seashore? How much less reason shall the Saviour then have to reject a contrite and humble heart? It would certainly be entirely without warrant for the just man to give way to pusillanimity or discouragement on account of the assaults of hell or of the world or of the flesh. No, whoever we may be, sinners or just, everywhere and in all circumstances, in sufferings and temptations, in life and in death, we shall pray with the Psalmist, "In thee, O Lord, have I hoped, let me never be confounded."[1]

[1] Psalms, xxx., 2.

CHAPTER XXIV.

THE SECOND WORD OF CHRIST ON THE CROSS

"Amen I say to thee, this day thou shalt be with me in paradise." (St. Luke, xxiii., 43).

Two great criminals were crucified along with Our Saviour. We are told that they were robbers and murderers. Tradition is not unanimous as to their names. The penitent one to the right of the Lord is usually called Dismas, and the impenitent one to the Lord's left, Gesmas. They were nailed to their crosses as was the Lord; they were not fastened to them with ropes as is often represented in pictures. Holy Writ contains nothing which would favor a contrary opinion. When the Gospel speaks of the crucifixion of the thieves, it uses the terms in which it speaks of the Lord's crucifixion. The circumstance, furthermore, that Pilate's permission was asked to break the bones of all three crucified, suggests the thought that all three had also been crucified in like manner. Then, Saints Augustine, Gregory and Ambrose expressly state that the nailing to the cross of the thieves was a matter of old tradition. Decisive, finally, on this question is what history tells us of the condition of the three crosses as found by

St. Helena in the reign of Constantine the Great. All three showed similar traces of blood, all three were similarly pierced with nails. Had the thieves not been nailed to the crosses and, for that reason, had there been found only one cross pierced with nails, it would not have required a miracle to identify the cross of Christ and to distinguish it from the others.

To prevent the crucified from insulting their executioners, the authorities and the emperor, their mouths were often closed by means of hooks. Cicero tells us [1] that a slave called Strato had his tongue torn out before his crucifixion, because Sassia, a notorious woman who had assassinated her husband, feared to be betrayed by the last words of the dying slave. It was surely the special Providence of God which prevented the application of such inhuman treatment to the Redeemer and to the two thieves.

The second word of Christ on the cross was addressed to the thief on the right: "Amen, I say to thee, this day thou shalt be with me in paradise." Let us consider: [2]

I. The occasion, and
II. The contents of this word.

I.

The second word was occasioned by Dismas, the thief on the right side, who reprimanded the thief

[1] Cic., pro Cluent. 66, Sepp., vi., 358.

[2] St. Luke, xxiii., 39–43; St. Matthew, xxvii., 44; St. Mark, xv., 32.

on the left for his blasphemies, and who confessed himself a sinner, defended Christ the Lord and, finally, begged for His mercy after He would arrive in His Kingdom.

It was only the thief on the left who blasphemed the Redeemer. The words of the evangelists St. Matthew and St. Mark that they who were crucified with Christ reproached Him, do not justify the conclusion that *both* blasphemed Him. For the evangelists, in their report, cite the different *classes* of people who ridiculed Christ, such as the passers-by, the scribes, the pharisees, the executioners and the thieves. However, it is certain that not all the passers-by without exception ridiculed Him and, for the same reason, we cannot conclude that both thieves did the same. Furthermore, as St. Augustine remarks, the Scriptures often use the plural number for the singular. Thus, for instance, St. Paul says of the Prophets, "They stopped the mouths of lions, they were stoned, they were cut asunder."[1] And still David alone stopped the mouth of the lion, Jeremias alone was stoned and Isaias alone was cut asunder. Besides, it is not likely that the thief on the right would have chidden his suffering companion with such freedom, had he, immediately before, committed the same sin himself, or else he certainly would have mentioned this sin in express terms in his self-accusation. Then, finally, the thief on the left would have thrown back at his monitor

[1] Hebr., xi., 33, 37.

in bitter irony his own blasphemies, which, however, did not happen. Now, as St. Luke expressly states that "one of these robbers who were hanged, blasphemed him," we must declare the thief on the right innocent in this regard.

The words of the bad thief, "If thou be Christ, save thyself, and us," denote a fearful hardheartedness and a meanness beyond description. For what is more unnatural, what is more repulsive to human feeling than that an unfortunate man should cast slurs at a companion in misfortune? Such a thing, usually, happens only in hell. The suffering, as a rule, rather console one another. These words, furthermore, contain an impudent blasphemy, inasmuch as Gesmas not only commanded the Saviour what He should do if He were the Christ, but also demanded that Christ enable him by a miracle to continue his sinful life. But if, as some commentators opine, Gesmas really recognized Christ as the God-Man, then, of course, his blasphemy was made worse by his doubting the divinity and power of Christ. This infamous wretch could no longer use hands and feet in the service of sin, for they were nailed fast. To fill the measure of his iniquities, he used his tongue. He died as he had lived, and his soul was buried in hell. This is usually the case when a man, from his youth up, heeds not the voice of conscience and adds crime to crime; he will finally grow attached to sin, which will become a strong habit; he will grow blind and obstinate and die a horrible death.

Impelled, partly by righteous indignation and partly by love for his obstinate companion in vice, whom he wished to bring to repentance, Dismas said, "Neither dost thou fear God, seeing thou art under the same condemnation?" which may be amplified as follows: that the Jews below us do not fear God, I can understand. They see Christ on the cross, and no punishment has yet reached them; wherefore they think themselves in control. But that thou shouldst not yet begin to fear God who, like Christ, art hanging on a cross and hurrying to eternity, is beyond comprehension. But as if this comparison had somewhat hurt the honor of the Redeemer, Dismas adds, "And we indeed justly, for we receive the due reward of our deeds: but this man hath done no evil."

Finally, then, at least one voice is heard in favor of the Saviour. The apostles are silent; the Jews are shouting, "He is deserving of death"; the Romans are executing the unjust sentence; but an old robber proclaims Christ to be innocent and declares Him free of guilt. Hear it then, O Pilate! Hear it, ye executioners! Hear it, ye pharisees, ye scribes, ye chief-priests! Learn of this robber, "this man hath done no evil." Recognize at least now your awful error, acknowledge, at least now, the mistake you have made, contritely ask Christ's pardon, embrace the cross as Magdalene does, and ye shall be saved through the power of the innocent blood shed by you. But they raved in anger and they fain would crush the head of the robber who was publicly branding them.

The thief on the right, however, acknowledges himself to be a sinner. He does not, like Adam and Eve, excuse himself, he acknowledges his errors, he makes his confession. Besides, he recognizes that his death on the cross is a just punishment of heaven. It is, indeed, a sign of true conversion when the sinner praises and blesses the chastising hand of God; it is a sign of predestination when the sinner, in a spirit of penance, supports all sufferings imposed on him, patiently and joyfully, without complaint or murmur. Judas had also confessed a few hours before, but not, as the thief, to Christ but to Christ's enemies. For which reason he despaired. But this thief was not driven to despair by the thought of his sins. No, it was consoling to him that "this man hath done no evil." The innocent Jesus was his solace, Who, as he confidently hoped, would give satisfaction also for him. Therefore, without any preliminary, and without even considering that Christ in His sufferings was hardly able to pay attention to others, he in child-like confidence added the request, "Lord, remember me when thou shalt come into thy kingdom." He does not, then, wish as did the other thief, to be freed from the cross; he requests something better. But how modestly he requests it. Unlike the sons of Zebedee, he does not wish to sit at the side of the Redeemer and to rule with Him. No, like the prodigal, he deems himself unworthy of God's sonship. He merely asks that the Redeemer, when upon the throne of His glory, should remember him.

Here the question presents itself how this thief could arrive, not only at the knowledge of the Saviour's innocence, but at the knowledge of the divinity of Jesus Christ and of His kingdom. He had not been a witness of the Redeemer's miracles. He had not beheld Him in His glory on Mount Tabor. He had not seen His transfigured countenance, nor His snow-white garments, nor the splendor that surrounded Him. He saw only His disgrace, His humiliation, nothing but a body covered with wounds, the eyes already glassy from approaching death. Can He then be a king Whose throne is a cross, Whose diadem is a crown of thorns, Whose court following are two murderers? Usually kings rule only as long as they live; when they cease to live, they cease to rule. How then, I ask again, could the thief recognize a king, the Son of God even, in such a Christ Who bore no resemblance whatever to a ruler? It was the result of a short but good meditation on the sufferings of the Saviour, united with an inward grace which the Redeemer grants fully and abundantly to all those who devoutly take to heart His bitter passion. "The thief," writes St. Ambrose, "came to the knowledge that Christ bled for him and not for Himself, and this knowledge enkindled in him the fire of Divine Love." "O eternal light," exclaims St. Cyril of Jerusalem,[1] "which enlighteneth those who are in darkness."

[1] Cath. 13, C. 31.

The thief on the right had, then, presented his petition to the Saviour. Christ thereupon spoke the second word, "Amen I say to thee, this day thou shalt be with me in paradise." After having considered what prompted this word, let us now examine its import.

II.

The second word of Christ contains the fairest promise ever made to a sinner. Christ promised the thief an entrance into paradise, on that same day, as an associate and in the company of the Redeemer Himself.

The paradise, which Christ promised the thief for that day, must not be understood as the place called heaven. It means the direct vision of God and the felicity resulting therefrom. It should not seem strange to us that one may see God without being in heaven, in the dwelling of the blessed spirits. No created spirit, not even the soul of Christ, is present everywhere. It is, then, possible that souls and spirits behold the omnipresent God face to face, without, therefore, being themselves united in the same place. The soul of Christ, indeed, enjoyed this beatific vision from the first moment of its existence. But, as we have mentioned before, it was subject to suffering, for other causes, as long as Christ lived on earth. But as soon as by death His soul separated itself from His Sacred Body, it became unspeakably happy. Then it descended into Limbo to communicate a similar happiness to the souls of the just of the

Old Testament. In their presence and amidst their rejoicings and jubilations, Christ arose gloriously from the dead on Easter morning. During the forty days of the Redeemer's sojourn on earth after His resurrection, they were His constant, invisible companions, until, on the day of His ascension, He finally led them into the heavenly Jerusalem, to the home of the holy angels. When, therefore, Christ promised paradise to the thief for that same day, He promised him that on this day he would be associated with the happy number of the souls in Limbo. And Christ could in truth call Limbo a paradise. For when His Soul arrived there, it was changed into a paradise, as the essential happiness of paradise or heaven consists precisely in the immediate vision of God.

To his petition, the thief did not expect the answer he received, "To-day thou shalt be with me in paradise." It went far beyond his most sanguine hopes. Until now this man had been a man of blood. He had lived on murder and rapine, he had grown old in malice. He still is clad in the robber's garments and, lo! he is to enter paradise. Where, then, is his nuptial garment? To achieve paradise, the saints distributed all they had among the poor, princes and kings resigned their crowns, went into solitude and retired into quiet cloisters. To gain paradise, young men and maidens battled strenuously for years against the world and the flesh. To render themselves worthy of paradise, confessors deplored their smallest faults with most bitter tears and performed the most painful works of penance. Now this grayheaded sinner merely says, "Lord, remember me," and paradise is assured to him. A clever robber, indeed. A few moments more and he will seize his booty. He will be a robber to the end. Even in death, he cannot desist. He is a fortunate robber. After all that he has hitherto acquired by pillage and rapine, he in the end seizes upon the treasures of heaven.

And the possession of paradise is promised him for that same day. "To-day thou shalt be with me in paradise." Not, then, on the last day, not after long sufferings in purgatory, no, to-day, before the sun goes down, shall he see God face to face. Such was the reward of his heroic profession of the Divinity of Jesus Christ, of his glowing love and of his immeasurable penitential sorrow. He died a martyr of love. Yea, that was given to him which was denied to the patriarchs and prophets, even to St. Joseph and St. John the Baptist. For, though these died without guilt and immune from temporal punishment, they had to wait in Limbo for years and even centuries for the hour of their deliverance. But when the soul of the good thief arrived in Limbo, it was already changed into paradise. He was the first whose soul obtained the beatific vision immediately after death.

What, finally, must increase our astonishment is the fact that this robber accompanied as it were, the Redeemer in His entry into paradise. "*With me* thou shalt to-day be in paradise." It would seem that Christ would have reserved such an honor for His Blessed Mother, for St. John or for other innocent souls. One might almost say that Christ owed it to His own honor to select a choicer escort when entering into the heavenly kingdom. But how could He in a more brilliant light have shown to the souls in Limbo the infinite fruits of the work of His Redemption and the power of grace merited by Himself than by introducing into their midst a hoary-headed sinner whom, a few hours before, He had delivered from the thraldom of Satan. A converted robber and murderer! That was, indeed, the most glorious first fruit of His precious Blood; it was a trophy of victory becoming the Redeemer of the world, the conqueror of hell.

However, as the promises made by Christ to the thief were so extraordinary while He Himself was the picture of the greatest weakness and impotence, He confirmed them with a solemn declaration. "*Amen I say to thee,* this day thou shalt be with me in paradise." At these words the pharisees and chief-priests burst into an infernal shout of scornful laughter and asked each other in all seriousness whether or not the man on high had lost His reason and become distracted.

However, no matter how much this second word of Christ on the cross, as is clear from this meditation, may enliven confidence in Him and dispel from the heart of the greatest sinner all discouragement and despondency, we should still not forget the remark of St. Augustine: "It is one who in his last hour became converted and found grace, in order that thou mayest not despair; but it is only one, that thou mayest not sin by presumption.'' In view, therefore, of the happy death of the thief on the right, no one ought to postpone his conversion to the time of death. Whoever would act thus, would be most unlike to that thief. He had indeed committed many crimes and disgraceful acts; but he had not deliberately remained impenitent. On the contrary he made use of the extraordinary grace he received, at the very moment it was offered him. Illumined by this grace, he had hardly recognized the seriousness of his aberrations, when he began his confession and was converted. Whoever deliberately puts off his conversion to the hour of death, really entertains the sentiments of the thief on the left, who desired nothing more than to continue his life of rapine. For this reason such a one is, like the thief, in the greatest danger of dying in final impenitence.

We can draw another practical application from this meditation. Before us we behold three who are crucified. One is the innocent Saviour, the second is a penitent sinner and the third, an impenitent one. Therefore, whoever we may be, it will be impossible for us to shirk the cross in this world or to descend from it. We all, without exception, must die on the cross. But what an immense difference there was between the cross of the bad thief and that of the good one. The cross of the bad thief was heavy; without any solace whatever, cursing and blaspheming, he rebelliously endured the most cruel torments. It was a sterile cross; he could not expect even the least reward for all his sufferings. It was a cross without end, from which he plunged into the eternal flames of hell. On the contrary, the cross of the good thief was a light one; he would not for the whole world have descended from it. It was a fruitful one; he gained heaven thereby. It was of brief duration; in a few hours, he was with Christ in paradise. Let us resolve then, like the good thief, patiently to persevere on the cross in a spirit of penance. According to his example, we should draw the necessary strength and power from the sight, the words and the wounds of the crucified Redeemer, and then the cross shall be also for us the royal road to the heavenly paradise.

CHAPTER XXV.

THE THIRD WORD OF CHRIST ON THE CROSS

> "When Jesus therefore had seen his mother and the disciple standing, whom he loved, he saith to his mother: Woman, behold thy son. After that, he saith to the disciple: Behold thy mother."
>
> (St. John, xix., 26, 27.)

The first word of Christ on the cross concerned His enemies, who, however, instead of being converted, continued to offend Him. They, indeed, more than others, needed His pity, His help and His prayers. The second word was addressed to a repentant sinner to whom Christ bequeathed paradise. Not until He spoke the third time did He address His relatives and friends.

St. John records this incident in the following terms: "Now there stood by the cross of Jesus his mother, and his mother's sister, Mary of Clephas, and Mary Magdalene. When Jesus therefore had seen his mother and the disciple standing, whom he loved, he saith to his mother: Woman, behold thy son. After that, he saith to the disciple: Behold thy mother. And from that hour the disciple took her to his own."[1] If, in ap-

[1] St. John, xix., 25-27.

parent opposition to St. John's narrative, the three other evangelists write that the above mentioned persons and a few others were standing at some distance from the cross,[1] it is to be remarked that they refer to a different time. In the beginning, at the crucifixion and the raising of the cross, the women stood at some distance. It was the only thing they could do. Later the Blessed Virgin, John, Mary, the wife of Cleophas, and Magdalene approached nearer to the cross.

Let us now consider

I. The persons to whom Christ addressed the third word and

II. The word itself.

I.

The persons to whom Christ addressed the third word were His holy mother and the disciple whom Jesus loved.

The mother of Jesus, then, stood under the cross, a fact which was indeed astonishing. Was it not unheard of for a mother of her own volition to assist at the execution of her son, especially when the execution was not a hurried one, such as decapitation, but one accomplished by a slow process of terror-inspiring torture? Still, the mother of Jesus was present at the place of execution; she even looked attentively upon the different scenes. She did not, like Agar, turn away her eyes so that she might not behold her Son dying.

[1] St. Matthew, xxvii., 55, 56; St. Mark, xv., 40, 41; St. Luke, xxiii., 49.

No, like the mother of the Maccabees, she had her eyes fixed constantly on her dying Son. That such was the case is clearly indicated in the Scriptures. For when the Saviour said, "Woman, behold thy son," it was only by His look that He could show His mother that He meant her and not one of the other women. Their looks, then, must have met. Mary, therefore, beheld the thousand wounds from which the blood flowed to the ground; she saw the hands and feet pierced with nails; she saw the cruelly lacerated body; she heard the blasphemies and the jeers of His enemies. She heard and saw all this, and it must indeed have caused indescribable pain to her maternal heart. Besides, she could do nothing to allay the sufferings of her Son. The wounds were open; she could not bind them. The lips were parched with a burning thirst; she could not hand Him a refreshing drink. The Holy Face was disfigured by spittle and blood; she could not refresh it. The honor of her innocent and suffering Son was attacked; she could not defend Him. He was forsaken by heaven and by earth, and she could give Him no comfort. What a difference between times gone by and the present, between the manger and the cross! Certainly even then, His couch was not strewn with roses, but she could at least take care of Him, she could, in her maternal love, dry the tears of the moaning Babe, she could fold Him in her maternal arms. What a difference between the crib and the cross! There was life, here is death; there the adoring shepherds and the Magi, here the blaspheming Jews and the Gentiles. There the songs of angels abounded, here all is total abandonment. Even the very honor of the mother of God was attacked by the Jews. Instead of sympathy and consolation, she received from them railings and ridicule. "She thought herself," we may suppose they said, "the mother of the Messias. Now she can see to what sort of a Messias she has given life." But more than all this, the thought grieved her that these cruelties to Her Son were offenses against the Heavenly Father. The thought, finally, that the Blood of Her Son was being shed in vain for millions of people, filled the measure of her woe and made of her a sorrowful mother indeed.

However, Christ was to suffer death for the welfare of mankind; such was the will of the Heavenly Father, and not one human soul could be saved otherwise. She, therefore, bore her mental anguish with the utmost resignation, with heroic patience. She *stood* beneath the cross, says the Gospel. She did not faint and drop from exhaustion, as some pictures represent her. Nor did she lacerate her flesh in the greatness of her sorrow, says St. Anselm; she murmured not, she did not appeal to God's vengeance, she did not tear her hair, nor did she fill the air with her cries. No; she *stood* beneath the cross, erect, subdued, modest, her eyes filled with tears and her heart with woe, our true model when we assist at the death of relatives. We may then, indeed, be sad, but not like to those who have no hope. Our sadness should partake of a Christian and not of a pagan character. Mary *stood* under the cross; she bore all her sufferings with a heaven-born patience. Even more; she took part, as much as a merely human being could, in the sacrificial act of Christ. For, whilst her Divine Son, as the High-Priest of the New Law, offered up to Heaven His Blood and His Life, she made the offering with Him. She put her heart and all its sorrow into the chalice of the Redeemer. "It was well," once remarked a mother after listening to the narrative of Abraham's sacrifice, "that God demanded this sacrifice of the father, for the heart of a mother would never have been equal to it." Mary, however, subdued even the power of her own maternal heart. Thus did the second Eve re-establish what the first Eve, standing beneath the tree, had destroyed.

The other person to whom the third word was addressed was St. John. His presence beneath the cross is also a cause for wonder. For, at the seizure of Christ, he with the other apostles had lost courage and had hastily fled. But, after his first fright had subsided, he soon, happily for him, joined Mary, and sought refuge with her. At her side, and led as it were by her motherly hand, he courageously ascended Calvary. Mary led the deserting apostle back to the Redeemer.

Thus John arrived near the cross where a threefold and very painful trial awaited him. First, his *humility* was put to the test. He was recognized as an adherent and disciple of the Crucified

One. "It had been better for him," they said, "had he remained at his nets instead of joining an impostor; but undoubtedly he thought he would obtain, through him, something worth having." Then his *faith* was tried. Nothing of what he saw on Golgotha, betrayed the only-begotten Son of God, the wonder working Master. What he did see in the Crucified One, wounds, ignominy and weakness, apparently militated against His Divinity. But John held in abeyance his reason and his senses. He doubted not, neither did he take umbrage nor was he scandalized at his Crucified Master. The most painful trial was reserved for his *love*. What torture for his loving heart to behold his Redeemer in such torments and to know that the hour of separation was fast approaching! However, John, like Mary, *stood* beneath the cross, his eyes unceasingly turned on the Holy Face. The humility he shows in speaking of his steadfastness is truly touching. He does not mention his own name; he merely says, "There stood the disciple whom Jesus loved." He wished to intimate thereby that he owed his steadfastness not to his own power, but solely and alone to the love and grace of the Redeemer, upon Whose breast he had reclined at the Last Supper.

When Jesus, therefore, says Holy Writ, had seen His mother and the disciple standing whom He loved, He said to His mother, "Woman, behold thy son." After that He said to the disciple, "Son, behold thy mother." Let us examine this third word more closely.

II.

The first part of the third word of Christ was addressed to His mother. For He took deeply to heart her sorrow and sadness. He alone, Who knew the greatness of her love, could know the greatness of her sorrow. She had, indeed, a powerful claim on His filial love and gratitude. For thirty years He had grown under her watchful care. The unceasing industry of her hands had provided, in His infancy, for His daily sustenance. Then all the rude trials to which Mary had been subjected for His sake passed before His mind: the suspicion, albeit guiltless, of St. Joseph, the journey to Bethlehem, the contempt met with there, the flight into Egypt, the three days' search for the boy of twelve years, the meeting on the way to Calvary. And now His death is to inflict on her the hardest blow of all. It touched Him. From filial love and as an example to all children, to all sons and daughters, He provided as well as He could on His death-bed for His mother. He confided her to a man, who, He was convinced, would fill His place as far as was possible and who would lighten the sorrow of Mary at the loss of her Son. "Woman, behold thy son."

"But, O good Jesus," asks St. Bernard anent these words, "why art Thou ashamed to call Mary Thy mother, who bore Thee under her heart, who nourished Thee in Thine infancy, who clothed Thee and who cared for Thee so tenderly? Why dost Thou say so harshly: Woman, behold thy son?" We might remind the Saint that at that time the word 'woman' had not the contemptuous sense which nowadays is sometimes attached to it, but that it had an honorable meaning. But it still remains true that it has not the significance of the word 'mother.' Why, then, did not Christ call Mary mother? Because, in the first place, He would not increase her suffering nor render more acute her sorrow by pronouncing the sweet name of mother. For separation from dearly beloved persons is made lighter by showing apathy and want of feeling and by refraining from marks of tenderness. Then the Saviour avoided mentioning the name of mother in order not to excite and embitter against the mother the enemies of the Son. He, as it were, represented her to the Jews as being a stranger to Himself. These words, moreover, contain a mysterious reference, filled with solace and comfort for Mary, to the glad tidings which God announced to our first parents when He spoke of the *woman* who should crush the serpent's head. Finally, the words of the Saviour enfolded another great mystery. For, whenever He acted as God, as for instance, at the marriage feast of Cana, or before that, when He was found by His parents in the Temple, He never called Mary mother; He rather considered her as His creature. And now Christ, the Eternal High-Priest, was about to redeem Mary, as well as the rest of mankind, by His death.

No matter how considerate and forbearing the

Saviour meant the words to Mary to be, many holy Fathers nevertheless opine that at this word the prophecy of Simeon was accomplished: "Thy own soul a sword of sorrow shall pierce;" that, at this moment, Mary became the queen of holy martyrs. For at this moment she sacrificed the last claims of her maternal love. It was indeed a sad exchange. The servant should now be her son instead of the Lord; the disciple, instead of the Master; the son of Zebedee, instead of the Son of God; the mere man, instead of the true God. "My son," Mary could well exclaim, "why hast thou done so to me?"[1] "Call me not Noemi (that is, beautiful,) but call me Mara (that is, bitter,) for the Almighty hath quite filled me with bitterness."[2] But in all humility she now received the sad message as she formerly received the glad tidings of the angel. "Behold," she said, "I am the handmaid of the Lord. Be it done to me according to His word."

The second part of the third word was addressed to St. John. The Saviour was touched also by the grief and sadness of this disciple who so faithfully stood beneath the cross. To console him for the dire loss which he was to suffer in His death, Christ gives him His own mother as a compensation: "Son, behold thy mother." Hereby Christ reminds the disciple of his duty to care for Mary as a good child ought. And John, from that hour, took her unto his own.

[1] St. Luke, ii., 48.

[2] Ruth, i., 20.

By these words of the Redeemer an extraordinary distinction and honor was conferred upon St. John. How a minister feels honored when representing a mighty king or emperor at a foreign court! But what is all that in comparison with the distinction accorded to St. John, who, in relation to Mary, was to represent the King of kings, the Son of God? What an honor, besides, was it not for St. John to be permitted to greet as his own mother, the mother of God. It was certainly a glorious feast in heaven when Christ, some years later, took Mary, body and soul, into heaven. All angels and archangels, all cherubim and seraphim felt honored when greeting her as their queen. In honor, therefore, of their mistress and queen they chanted their most beautiful lays. They saluted her as the Queen of glory, as the exalted Queen of heaven, but as their mother—never! They durst not call the Blessed Virgin mother, that was the privilege of St. John.

This distinction was, furthermore, richly fraught with grace for St. John. And did not Christ owe it to His mother, ay, to His own honor, to adorn His representative with virtues and heavenly gifts? Most certainly He did. And what an increase was added to these graces through the intercession and the example of the Blessed Virgin! We may truly apply to St. John what St. Thomas of Villanova says of St. Joseph: "If a single salutation of this Virgin could sanctify the precursor of the Lord before his birth, what, think you, did the society of Mary during many years, effect in St. John?" But if we ask for the reasons why it was St. John who received this great distinction, the holy Fathers are unanimous in answering that it was above all the virginal purity of this apostle which attracted the heart and the eyes of Christ. We ought, then, to preserve unsullied the purity of our state of life. "It is good and wholesome also," says one holy Father in reference to this distinction, "to stand under the cross of Christ and to persevere beneath it."

"Woman, behold thy Son! Son, behold thy Mother!" Although these words of the dying Redeemer fill our hearts with sadness at Mary's afflictions, although they spur us on to assure the mother of Jesus, standing under the cross, of our admiration and of our sympathy, still they are for us, as they were for St. John, words of the sweetest consolation. For in saying these words, Christ also thought of us. Undoubtedly John was privileged, inasmuch as he alone took the mother of Jesus into his own house and cared for her as for his own mother. But it is the conviction of Holy Church that, at that moment, John also represented the entire human race. In the name of us all, John received the consoling message. By consenting to the incarnation of the Son of God, Mary had already become our mother. But, before departing, Christ wished solemnly to declare her as such and to recommend the care of her spiritual children to her who is the second, better Eve and the true giver of life.[1] Therefore the words of the Saviour, "Behold thy mother," are to be taken not merely as an instance of tender, filial solicitude, but also as a last act of love on the part of the dying Redeemer, intended to embrace the whole world.

According to the will of Christ, then, Mary should be our spiritual Mother and we should be her children. For which reason we ought to render ourselves worthy of such a great honor by daily greeting her as our mother, by loving and revering her and by imitating the glorious example of virtues she gives us, especially of steadfastness in suffering. But she ought to be the mother not only of each one in particular, but also of all Christian families. Every Christian family should take her, as John did, and receive her joyfully into their house. Especially should we invoke the Mother of Sorrows at the hour of death. She assisted so lovingly at the death of her Divine Son, she will also assist us maternally at our demise and obtain for us the grace of a happy death.

[1] Scheeben, Handbuch der Dogmatik, 3 Vol. Part I, ch. 5, No. 1626—1630, No. 1813—1817.—Kolb, S. J. Wegweiser in die Marianische Litteratur (Freiburg, Herder, 1888), pp. 15—18, 77—79.

CHAPTER XXVI.

THE FOURTH WORD OF CHRIST ON THE CROSS

> "And about the ninth hour Jesus cried with a loud voice, saying: My God, my God, why hast thou forsaken me?"
>
> (St. Matthew, xxvii., 46.)

After Christ had addressed the third word to His Blessed Mother and to St. John, there occurred an eclipse of the sun of three hours' duration. In order not to interrupt our subject, we shall, later on, pay some attention to this wonderful event of nature.

Towards the end of the eclipse, at the ninth hour, according to our time about three o'clock in the afternoon, Christ broke the solemn silence and exclaimed with a loud voice: "My God, my God, why hast Thou forsaken me?" Now the long desired hour had arrived, the ninth hour, which was to mark a turning point in the history of mankind: the hour in which error's shadow was to recede before truth, and the day of salvation was to begin.

But what a remarkable outcry! What an astonishing complaint! Such a reproach had certainly never been heard as long as the world existed, nor shall another like it be heard until the end of time. We need all the power of faith to believe that it really happened, as reason would fain revolt and deem it impossible. We can easily understand that man might complain of man or that God might complain of man; but that Christ, the Son of God should complain of God is a mystery that goes beyond our comprehension.

However, let us make an effort to penetrate more deeply into these words by considering [1]

I. The meaning of these words,
II. The reasons for uttering them and
III. The different impressions they made upon the auditors.

I.

When Christ complained of abandonment, or of a kind of separation from God, He could have had reference only to His human nature. He therefore did not address Himself to the *Father,* but to *God,* showing thereby that He was offering His plaint not as the Son to the Father, but as man to God. Now the abandonment by God of Christ's human nature was not a separation of the latter from the second Person of God. For the union of the second Person of the Godhead with Christ's human nature was and is inseparable. If this union had been dissolved at the death of Christ, then not God, but a mere man would have died for us, and our redemption would not be accom-

[1] St. Matthew, xxvii., 46, 47; St. Mark, xv., 34, 35.

plished. Neither was the abandonment by God of the human nature in Christ a withdrawal of grace. On the contrary, the plenitude of grace at all times existing in Christ effected that fortitude which bore Him up on the cross as it had done in the Garden of Olives. The abandonment, finally, did not consist in depriving the soul of Christ for a time of the direct vision of God. Christ rather complained, not only that God refused to preserve His human nature from impending death, but also that He abandoned it to suffering without the least solace whatever. For His human nature might have been relieved in a twofold way; first, through a direct action on all that contributed to make it suffer: upon the thorns, the nails and the scourges, by depriving them of their power to inflict pain, upon the arms of the executioners by withering them, and upon the tongues of the blasphemers by paralyzing them. Secondly, God could have filled the soul of Christ with such consolation that He would not have felt external pain. Nothing of the kind happened, however. On the contrary, God abandoned the soul of Christ to repugnance, to fear, to sadness and to the excruciating knowledge that His Passion would be useless to so many human beings. He even allowed Satan whose hour was at hand, to employ this time of unnumbered sufferings in most cruelly torturing the Soul of Christ. God assisted Christ's human nature only in so far as was necessary to sustain it in the midst of these terrible afflictions. He appeared to prolong life only to make possible more suffering. This was the object and the cause of the reproach. It is hardly necessary to mention that Christ permitted this sense of abandonment with the full freedom of His Will.

No matter how painful this abandonment by God was to the Saviour, He did not, in those moments, suffer the abandonment of the damned in hell, as Calvin, the gloomy heretic, maintains. Not at all. The abandonment of the damned is without hope and full of despair. Not so the abandonment of the Redeemer. This appears clearly from the twenty-first psalm in which the prophetic spirit of king David describes the sentiments and feelings of the Redeemer at this moment. The prophet first shows us that when Christ asked of God the reason of the abandonment, He was not at all in ignorance of it. For after crying out: "O God, my God, why hast thou forsaken me?" Christ answers Himself: "Far from my salvation are the words of my sins," that is, the sins of men, laden upon Me, are the cause, why there can be no thought of My salvation or of My escape from death. They are the cause why, besides being the reproach of men and the outcast of the people who have numbered all My bones, I am also forsaken by heaven and deprived of all consolation. Then, however, Christ rises to the joyful confidence that after His death, not only the Jews, but all the nations of the Gentiles shall return to the Lord and in His Church shall be satiated with the meat of His sacrifice.

Whether or not, as some theologians opine, Christ said the entire psalm in a subdued voice, we may not decide. Thus much is certain, that the psalm expresses the feelings and sentiments of the Redeemer and that the first words thereof, "God, my God, why hast thou forsaken me?" were pronounced by Christ in a loud tone of voice.

Let us now examine the reasons for uttering this reproach.

II.

Three reasons urged the Saviour to utter it. First he was impelled by the humility of His Heart. Then He uttered the plaint for our manifold instruction and, lastly, for our consolation.

In the first place, the humility of His Heart urged Him to perform, before His demise, the most heroic act of self-humiliation. The humiliations heaped upon Him by His enemies were indeed very great and burdensome beyond expression. But they rebounded from His Divine Patience and Majesty as from a shield and, at least, Christ did not therefore lose the respect of well-meaning people. But by complaining of being abandoned by God, He, as it were, abandoned Himself. It was the greatest act of self-abasement and of self-renunciation which can be imagined. For, indeed, O Saviour Jesus Christ! if God hath abandoned Thee, as whom should we consider Thee? Thou hast, in the past, worked thousands of miracles to prove that Thou art true God, as is the Father, and now Thou complainest that God hath forsaken Thee! Thou hast publicly proclaimed to the people that "what things soever the Father doth, these the Son also doth in like manner."[1] David, the prophet, once said that he had never seen the just forsaken. But of the sinner it is said, "We know that God doth not hear sinners."[2] I therefore ask again, if God has abandoned Thee, whom should we consider Thee to be? How can John, standing at the foot of the cross and hearing Thy complaint, still write, "We saw his glory, the glory as it were of the only begotten of the Father?"[3] However, by this self-abasement, by this obscuring of His Divinity, of His Divine Power and Sanctity, the Redeemer would atone fully for the pride and self-deification of our first parents, which had brought all evil into the world.

Secondly, Christ complained of being forsaken for our manifold instruction. Above all, He wished to forestall an erroneous and mischievous idea of His Passion. The wonderful calm and patience which the Saviour had shown throughout the day amid so many and such various sufferings, might lead those who had witnessed it to the opinion that He was entirely devoid of feeling or sensation. In view of all these facts, we ourselves might be tempted to assume that the Soul of Christ, in the last hours of life, was plunged in a sea of heavenly consolation, as was the case

[1] St. John, v., 19.
[2] St. John, ix., 31.
[3] St. John, i., 14.

with many martyrs, who were thereby rendered insensible to pain. The sufferings of Christ, to a certain extent, would then have been such in appearance only. Such a conception of them would naturally cloud our knowledge of His Love and of the horrors of sin for which He had to suffer, whilst it would also lower the value of the grace and the glory purchased by these sufferings. Therefore Christ, from Whose lips a complaint had never been heard, complained at the end of His life of being forsaken, and that in a loud voice, so that all men might know the enormity of His Soul's sufferings. The joy and the exultation of a St. Lawrence and of so many other martyrs in the midst of the most terrific tortures were fruits of this abandonment of the Redeemer.

Then again, Christ's complaint of being forsaken demonstrates to us the greatness of that punishment in hell which consists in the loss of God. For there are Christians who fear hell on account of the eternal fire only. To be separated from God and to be deprived of His society seems to them trifling and tolerable enough. Now, if the abandonment by God caused Christ such fearful torments, although His release was so near, what then, we are constrained to ask, must be the abandonment in hell, accompanied as it is, by God's curse, combined with despair and lasting forever?

Thirdly, Christ wished to direct our attention to the chief object to which our plaints ought to refer. We complain often and of many things, but, alas, not always of what it is worth our while to complain of. We should send up our cries to God when we are forsaken by Him, and this takes place when mortal sin is committed. Indeed, when mortal sin has brought about the most fearful abandonment by God, when the fires of hell are burning underneath one's feet, then it is high time to cry out with a loud voice, "O God, my God, why hast Thou forsaken me?" Then not a stone should be left unturned in the effort to be freed from that awful condition; then the sound of our wails and of our prayers should ascend to God that He may grant us the grace of conversion and pardon of our sins.

Finally, Christ, complaining of abandonment, wished to be the comfort and model of all the just in their disconsolate hours. It does not seldom happen that God, after having filled with joyful solace a soul in its devotions in order to draw it closer to Himself, quite unexpectedly ceases to bestow such marks of favor and, like the sun, appears to hide himself behind clouds. The sweet sense of God's presence and of pleasure in prayer vanish, until finally the soul feels as if God has withdrawn His grace, forsaken it entirely and abandoned it to eternal ruin. In this condition, which is more painful and more torturing than any other kind of suffering, Christ ought to be our consolation and at the same time our model. In such moods of the soul we should, according to His example, humbly and confidently address our complaints to God. But we ought to be honest enough to add with Christ, "Far from my salvation are the words of my sins." In the case of great saints such as St. Francis of Assisi and St. Catherine of Siena, it was a special privilege granted them by Almighty God that they shared these particular sufferings of the Lord. For us poor sinners, however, such tortures are usually a punishment. They are a punishment for our venial sins, for our lukewarmness and for our attachment to the honors and pleasures of the world. Ah! indeed, to go with the world and to enjoy its pleasures as much as we can without grievous guilt, and at the same time taste of the sweets of heaven, is something impossible. We should, therefore, bewail our lukewarmness and our venial sins, we should, in our abandonment, cry to God with the loud voice of prayer and of works of penance, and He, then, will disperse the dark clouds and again turn to us His countenance full of favor and of love.

There yet remains the consideration of the different impressions produced upon the by-standers by the cry of the Redeemer.

III.

The great mass of the people remained cold and indifferent; they cared very little about the Saviour's words.

Others, notably the chief-priests and scribes, were seized with a frenzy of anger at this fourth word of Christ. Undoubtedly, when these men, well acquainted as they were with the scriptures of the Old Law, especially with those which referred to the Messias, heard the cry of Christ, "My God, my God, why hast thou forsaken me?" they were involuntarily reminded of the abovementioned twenty-first psalm, of which those words are the beginning. And if they had been of a good will, even to the slightest extent, they would have been forced to admit that He who was hanging on the cross, was truly the Messias. For He was indeed a worm, and no man; those who saw Him were laughing Him to scorn; His tongue was cleaving to the roof of His mouth; His hands and feet were pierced; all His bones could be numbered; His garments were divided among the soldiers and upon His vesture they had cast lots. Every thing was just as the prophet had foretold. But they would not hear the truth; they resisted the truth, and they were greatly vexed at the Crucified One for daring to proclaim the truth to them, as Christians sometimes are when from the pulpit they hear unpleasant truths. The anger of the chief-priests and scribes grew as, in remembering this psalm, they made a discovery not very flattering to themselves. As we have already stated, they clearly understood that the Crucified One applied the psalm to Himself and thereby declared Himself to be the Messias. Therefore, they necessarily had to admit that they were the dogs of whom it is said in the psalm, "Many dogs have encompassed me; the council of the malignant hath besieged me."

It is proper to malice and impiety, coupled with

hypocrisy, to find a way out of embarrassment, when attacked or discovered, by resorting to ridicule and sneers. Thus the high-priests and scribes misrepresented the words of the Redeemer, "Eli, Eli" or "Eloi, Eloi," i.e., "My God," and exclaimed with peals of laughter, "Behold, he calleth Elias." And, like an echo, the words came back from the soldiers, "Behold, he calleth Elias."

To understand the cutting sarcasm contained in these words, we must consider that, as the Talmudists say, the Jews venerated Elias as the janitor of heaven and as the greatest helper in need generally, and when in dire straits, they were wont to invoke him. The sense, then, of the words, "Behold, he calleth Elias" is, now finally this man is coming to his senses; now finally he acknowledges his weakness and impotence; now he is surrendering; now finally the hypocrite is unmasked; now, undoubtedly, there will be an end to his pompous promises, "This day thou shalt be with me in paradise;" now he would be glad were Elias to open to him the gates of heaven or help him down from the cross.

The feelings, lastly, of the sorrowful Mother and of the friends of Christ at the Saviour's complaint and at the jeers following it, cannot be described. The pitiful cry of Christ penetrated deeply into their hearts. Their countenances, already pale, became paler still, and floods of tears streamed from their eyes.

Let us bewail with the sorrowful Mother the abandonment of her beloved Son. But we should also resolve never to forsake Him by mortal sin and thus increase His suffering. Let us, moreover, renew our sacred oath of eternal fealty to Him. If we find ourselves weak and tottering, let us pray for the grace of Christ. Let us pray with the disciples who went to Emmaus, "Lord, stay with us because it is towards evening."[1] Especially at the hour of death shall we cry from our inmost heart, O Jesus, forsake me not! O Jesus, reject me not! O Jesus, condemn me not! Then, through the Redeemer's goodness, we shall be saved from the eternal abandonment of hell and be united to Him in heaven forever.

[1] St. Luke, xxiv., 29.

CHAPTER XXVII.

THE FIFTH WORD OF CHRIST ON THE CROSS

> "Afterwards Jesus knowing that all things were now accomplished, that the scripture might be fulfilled, said: I thirst."
>
> (St. John, xix., 28.)

In the crucified, as in the case of all seriously wounded, the great loss of blood produced such an extraordinary inner heat that they felt as though consumed by fire. The thirst arising from this immense heat was, without doubt, the greatest of all the sufferings which these unfortunates had to endure. As eye and ear witnesses relate,[1] they would, after hanging a little while on the cross, complain of nothing except their burning thirst. They seemed dead to all other pain.

This historical fact puts the complaint of the Saviour, "I thirst," in its proper light. After a superficial consideration one might think that Christ was complaining of a pain slight and unimportant in comparison to His other sufferings. And, if He intended to speak of physical anguish, one would rather expect a complaint of the pains in

[1] Sepp vi, 379. Friedlieb, Archæologie der Leidensgeschichte, p. 155.

His hands and feet or in His sacred head. But such a view is wrong. As the Saviour in the preceding sentence gave utterance to the greatest of all the sufferings of His soul, the abandonment by God, so now He expresses the worst bodily pain which He experienced. This thirst was more painful than the scourging or the crowning with thorns or the crucifixion itself; in it all the physical sufferings reached their climax. When, therefore, the Redeemer complained of thirst, He included the inner fever which consumed Him. It is as if He said, "My entire body is being consumed by fire."

That through this torture of thirst the Redeemer intended to atone for all sins of intemperance and of the taste generally goes without saying. Especially did He have in view the sin of our first parents. This sin began with pride and self-deification; therefore did He undergo the torture of being forsaken by God. It ended with gluttony; for this reason He completed the work of satisfaction by suffering the torture of the most painful thirst and so re-establishing the order which had been disturbed. Let us now consider[1]

I. The reasons for uttering this complaint,
II. Its circumstances and character and
III. The granting of the petition contained in it.

[1] St. John, xix., 28–30; St. Matthew, xxvii., 48, 49; St. Mark, xv., 36; St. Luke, xxiii., 36.

I.

Until now Christ had not complained of any bodily pain. The reason why He did it now at the end of His life is given us by Holy Writ itself. "Afterwards," says St. John, "Jesus knowing that all things were now accomplished, that the Scripture might be fulfilled, said: I thirst." Everything, then, was accomplished that the prophets had foretold; one thing only was wanting: that, in His thirst, He be given vinegar to drink. In order that this prophecy also might be accomplished, He revealed His thirst to the torturers. Otherwise they might not have thought of giving Him vinegar. Of course, we know that the different mysteries of Christ's Passion were not accomplished because they were prophesied, but that rather these mysteries were themselves the causes of the prophecies. For these things which happened through the free will of men, just *because* they really happened, were foreseen by Almighty God from all eternity and were foretold by the prophets centuries before they happened. Now, as it was written in the Scriptures that Christ was to be given vinegar to drink, St. John shows us the Saviour as if in anxiety that nothing remain undone and that the will of the Heavenly Father be accomplished even to the minutest detail. Hanging, then, on the wood of martyrdom, plunged in a sea of bitterness and overwhelmed with pain, the Saviour attends primarily to the accomplishment of God's will. That God's will be done, is

His most ardent desire. Therein is contained a lesson for us; how we should strive to accomplish even to the smallest detail the will of God revealed to us in Holy Writ. But how many Christians confine their efforts to that which is absolutely necessary and which is prescribed under pain of eternal damnation! How rare is faithfulness in little things! How scarce is true zeal in the service of God at every moment in our lives! How truly rare it is in sufferings. The slightest ailments often furnish pretexts for neglecting the most serious duties.

Then Christ said, "I thirst," for two reasons which had also impelled Him to complain of his abandonment. On the one hand, He wished to teach the Jews and us that He suffered bodily pains in reality and in the highest degree, and, on the other, He wished to draw our attention to the fires of hell. For if the inward fire that consumed Him could draw such an outcry of pain from the patient Saviour, who, then, would dwell with everlasting burnings? [1]

The last reason was the desire of the sacred Heart of Jesus to suffer even more for us. For He knew that the jeering bystanders would offer Him vinegar as a refreshment and that thus His cry would bring upon Him a new humiliation. This fact alone proves the truth of what the Holy Fathers say, namely, that at the end of His life, Christ was ready to undergo even more sufferings, for our sake, if God had demanded it.

[1] Is., xxxiii., 14.

Thus did the Redeemer of the world end His life in the most perfect manner; on the one hand, as we have seen, with an act of the greatest self-humiliation and, on the other, with an act of the most heroic charity. For, by revealing His thirst after He already had reached the most intense degree of pain, He brought about new sufferings, and thereby showed His willingness to suffer even more for the glory of God and for the salvation of our souls. We, on the contrary, are glad when pain has left us. To offer ourselves to God for new and greater afflictions never enters our mind. We rather study how to shake off or lighten our present cross or avoid impending sufferings.

Let us now consider the circumstances and the character of the fifth word.

II.

Three circumstances here merit our attention. Christ did, indeed, complain of bodily sufferings, but only after He had complained of sufferings of the soul. Whilst, therefore, we are not forbidden to complain of bodily ills, the ills of our souls should, above all and in the first place, be nearest to our heart, especially that abandonment by God which is caused by mortal sin. There are Christians, however, who are never aware of these spiritual ills and who, therefore, never feel the need of complaining of them, not even to those who are empowered to heal the wounds of the soul.

Christ did, indeed, complain of His bodily ills, but not with a loud voice, as He did in His abandonment. Thereby we are taught that we should never loudly complain to God of our bodily sufferings. It would be improper, as these sufferings, no matter how grave they may be, are capable of producing, with God's grace, much that is good and salutary. For, with the help of grace, they lead sinners to conversion, they detach the heart from earthly things, they purify the just, they offer him opportunities of gaining much merit, and they unite him most intimately with the Crucified One Himself. If, however, one be forsaken by God through mortal sin, then it is proper to loudly invoke the mercy of God.

Christ did, indeed, complain of bodily ills, but only when they had reached the greatest intensity. I am certainly not in favor of unreasonable exaggeration in this matter, nor do I mean to say that one should not look for remedies until in the throes of death. Some, even, ought to be advised to take more care of their health. On the other hand, it is wrong to fill the air with lamentations at every slight indisposition, especially as the entire ailment is sometimes merely a figment of the imagination.

Two qualities of Christ's plaint are to be conspicuously mentioned: its brevity and its unassuming tone. The plaint consisted of only one word: "Sitio," "I thirst." This is all Christ has to say about His great affliction. How unlike the Redeemer are those Christians who draw the most pitiful descriptions of their bodily infirmities, unimportant as they sometimes are, and who can never reach the end when they have once begun their story.

Then the complaint of Christ was entirely without presumption. He merely states what He suffers without asking for anything. He left it to the bystanders to determine whether and how His excruciating thirst was to be quenched. I will not affirm here that the sick ought to be prohibited from asking for this or that relief. But there are sick people whose demands, in this particular, go beyond all reasonable bounds. Now they want this, then that; and with the best of will, one cannot satisfy them. They are continually in a bad humor, stubborn and a real cross for all who are around them. Such sick persons should remember Our Divine Saviour who patiently took even the vinegar which was offered Him in ridicule to quench His thirst. The saints must have thought of it, for they rejoiced on their sick beds, when they met with forgetfulness or even wilful neglect.

Now, what kind of a response did the request contained in the Saviour's complaint meet with?

III.

After Christ had spoken the word, "I thirst," one of the bystanders, probably a soldier, ran for a sponge, filled it with vinegar, stuck it on a pole and, assisted by several others, gave Him to drink. At crucifixions the Roman soldiers always had in readiness a vase of vinegar, from which to refill the leather bottles from which they drank, and also to offer to the crucified. Sponges were likewise at hand for the executioners to use in washing off their blood-stained arms and clothes.

To the narrative of the evangelists St. Matthew and St. Mark, St. John adds the item that it was a rod of hyssop to which the sponge was attached. The motive of St. John in completing the report of the other evangelists by this detail can readily be surmised. In times gone by the Israelites were commanded by God to dip a bunch of hyssop into the blood of the lamb and with it to sprinkle the sills and posts of their doors in order to keep away the destroying angel.[1] When, later on, Moses had concluded on Mount Sinai the covenant between God and the people, he used for sprinkling the altar and the people a bunch of hyssop dipped in the blood of the immolated calves. Hyssop was also to be used in preparing the waters of purification and of reconciliation. Wherefore David exclaimed, "Thou shalt sprinkle me with hyssop."[2] Finally, because of its intrinsic purifying virtue, hyssop was used to heal leprosy, which is a type of sin. Hyssop was therefore hallowed by religious observance; its properties rendered it full of significance, and by its use in connection with the first paschal lamb as well as with the making of the Old Testament, it had acquired a peculiar relation to the purifying Blood of the Paschal Lamb of the New Testament.

When the soldiers made a move to approach the

[1] Exod., xii., 22.

[2] Psalms, l., 9.

Redeemer with the sponge attached to the reed, they were arrested by cries of "Halt!" coming from different directions. "Halt!" they cried, "Wait, do not yet give Him the vinegar. Let us first see whether Elias will come to refresh and help Him." For the chief-priests and pharisees had sneeringly exclaimed, "Behold, he calleth Elias." Now, although the pagan soldiers had not heard much of Elias, the helper in need, still they quickly entered into the spirit of the insolent jest of the Jews and joined them in jeering at the expiring Saviour. But the soldier did not waver in his purpose. "Hold!" he cried, adding his cruel jest to theirs, "Let me give Him the vinegar and prolong His life until Elias arrives. Otherwise He might perish before Elias has time to put in an appearance."[1] Elias came not, and the Redeemer who had not drunk the wine mixed with myrrh offered Him to diminish His pains, now drank the vinegar because it was given in jest and ridicule. He drank because He wishes to accomplish the last prophecy yet to be fulfilled and because He, the Lord of life and death, now wished to die.

Ah, indeed, the Son of God had not deserved such treatment on the part of men. That they might not lack wherewith to quench their thirst, He had, in the beginning of time, created the rivers and caused to spring forth from the earth's recesses everywhere the clearness of many waters. And if, notwithstanding, water sometimes failed,

[1] See note 18.

He was ready to work miracles to remove the consequent distress. Ismael thirsted, and He showed Agar a fountain; the people of Israel were perishing with thirst, and He drew from the rock a refreshing source; He gave Moses a rod to make bitter water sweet. When, in the fulness of time, He had become man and dwelt among men, He proclaimed to all who were thirsty, "If any man thirst, let him come to me, and drink."[1] But to Him, the bountiful Creator, His chosen people refused even the smallest drop. They stood calmly by, they grinned cruelly at the scene of the mockery. Truly, the vineyard from which Christ expected sweet grapes had brought forth wild ones.[2] The Samaritan woman at Jacob's well had, in truth, been more compassionate. When He was thirsty, she did not refuse Him the drink of water. But if, as we have seen, the Lord's bodily thirst was great, the thirst of His soul for our salvation was still much greater. He was therefore more anxious that the latter thirst be quenched than that the parched mouth and the withered tongue be again moistened. Christ thirsts for our souls, He thirsts for our conversion, He thirsts for our good works, He thirsts for our perfection. Let us quench this thirst of our Redeemer to our utmost power. Let us sanctify our own souls and lead other souls to Him. Then His Sacred Heart will be to us a fountain of water springing up into life everlasting.[3]

1 St. John, vii., 37.
2 Is., v., 4.
3 St. John, iv., 14.

CHAPTER XXVIII.

THE SIXTH WORD OF CHRIST ON THE CROSS

"When Jesus therefore had taken the vinegar, he said: It is consummated." (St. John, xix., 30.)

The last painful moment of His life permitted the Redeemer to express what He could no longer say after death had paralyzed His tongue: "It is consummated." Solemnly, before heaven and earth, before God and the world, the dying Redeemer declares that the mission of His life has been fulfilled and that everything referring to Him and promised in the Scriptures of the Old Law, in prophecies and prototypes, has been accomplished to the very last.

Inasmuch as these prophecies relate to the history of the Passion, we have repeatedly referred to them in the course of the preceding chapters. One thing more, however, was promised in the books of the Old Testament, the accomplishment of which needs a special exposition. It is the main and central point in the whole history of the Passion. According to the prophet Isaias[1] (liii., 10) through the future Redeemer, in fact, through His death, there would be offered to God

[1] See note 19.

a real and the most valuable sacrifice, reconciling God and the world. This was the hope of the human race languishing in the slavery of Satan. And now this hope was also realized, this *sacrifice* was consummated. As the fruit of this propitiatory sacrifice of Christ, Isaias mentions an eternal, spiritual progeny, i. e., the entire multitude of the elect whom no one can number.

Let us now bring forward the arguments to show that Christ's death on the cross was

I. A real sacrifice in the strictest sense of the word and

II. A sacrifice of infinite value.

I.

We will briefly summarize the external proofs of the truth of our first proposition. That Christ's death on the cross was a sacrifice in the strictest sense of the word is evident from the fact that the main object of the bloody sacrifices of animals in the Old Law was to typify and represent the giving up of the life of Jesus in a violent death. Now the bloody sacrifices of animals were real sacrifices, and therefore it was necessary that Christ's death on the cross, typified by them, be a real sacrifice. For reality cannot be less true than its shadow, nor fulfilment and accomplishment than their types and figures. Then, coming to the New Testament, we find, in the first place, that Our Divine Saviour is often called a Lamb. "Behold the lamb of God, behold him who taketh away the sin of the world," writes St. John (i., 29). "Christ, our pasch, is sacrificed," joyfully exclaims St. Paul.[1] "You were redeemed with the precious blood of Christ, as of a lamb unspotted and undefiled," St. Peter teaches us.[2] Now, if we remember that in the Old Law the lamb was one of the animals most frequently offered in sacrifice, we easily understand that the writers of the books of the New Testament, in calling Christ a lamb, were convinced that He offered a true and real sacrifice. Furthermore, what they merely suggest by this comparison, they elsewhere state in express terms. St. John writes: "Jesus is the propitiation for our sins: and not for ours only, but also for those of the whole world."[3] Paul the Apostle represents to the Ephesians how Christ had delivered Himself as an oblation and a sacrifice to God for an odor of sweetness.[4] Finally, the doctrine of Christ's vicarious and propitiatory sacrificial death is repeatedly laid down, in clear and most definite terms, in the epistle to the Hebrews. Christ sacrificed Himself once for the sins of the people.[5] "Christ was offered once to exhaust the sins of many."[6] And this doctrine of Holy Writ is the doctrine of the Holy Fathers, the doctrine of the Catholic Church and the conviction

[1] I. Cor., v., 7.
[2] I. Pet., i., 19.
[3] I. John, ii., 2.
[4] Eph., v., 2.
[5] Hebr., vii., 29.
[6] Ibid., ix., 28.

of the whole Catholic people. "What sacrifice," asks St. Leo,[1] "was ever holier than that which the true High-Priest laid upon the Altar of the Cross by sacrificing His own Body?" And joyfully does the Church sing on the holy eve of Easter, "O wonderful condescension of Thy goodness towards us, O God! O inappreciable favor of Thy Love! In order to redeem the servant, Thou hast delivered the Son."

But let us enter more deeply into the subject by showing that in Christ's death on the Cross every thing is found which belongs to a real sacrifice. For this purpose, however, it is absolutely necessary first to define the idea of a sacrifice briefly but thoroughly. By the word sacrifice in its strict sense we understand a religious act by which a visible gift is offered to God and destroyed in some way, so that God may be honored and worshiped. First, then, there is required a *visible gift,* something that is material and tangible. Sacrifices of prayer, of self denial and of the heart are sacrifices only in a figurative and free sense of the word. Secondly, this visible gift must be *offered up.* For the sacrifice does not consist so much in the visible object as in the offering of it. The sacrifice is not the object in itself, but an *act* which, of course, presupposes a sacrificial gift. Then, the object must be offered directly to *God.* If, for the love of God, one were to offer to a poor man a lamb or a loaf of bread, it would be an

1 Sermo 13 de Pass. c. 3.

alms but, properly speaking, not a sacrifice. Then the visible gift must be offered to God by being *destroyed in some way.* Thus, in the Old Law, animals were slain and burned, incense was likewise burned, liquids were poured out. For this is the only possible way of offering them directly to God. In fact, sacrificial gifts cannot be carried into heaven to Him. By being destroyed or, at least, withdrawn from every earthly and profane use, they are, as it were, given back to the Creator. The intrinsic reason however, why the offering is made by destruction, entire or partial, is contained in the end of the sacrificial act, namely, solemnly to acknowledge God's supreme dominion, especially to worship Him and to subject ourselves entirely to Him as to the Lord of life and death. The best expression of this inner disposition would indeed be to offer life itself, as was done in the death of Christ on the Cross. But according to a Divine ordinance, man has no right to dispose of his own life. Wherefore, in ancient times, instead of life itself, such objects, animate and inanimate, were offered as contributed directly to the sustenance of human life and which, for this reason, best represented the sacrifice of human life itself.

With this first object of the sacrificial act, namely, the praise and worship of God, is intimately connected the intention of showing Him our gratitude in an external and efficacious manner, as well as to beg of Him new gifts and graces. After the fall of man, the sacrifices assumed very plainly the character of being *propitiatory.* To placate God, the animal of sacrifice must surrender its life in place of the sinner who had forfeited life and merited death.

The right and, in a certain sense, the duty of offering sacrifice originally belonged to all upon whom the duty of external religious acts was incumbent, that is, to the individual, to the family and to human society. Thus Cain and Abel offered sacrifice. The father would sacrifice in the name of the family, and, in the name of a community, a priest appointed for that purpose by the civil authority. Sacrifice, however, being the most sublime and most perfect act of religious worship, was soon exclusively reserved for public worship held in common. By taking part in this public worship, the individual perfectly satisfied his personal obligation. With the Jews especially, Almighty God, as it were, took this matter into His own hands. He not only determined the various sacrificial gifts, but He also appointed the priests who had to offer them in the name of the people. For, if a man, especally a sinful man, wishes, in the name of the people, to stand as an agent of mediation and reconciliation between God and sinners, it is proper that he be empowered for the purpose by God and that, at least by his office and his dignity, he be segregated from sinners and consecrated. But when the plenitude of time arrived, all men were deprived forever of the right to offer sacrifice, because the Son of God Himself was to appear, according to

His human nature, as the Priest of sacrifice, as the High-Priest of the new dispensation. The burning of incense is therefore no longer a sacrifice, but merely a sacred ceremony.

Thus, by the order of the heavenly Father, the Lord of life and death, Christ, by His bloody death on the cross, freely offered to God His human life, instead of ours, to honor Him and to placate Him, and He renews this sacrifice in an unbloody manner at every holy Mass. Christ's death on the cross was therefore a true and real sacrifice. Everything pertaining to the essence of a sacrifice was there: a visible gift, namely, the sacred humanity of Jesus Christ; the offering of this gift by a High-Priest appointed by God; the destruction of this gift by death and the intention of honoring and glorifying God through this same destruction.

But, one might ask, did not the executioners put Christ to death and deprive Him of life? Ought not therefore the executioners to be considered the sacrificing priests at Christ's death on the cross? Such a conclusion would be false. It is true, the executioners inflicted upon the Saviour tortures which naturally could but bring on death, and, in consequence of these tortures, Christ finally died. However, notwithstanding these tortures, even had they been a thousand times greater or had they lasted thousands of years, Christ would not have died, had He not Himself willed it. Even at the very last moment of the Saviour's life, it lay within the power of His human will, united as it was with the second Person of the Godhead, to avoid death entirely. Such was not the case with the holy martyrs. Joyfully, indeed, and exultingly, their will in complete submission to the will of God, did these heroes approach death; but they approached an inevitable death, a death whose coming they could not delay for a single second with all the powers of their will. Christ, on the other hand, died because He willed it and when He willed it. By a resolve of His own human will, He effected the separation of soul and body, inasmuch as with perfect freedom He permitted the tortures to now finally produce their fatal effect. In this, and in this alone, did the sacrificial act of Christ's death on the cross consist. Christ was therefore not only the Victim, but also the sacrificing Priest. Far from being sacrificing priests, the executioners rendered themselves guilty of the crime of deicide. Christ's death on the cross is, therefore, a real sacrifice. It differed from all other sacrifices, not only because in it, as the only genuine sacrifice, the First-Born of humanity was offered, whilst in the others animals of lower rank were immolated in the stead of human life, but also because it was a sacrifice of infinite value.

II.

The infinite value of the sacrifice of the cross is deduced first from the infinite dignity and holiness of Jesus Christ, the sacrificing Priest, and, secondly, from the infinite treasures of satisfaction and merit which it contains. Let us explain more fully these two thoughts.

The value of a sacrifice depends first of all on the value of the sacrificial gift. Under this aspect, a sacrifice of one thousand lambs would have more value than one of ten lambs under perfectly similar circumstances. Now the most valuable gift ever offered to God was the body, the blood, the life of the God-Man. This gift was in itself of absolutely infinite value, and it caused the sacrifice of the cross to be immeasurably superior, in intrinsic value, to all the sacrifices of the Old Law. Nevertheless the infinite value of Christ's sacrifice is owing more to the infinite dignity of the Sacrificer than to the infinite value of the gift. Does not, in every day life, the personality of the giver add to the gift a special value? In your prayer-book you have a small, insignificant picture. It is torn and soiled. And still it is dear to you, and you would not give it for any price. Why? You received it from a good friend or from some exalted personage, perhaps the Holy Father gave it to you when, prostrate at his feet in the Holy City, you implored his papal blessing. Does not a mother take more pleasure in a simple bouquet given to her on her namesday by a good and pious child than in a more pretentious gift offered by a wayward son? Thus the personality of the giver can impart a great value to a small gift. That is why the infinite dignity and holiness of Christ gave to His sacrifice an infinite value. This is so true that if Christ, instead of offering

Himself to God, had offered only a lamb, for instance, the sacrificial act of Christ would have had an infinite value owing to the personality of the sacrificing Priest.

The sacrifice of the Cross is, therefore, the greatest, holiest and most valuable act which was ever performed since the creation of the world. Whatever the patriarchs and prophets, the confessors and virgins, the martyrs and apostles, all the saints and even the Blessed Virgin did that was good and holy, all of it put together, being finite, cannot be compared with the value of the sacrifice of the Cross.

The infinite value of the sacrifice of the Cross is derived, secondly, from the infinite treasure of satisfaction and merit which it contains. This treasure is so infinitely vast that, notwithstanding the untold wealth distributed therefrom to men for centuries and daily flowing to them even now, it is not only not exhausted, but it has not even been diminished. It could not be diminished even if there were a million times more human beings, even if this out-flowing wealth were a million times greater, and if the world were to last for all eternity.

But what is this glorious and manifold wealth, which is the product of the sacrifice of the cross? It can be divided into two kinds, viz., perfect reconciliation and perfect restoration to grace. In the first place, Christ has satisfied for the guilt of sin. By His sacrifice He has rendered to His heavenly Father an honor infinitely greater than that which was withdrawn from Him by the sins of the whole world. Then He also more than plentifully atoned for the penalties of sin. To prevail on God to waive His right of punishing us, He took upon Himself sufferings of infinite atoning power. But Christ merited for us not only the remission of guilt and of punishment, He also gained for us a perfect restoration to grace, a superabundance of life, the entrance "into the Holies," as the Scripture has it. To the redeeming death of Christ we owe each and every grace which we have ever received from God, the grace of the true faith, the grace of prayer, the grace of our heart's conversion, the grace of the victory over temptation, and from it alone can we expect the grace of final perseverance. From each one of these graces, there hangs, as it were, a drop of Christ's precious Blood with which it was purchased. But not only did Christ merit for us the plenitude of actual graces, but He also merited sanctifying grace, the infused virtues, the gifts and fruits of the Holy Ghost, the celestial transfiguration of soul and body; in a word, all the glories of grace in the children of God, which glories are indeed hidden here below, but, in the next world, shall be unfolded in most wonderful splendor. The establishment also of the Holy Church and her endowment with all the gifts and means of salvation are fruits grown upon the tree of the Cross. Wherefore, in holy inspiration and filled with joy and rapture, the Church sings in her Passion hymn:

"Cross of faith, among all others,
Tree most precious, wondrous rare;
None e'er yields such leaves, such flowers,
Nor such fruit, divinely fair."

Now by the fruits the tree is known. Therefore, from the infinite satisfaction and merit of the sacrifice of the Cross, we rightly infer its infinite value. It remains for us to participate in the fruits of the sacrifice of the Cross to an always increasing extent by prayer, by good works, by the reception of the sacraments and by assisting at holy Mass.

The sixth word of Christ on the cross is, then, full of meaning when taken to signify, "The sacrifice is consummated." His death on the cross was really the sacrifice of the New Law, promised by the prophets and prefigured by the sacrifice of the Old Law; it was a sacrifice of infinite value. Christ's mission in life was now fulfilled. Justly, therefore, and as if in holy enthusiasm, does a celebrated Father of the Syrian church [1] cite all the prophets to appear upon Calvary, there to gaze on the Messias and to testify before the entire world that their prophecies concerning Him have been fulfilled to the letter. "Approach," he exclaims, "Isaias, and behold the Lamb offered to the Divinity, immolated, suspended on the cross and covered with blood! . . . Zachary, look

[1] Jacob of Sarug. First discourse on the passion of Jesus. Translated by P. Zingerle. Theol. Quartalschr. (1891) p. 410.

upon His hands and see the wounds! . . . David, whose son He is, come and behold Him on Golgotha: they have pierced His hands and driven nails through them, they have given Him vinegar." . . . The Redeemer could therefore confidently close His eyes.

Happy the Christian who, in death, can say with the Saviour, in holy joy and with a cheerful heart, "It is consummated." Consummated is the work which the heavenly Father hath given me, the sacrifice of mine own self is consummated. Past are now the days of labor, the days of tribulation and of temptation; they are past forever. Past is the horrible, dark night of tempests, and lo! I already behold the dawn of the eternal day of light and heavenly brightness. Nothing now remains but to receive the crown of justice.

But if our last hour were to come to-day, could we say with as much confidence as the Saviour, "It is consummated"? Alas, how many are far behind in the work of their lives! How many have not even begun their work! How many, after having begun, have again folded their arms in idleness! It were terrible, however, if in such a condition, one were forced by approaching death to exclaim, "It is consummated." Consummated is the life of sin and vice! Gone are now all those sweeping pleasures, those vile passions. Gone now is boastful wealth, gone is the vanity of worldly honor. Past are now the hours of grace, the hours of salvation and of mercy. Now the hour of vengeance is striking. Time is at an end, eternity is beginning, eternity with its everlasting pains.

However, the Heart of Christ is good and full of love. The Redeemer still gives us time for life, time for work and for penance. Let us, then, with all our hearts, deplore our past neglect in the service of God and, with redoubled efforts, strive to retrieve past omissions. Let us by ceaseless work redeem lost time and thus make haste to enter into eternal rest.

CHAPTER XXIX.

THE SEVENTH WORD OF CHRIST ON THE CROSS

"And Jesus crying with a loud voice, said: Father, into thy hands I commend my spirit. And saying this, he gave up the ghost."

(St. Luke, xxiii., 46.)

All things which Holy Writ had predicted regarding the life and Passion of the Redeemer, were fulfilled. His thirst was to be quenched with vinegar. As soon as Christ had taken the vinegar, He said, "It is consummated." All was consummated that the heavenly Father had entrusted Him with; everything that was demanded by Divine Justice, everything to which the Redeemer's love had impelled Him, everything necessary or conducive to man's salvation, everything was now consummated. Consummated was now the work of the bloody Passion, the chalice was drained to the dregs, and whatever evil hell and the world could inflict on Christ, was now overcome. Consummated was now the Old Testament with its onerous laws and bloody sacrifice of animals, its prophecies were fulfilled, its figures had passed into reality, and the synagogue now came to an end. "It is consummated!" This sixth word of the Redeemer was the prayer of thanksgiving in the evening of His life, the message of joy for all the elect, the announcement of victory over hell and the cry of triumph at the moment of death. The work of redemption, the sacrifice of the New Law, was consummated. Nothing else remained but to die. Wherefore the Redeemer cried out with a loud voice, "Father, into thy hands I commend my spirit." Let us consider [1]

I. The meaning of the seventh word and

II. The circumstances of its utterance.

I.

In the last moment of His life the Redeemer thought almost exclusively of His heavenly Father and of His own soul. In the seventh word He addresses God with the word "Father." This was the last declaration of His own divinity. During His public life, He had often and in various ways declared Himself to be the Son of God, and He had worked many miracles to prove the truth of His declaration. Before Caiphas He had maintained this same declaration although He foresaw all the tortures it would cause Him. He held to this declaration until death. In the Crucified Redeemer we must therefore adore the Son of God and bend our knee before Him.

He furthermore called God His Father to show once more that His will was in complete subjec-

[1] St. Matthew, xxvii., 50; St. Mark, xv., 37; St. Luke, xxiii., 46; St. John, xix., 30.

tion to the will of the Father and that He was obedient unto death, even unto the death of the Cross. The word, "Father," was at the same time the expression of filial love and of strongest confidence. It was not, as we have seen, from diffidence or pusillanimity that, immediately before, He had not called upon the Father as such but rather had exclaimed, "My God, my God, why hast thou forsaken me?"

Besides the Father, His soul was also the subject of Christ's thoughts. He had no more earthly goods to dispose of. His garments had been distributed and the lot cast upon His vesture. He had early provided for His Blessed Mother. He gave no directions as to the place and manner of His burial; that He left to others. But he now recommended His soul to the Father. He did it for a threefold purpose. First, this recommendation of the soul was, in a manner, an offering of it. He had already shed and offered His blood, but His soul was still His own. In grateful recognition therefore, of all natural and supernatural gifts with which it was endowed, He laid in the hands of its Creator this soul which was the master-piece of Divine Love and Power, and He offered it to the Father. Secondly, He recommended His soul to God in order that God might now finally free it from its sufferings and thus allow it to enjoy unmolested all the delights and pleasures resulting from the immediate vision of God. Thirdly, He recommended His soul to the Father in order that He might, as it were, take it in charge until the day of the resurrection.

Strictly speaking, there was no need of a recommendation on the part of Christ. He might have appealed to the innate right He had of enjoying, free from every suffering, all the delights of heaven, of being preserved from bodily corruption and of speedily rising from the dead. He might also have reminded the Father of the infinite merits of His life and passion. But the Saviour was humble of heart. And, to give us also an example, He used the language of humility.

Then again, the seventh word is very *instructive for us.* We may learn from the Redeemer the right manner of preparing for death. One should arrange early all temporal affairs and whatever concerns his family and relatives. There should be no unreasonable anxiety about the body and its burial nor about the grave and its adornment. For, when the house is in flames, it would be foolish to worry about some thread-bare garment and to forget to save the gold and the jewels. No one was ever less attentive to these matters than the Redeemer. But no tomb ever became more glorious than His. On the approach of death we should think of and turn to Divine mercy and love. To this mercy should we recommend our poor souls and not pay attention to our merits. For whatever good we have done, we owe it to Divine grace, whilst many of our good works are faulty and need cleansing. Such humility will surely crown our merits. We should commend our soul into the hands of the Father, into those hands which have formed us, into those hands which hold our destiny and from which no one can ever snatch our souls.

While the seventh word of Christ on the cross is instructive, it is also very *consoling*. For, recommending *His own* spirit to the heavenly Father, the Saviour recommended all *those* who are one with His spirit. "But he who is joined to the Lord, is one spirit," says St. Paul,[1] i. e., whoever is in possession of sanctifying grace is one spirit with Him. Whilst, therefore, in the last hour we may have to face much that might fill us with terror, if by sanctifying grace we are united with Christ, we may confidently close our eyes in death. For by more than eighteen centuries a recommendation to the heavenly Father has preceded us. On account of the prayer of Christ in which with His spirit, He also recommended ours to the Father, we may expect a merciful reception.

Let us now direct our attention to the circumstances of the seventh word.

II.

The first circumstance meriting our consideration is the fact that Christ spoke this word with a loud voice. It is unheard of in history that

[1] I. Cor., vi., 17.

any one who was crucified spoke in a loud voice just before death. The fearful fever which made the tongue cleave to the palate prevented it. At most, it may have happened that a person dying on the cross, uttered a loud groan or sigh. But to distinctly pronounce an entire sentence with a loud voice, was impossible except by a miracle. This must impel us the more to examine the reasons why Christ worked such a miracle.

In the first place the Redeemer wished to show by this wonderful demonstration of strength that He was even then capable of removing or postponing the natural effects of His sufferings and that, as St. Augustine says,[1] He died not from weakness but by power. "To die," St. Bernard therefore says,[2] "means great weakness; but *thus* to die, means immense strength." As, then, the word itself was the last declaration of His divinity, just so, as the pagan centurion acknowledged immediately afterwards, the loud voice was the last miracle in confirmation of it.

Then, by His loud cry, Christ manifested the whole natural pain felt by the soul when it must leave the body. This pain was especially severe in the soul of Jesus Christ. How hard is it not to take leave of a good friend? Now the soul of Christ saw in its Sacred Body the best and most lovable friend with whom it had been most intimately united in weal and woe for thirty-three years. Besides, this body had assisted the Sav-

1 Serm. 218, c. 12. Migne, P. L. t. xxxviii., col. 1087.

2 Serm. de Pass. Domini, n. 4.

iour's soul with the utmost self-sacrifice, in the work of Redemption. It had suffered hunger and thirst, it had become fatigued through the labors and heat of the day. It had been cruelly scourged; it had allowed hands and feet to be pierced and the head to be crowned with thorns; it had given all its blood; it had, in a word, borne the expenses of Redemption. Now the soul of Christ had to part from this body, and therefore He loudly expressed His sorrow.

The parting of the soul from the body, with which it has been intimately united for twenty, fifty or perhaps seventy years, is also with us the saddest event of all. It is sadder than the parting from worldly possessions, sadder than the separation from relatives, especially when the body with its five senses has been to the soul only a companion in sin and an instrument for sin. Indeed, to be forced to leave such a body which has been the chief source of enjoyment for the sinner and profligate and to leave it with the prospect of again being united to it forever in the flames of hell, has thrown many a soul into despair and has forced from many a dying person a cry of desperation.

Through the loud cry, the Redeemer also gave expression to another sorrow. *His* death, namely, was *our* spiritual birth. Whatever the sacred humanity of Christ suffered thereby, was to be made known to the entire world. Rachel of yore called the son whose birth caused her death, "Benoni," that is, "son of my sorrow." The father, however, called him Benjamin, that is, "son of my right hand." May we, whose regeneration cost the Saviour His life, be also recognized by our heavenly Father as "sons of His right hand," that is, as such upon whom He may confidently place His right hand, as if for support, in all that concerns His greater glory and the salvation of souls.

Furthermore, Christ cried with a loud voice in order to encourage death to approach Him. Death sat at the foot of Calvary and steadily gazed upon the three crucified ones. He dared not approach the Redeemer. For he well knew that he had no rightful claim on Him Who was the author of life and Who had not sinned in Adam. Wherefore the Redeemer, by crying loudly, enticed him to approach, and death was heedless enough to heed this voice. For he had no idea that by devouring this prey, he himself would lose his life and find his death.

Christ, finally, cried with a loud voice, just as the lion roars when going forth to seize his prey. Now the moment had arrived when Christ, always so hungry for immortal souls, was to go forth from Golgotha to satisfy His consuming hunger. With a loud voice He announced to the world the march of conquest which nothing should withstand. Therefore, in terror and in joy as well, the earth quaked, the rocks were rent, the graves opened; but the sun appeared in its full splendor. This cry of the Redeemer penetrated into the inmost depths of the earth. It was the signal of redemption to the souls in Limbo. But to the fallen spirits it was a clap of thunder which, in a moment, wrecked all their plans.

The second circumstance of the seventh word is the fact that it was the last word of the dying Redeemer. For, after saying this word, or rather whilst saying it, He bowed His head, and thereupon He breathed forth His soul. The bowing of the head was, therefore, not an effect of death already present; it was an act willed with full deliberation. It must, indeed, have a deep meaning. For when Christ addressed the Father at the last supper, He raised His eyes to heaven. Why then does He now bow His head, whilst He is speaking to the Father Who is in heaven? Although the crown of thorns may have prevented Him from raising His head, why did He not keep it in its former position, and why did He not at least raise His eyes to heaven?

First, the bowing of the head was the expression of His humble submission to the will of the Father. At the same time it denoted the powerful weight of sin burdening His shoulder and pressing Him down. Whoever walks along laden with a heavy burden always walks with a bowed head. Then this bowing of the head was the parting salute to His beloved mother, to St. John, to the pious women and to the thief on the right. Wherefore, according to tradition, the Saviour did not bow directly ahead but more to the right where all these saints were. Furthermore, He desired to breathe His spirit upon those to whom He was now about to descend in order to deliver them from Limbo's prison. The bow of the head was the sign of reconciliation; it was the sign that He breathed forth His spirit for the salvation of the world and that this spirit should always remain among men. Finally He bowed His head as if to implore a blessing.

After Our Divine Saviour had bowed His head, he gave up the ghost. Upon the cross we now behold only a corpse bleeding from many wounds. But the divinity dwells in it, it is inseparably united with the second Person, it is really the corpse of the Son of God. The soul, also inseparably united with the second Person, was immeasurably happy immediately after the separation from the body, and it descended into Limbo. No matter, therefore, how much we are entitled to mourn the death of the Saviour, we must congratulate Him also with all our hearts for such a happy death.

The Son of God, then, has died. Now the sinner may breathe easier. It must indeed, be terrible, as Holy Writ says, to fall into the hands of the living God. But a dying God, a God struggling with death, a God breathing forth His soul, is not to be feared. He can only be loved. In presence, then, of the lifeless body of the God-Man, let this be our resolve, that in future we shall no longer walk in the spirit of fear, at least not of servile fear, but rather in the spirit of love. Out of love for Him Who loved us until death, let us deplore our sins and avoid them in future.

Out of love to Christ crucified let us strive to become like to Him. Then, in death, we shall also be able to say confidently, "Father, into thy hands I commend my spirit."

CHAPTER XXX.

THE SUFFERINGS OF CHRIST ON THE CROSS

"O all ye that pass by the way attend, and see if there be any sorrow like my sorrow."

(Lam. i., 12.)

In meditating upon the seven words, we have already considered various great sufferings which the Redeemer had to undergo during the three hours that he hung upon the Cross. But there remain several others which merit our attention. And it appears meet and just, as well as useful and salutary, to summarize and group in one chapter all the sufferings of Our Lord on the Cross, in order to obtain as faithful a picture as possible of the crucified Redeemer. If the garden of Olives, the different courts, the place of flagellation and the stations of the way of the cross are sacred spots, then surely Mount Calvary ought to be for us, as it was for the saints, an abode of predilection. The contemplation of the Crucified Redeemer ought to be the daily bread, the consolation and the comfort of our souls. In grouping the various sufferings of the Crucified Saviour, we shall but briefly mention those which we have already meditated upon in detail. Let us consider the sufferings of the crucified Saviour

I. In His sacred Body,

II. In His honor and

III. In His soul.

I.

In describing the sufferings which the Crucified Saviour was called upon to bear in His sacred Body, I shall appeal less to the imagination, but I shall endeavor, by presenting some thoughts, to convince the reason that the bodily sufferings of the Redeemer must have been immeasurably great.

Of all deaths, that by crucifixion was held by the entire ancient world to be the most painful and the most cruel. The suspension alone from the arms stretched upwards for such a long time, was intolerable torture. History tells of certain English martyrs who, for the purpose of making them deny the faith, were suspended from beams by means of ropes attached to their hands and left several hours dangling between heaven and earth. When finally the ropes were cut, they fell to the ground as if dead. Now Christ was not attached to the cross with ropes but with nails. These nails were driven through the hands and feet, just where many sensitive nerves and tendons meet. Some of these were lacerated, others were violently bruised. It is true, as antiquarians show, that it was customary at crucifixions to fasten to the middle of the cross a prop upon which the main weight of the body should rest,[1] so that the hands would not be torn through. In regard to the cross of Christ, St. Irenaeus [2] and the holy martyr Justin [3] mention this support in express terms. But there was no trace of a foot rest to act as a support from below. The feet of Christ were nailed directly to the main beam of the cross. The main weight of the body, therefore, bore partly on the pierced feet and partly on the pierced hands. If Christ would relieve the one, the other suffered so much the more. Every move, every slight tremor brought about renewed pain penetrating to the very marrow. Owing to the wounded and terribly swollen hands and feet, and, yet more, to the unnatural lesion and tension of all the muscles caused by the strained position of the body, the circulation of the blood through the heart and lungs was rendered difficult and partly impeded. Thence resulted a difficulty of breathing which increased to a sense of suffocation accompanied by a sensation of fear and spasmodic contraction of the heart. Another result was that the blood rushed to the head with increased pressure, abnormally extending the arteries and immensely increasing the pains in the thorn-crowned head. And as the body, which the scourging had entirely covered with wounds, was exposed for three hours to the fresh and, be-

[1] Hence the expression: equitare in cruce.
[2] Adv. haeres. 2, 24, 4.
[3] Adv. Tryph. 91. Migne P. G. t. vi., col. 693.

cause of the eclipse, even cold air, inflammation and wound-fever set in, so that the sacred body assumed a livid color. These pains reached their climax in the burning and steadily increasing thirst.

If to this we add the condition of exhaustion and faintness induced by the preceding sufferings of Christ, the loss of blood from the scourging and the crowning with thorns, and the sensitiveness of His sacred body, then we have a faint idea of the bodily sufferings of the Crucified One.

There are Christians who deem it extremely difficult to love God with a perfect love. Ah, that they would consider the Crucified Saviour Who might have saved us with one sigh of His Sacred Heart, but Who, out of love for us, was willing to shed all His blood! Indeed, it is impossible devoutly to consider the sufferings of Christ, and not be penetrated with a perfect love for Him and a perfect contrition for our sins. It is impossible devoutly to consider the sufferings of Christ and not to renounce, out of love for Him, at least all the sinful and dangerous pleasures of this world. It is impossible devoutly to consider the sufferings of Christ and not bear patiently and even joyfully the sufferings of this life. "For," as St. Bernard says beautifully,[1] "the wounds of Christ are on the one hand sources of blood to teach us to suffer and, on the other hand, sources of fire to teach us to love."

1 Serm. 33, in Cant.

May, therefore, the picture of the Redeemer bleeding from a thousand wounds be continually present to our minds and impress itself deeply upon our souls.

Let us consider, secondly, the sufferings of the Crucified One in His honor.

II.

With infinite care the Holy Ghost once had sanctified the virginal body which was destined to clothe the Son of God with flesh and blood. Nothing but what was absolutely pure and holy might ever touch His blood. Now, however, at the death of Christ, this blood flowed upon a soil desecrated by the sins of men and sated, in the lapse of centuries, with their blood. Thus, as it were, did the blood of the Most Holy One mingle with the blood of sinners and become one substance with it,—an ignominy for the Saviour which we cannot sufficiently take to heart. But thus it must needs be. For the blood of Christ was to flow for the sins of the world. Such was His last will and testament. It must mingle with sinful blood in order to purify and sanctify it.

Besides, the Redeemer died the most disgraceful and most shameful of all deaths, the death of the Cross. Among the Romans, this mode of death was applied only to the most abject of criminals; to those who were considered as rejected by the gods; to those whose bodies were deemed unworthy of burial. Never was it permitted to inflict this penalty upon a free-born Roman. Then, as if He had been the leader and chief of a band of robbers and murderers, Christ was crucified between two incendiaries and homicidal robbers. Furthermore, He was deprived of all His garments except the loin-cloth. And all this was done, not secretly nor privately in an enclosed prison yard, but publicly, in open daylight, on a hill, before the whole people who had assembled to celebrate the pasch.

But what caused the greatest dishonor and shame to Christ, were the blasphemies and jeers with which He was overwhelmed while hanging on the cross. True, he had been forced to drink of this chalice of ignominy on former occasions. But it was here, on Golgotha's heights, that, according to the Lamentations, He was to be satiated with ignominy. Hence the evangelists are very explicit in the description of these scenes. They not only mention the different classes of people who blasphemed and scoffed at the Redeemer, but they also give the very words of derision which were spoken against Him.

First, as we have already seen when treating of the second word of Christ, it was the thief on the left who opened his mouth in blasphemy. Then it was the passers-by, that is, those of the people who came and went or happened to pass on the way leading by Golgotha.[1] In vain had the prophet, centuries before, appealed to the

[1] St. Matthew, xxvii, 39, 40; St. Mark, xv., 29, 30.

passers-by for sympathy: "O all ye that pass by the way attend, and see if there be any sorrow like to my sorrow." They blasphemed Him, says Holy Writ, they critically and sarcastically wagged their heads, and distorting the words of Christ as the false witnesses had done, they said, "Vah, thou that destroyest the temple of God, and in three days dost rebuild it, save thy own self: if thou be the son of God, come down from the cross." Thus do they express their joy that, at last, the great wonder-worker is unmasked as a boastful deceiver. Does not this last word of the Jews recall exactly the one which Satan once spoke to Christ, "If thou be the son of God, cast thyself down"? Indeed, here we have the key to the solution of the otherwise incomprehensible mystery. These blasphemies were no longer human; they were diabolical. Satan had put them upon the tongues of the passers-by. During all the preceding sufferings of Christ, Whom he held to be a mere man, he had in vain tempted Him to anger and similar sins. Now, in his despair, he again had recourse to the weapon of derision and contempt, but Christ, contemning contempt, remained on the cross.

Many Christians, alas! act differently. For years, perhaps, they have followed the way of virtue and piety, and they have even sacrificed and suffered a vast deal for their holy faith. Then the devil, in human shape, attacks them with ridicule and derision. They cannot bear it; they descend from the cross and make friends with their own aggressors.

Then the executioners also joined in the taunts of the passers-by. Whilst they offered the vinegar to the Saviour they also said, as St. Luke narrates (xxiii., 36, 37), "If thou be the king of the Jews, save thyself." As before this they pierced Christ with sharp nails, so now they pierce Him with sharp tongues. However, among all those who ridiculed Christ, they were the least guilty, for they knew not what they were doing.

The grossest insults, finally, were heaped upon Christ by the chief-priests, ancients, scribes and pharisees.[1] All the prominent people were present on Golgotha. It was right that they should be there, for on that day the King of the Jews was to take possession of His throne. But I must give utterance to my surprise that the chief-priests were also to be seen on Calvary at this time. For the ninth hour was fast approaching when they were to begin the slaughter of the paschal lambs. And still they remain in great numbers on Golgotha. "Behold," they shout, "he calleth Elias." However, for the time being, their main object was to celebrate their triumph over the Crucified One and, therefore, without scruples of conscience, they set aside their entire ceremonial. What a wonderful dispensation of God that the high-priests should abandon the typical paschal lamb, when the true Paschal Lamb was bleeding to death.

[1] St. Matthew, xxvii., 41–43; St. Mark, xv., 31, 32; St. Luke, xxiii., 35.

The language which the chief-priests, ancients, scribes and pharisees used on this occasion was the most vulgar both as to form and as to meaning. They did not, like the passers-by address themselves to the Redeemer personally. To show Him their contempt, they spoke to each other of Him as of a third person, of the man hanging there on the cross. Without looking at Him they pointed their fingers at Him over their shoulders whilst they exclaimed, "He saved others; himself he cannot save; if he be the king of Israel, let him now come down from the cross, and we will believe him. He trusted in God: let him now deliver him if he will have him; for he said: I am the Son of God." Their first words, we may note, were almost the same blasphemies as those uttered by the passers-by: "He saved others, let him save himself." A strange conclusion indeed! If He has helped others to any extent, He deserves better treatment now. To encourage the Redeemer, however, to descend from the cross, they sneeringly add the promise, "And we will believe him." What wretched hypocrisy and lying! The Redeemer had, before their very eyes, performed greater miracles than the one which they were now presumptuously demanding; only very recently He had raised Lazarus from the dead, and still they would not believe Him. Two days afterwards, when Christ worked the greatest of all miracles by rising from the grave through His own power, they remained as obdurate as ever. But now they will believe, if He descends from the cross. "Know ye," asks one interpreter, "what these men would have done if Christ had acceded to their demands? They all together would have fallen upon Him and beaten Him to death with their fists." In the last words which they spoke, "He trusted in God: let him now deliver him if he will have him," they blasphemed the mystery of the cross, inasmuch as they, like the friends of Job, designate the cross as the sign of God's anger and curse. This derision of the instrument of our salvation contained a protest against the work of redemption. But thus it was to be. For David (Ps. xxi., 9) had predicted that the Redeemer would be ridiculed by those very words. Wherefore, without either willing or suspecting it, the chief-priests, by their blasphemies, gave testimony to the Messianic dignity of the Crucified.

The shouts of the chief-priests, of the scribes and of the pharisees still resound in our own days. "If he be the King of Israel, let him come down from the cross and we will believe him," is peculiarly the language of modern unbelief. The Divinity of Jesus Christ has been proven by thousands of miracles, and the divine establishment of the Catholic Church emits a radiance brighter than that of the sun. Still proud unbelief will not submit; it keeps on clamoring for new miracles, for new proofs. But take off its mask, and you will find it full of lies and of hypocrisy. Unbelief cares nothing for truth. On principle it will not acknowledge as God One Who was crucified.

The sermon of the cross is to it foolishness and a scandal. And the language of unbelief is also the language of immorality. There might perhaps be no objection to believing in Christ, if only He would descend from the cross, if only He would cease to preach, from this pulpit, the crucifixion of the flesh and of vicious inclinations. It is, too, in a certain sense, the language of sloth and of half-heartedness. One would, with pleasure even, tread the path of virtue and of perfection if only Christ would descend from the cross, that is, if the practice of virtue were possible without continued mortification and self-denial.

The prediction of the prophet Jeremias, "I am made a derision to all my people, their song all the day long," was, then, fulfilled. At such derision David would have exclaimed, in sorrow, "Neither let my enemies laugh at me,"[1] and Job would have cursed the day of his birth. But Christ's sole answer to ridicule and blasphemy was silence and constant perseverance on the cross. By this He proved Himself to be the true Messias, the true Son of God, of Whom it had been foretold that He would die on the cross. "It was a greater deed," says St. Gregory the Great,[2] "to destroy death through the Resurrection than to preserve life by descending from the Cross."

Let us yet consider the sufferings of the Crucified One in His soul.

[1] Ps., xxiv., 3.
[2] Hom. 21, in Evang. c. 7.

III.

The first suffering of Christ's soul arose from beholding a scene the possibility of which would be incredible were the fact not substantiated by Holy Writ itself.[1] According to Roman usage, the clothes and other belongings of the executed became the property of the soldiers; it was their fee. They had hardly erected the cross when they fell upon the belongings of the Saviour. There were four soldiers, as we have already seen; four formed a detachment. They ripped the seams of those garments the parts of which were sewn together, as, for instance, the mantle, and each soldier received a fourth part. With the garment proper, however, of the Saviour, they could not well do this, for it was seamless and woven throughout from the top. St. Bonaventure relates that the Mother of Jesus had woven it with her own hands for her Divine Child, and it had grown with Him just as the garments of the Israelites had grown with them in their passage through the desert.[2] Had, then, the woven raiment been cut, it would have become entirely unwoven and the pieces would have been useless. They therefore said, "Let us not cut it, but let us cast lots for it, whose it shall be." They did so. Roman soldiers always had dice about them with which to beguile the time during idle hours. Thus, at

[1] St. Matthew, xxvii. 35; St Mark, xv., 24; St. Luke, xxiii., 34; St. John, xix., 23, 24.

[2] Deut., viii., 4; xxix., 5.

the foot of the cross upon which the God-Man was bleeding for the salvation of the world, and under His very eyes, the rattling dice were shaken around the circle. With vile shouts the losers acclaimed the winner. Then they settled down to their task of watching Christ and of preventing His being taken down.

As far as the transaction itself was concerned, everything went on smoothly and peaceably enough. Whatever could be divided, was divided; for that which could not be divided, they cast lots and they were all satisfied. There are times when things go differently in Christian families. Matters of inheritance are at times the occasion of most serious quarrels and of life-long enmities between brothers and sisters. The seamless garment of Christ, holy charity, which ought to be held sacred among Christians, is thereby rent asunder, torn and trampled in the mire.

The executioners, however, did not long remain in possession of the Redeemer's garments. For the Roman law which appropriated to them the garments of the executed, also empowered friends and relatives to purchase them from the executioners for a fair sum of money. Thus there ensued between the pious women and the two rich and good men who soon afterwards came to Calvary, a holy rivalry to redeem, at any price, the precious relics, and they were restored to the sorrowful Mother, who thereby was greatly consoled.

The second sorrow of Christ's soul arose from His complete abandonment by heaven and earth.

And first, the lack of sympathy on the part of the people saddened Him. A few days before, when He made His solemn entry into Jerusalem, they had acclaimed Him with Hosannas: "Blessed is he that cometh in the name of the Lord." Now, when He is in distress, now, when He is dying, they show no sign of compassion. They "stood beholding," says the Gospel.[1] And yet, among these people, there were so many whom the Saviour had loaded with benefits.

Christ, moreover, saw Himself forsaken by almost all his friends. It is true that Mary, His Blessed Mother, stood beneath the Cross, but the sight merely increased the pangs of His soul. But of the apostles, with the exception of St. John, all had left Him, all had made themselves invisible. One other, forsooth, who had belonged to the twelve, Christ could behold from the cross by turning His head to the left. It was unhappy Judas who had hanged himself on the declivity of the hill, and who was now burning in hell.

In His dereliction by men, the dying Redeemer raised His head to heaven and turned towards God. But heaven remained closed. No voice of approval was heard as when, in days gone by, He had humbled Himself before John. No angel came to serve Him as in the desert, after He had fasted forty days. Not even did an angel come to comfort Him as on the evening before in the Garden of Olives. This urged Christ to complain,

[1] St. Luke, xxiii., 35.

"My God, my God, why hast thou forsaken me?"

So much the more intense, therefore, was the third sorrow of Christ's soul at the thought of the partial friutlessness of His Passion. He had now been hanging three hours upon the cross whence He hoped to draw all things to Himself. The awful darkness should indeed have been sufficient to enlighten souls and to kindle hearts. But with the exception of the thief's conversion, the Redeemer saw no special effects. And when He looked into the future, He recognized that His blood was being shed in vain for millions of people and that, notwithstanding all His sufferings, millions of men would be eternally damned.

Now the measure of sufferings was full. Now the Redeemer could say, "It is consummated. Father, into thy hands I commend my spirit." Thereupon He bowed His head and died.

At the cross her station keeping,
Stood the mournful Mother weeping,
Close to Jesus to the last.

"No tongue shall ever be able to express," says St. Bernard,[1] "nor shall any mind ever be able to imagine what sorrow the loving heart of Mary endured at this moment. Now, O Virgin, on Golgotha thou art paying with interest what thou didst not experience in Bethlehem." "The pains which she did not endure at His birth," says St.

[1] In Lament. B. Mariæ. Migne P. L. t. clxxxii., col. 1137.

John Damascene,[1] "she endured at the time of His death when she had to see that He Whom she even then had recognized as God, was now being put to death as a criminal."

> Through her heart, His sorrow sharing,
> All His bitter anguish bearing,
> Now at length the sword had passed.

O Christian soul! we have already read the law which God had once given to the people of Israel. "When there shall be found in the land the corpse of a man slain, and it is not known who is guilty of the murder, the ancients of the (nearest) city shall come to the person slain, and shall wash their hands . . . and shall say: Our hands did not shed this blood. nor did our eyes see it. And the guilt of blood shall be taken from them."[2] See! Before our eyes there hangs the corpse of One slain on the Cross. Whoever among us knows himself innocent of the blood of this Just One, let him approach, let him lay his right hand on the wood of the Cross, and let him testify before heaven and earth, "My hands have not shed this blood, and I am innocent of the blood of this Just One." Ah, No! O sweet Saviour Jesus Christ! Penetrated with the sorrow of contrition, we shall rather confess that our sins have been the cause of Thy bitter Passion, that our sins have killed Thee. May Thy precious Blood be not lost upon us. Cleanse us with it, and, by Thy bitter death, grant us a happy death.

[1] De fid. orthod. lib. 4, c. 14.
[2] Deut., xxi., 1, 6–8.

CHAPTER XXXI.

WONDERFUL EVENTS BEFORE AND AT THE DEATH OF CHRIST

> "Now from the sixth hour there was darkness over the whole earth, until the ninth hour.—And behold the veil of the temple was rent in two from the top even to the bottom, and the earth quaked, and the rocks were rent. And the graves were opened: and many bodies of the saints that had slept, arose.
> (St. Matthew, xxvii., 45, 51, 52.)

The great drama enacted on the first Maundy Thursday and Good Friday in Jerusalem and in its vicinity, is gradually approaching its end. As we have considered in our meditations, both heaven and earth followed the destinies of the Divine Sufferer with close, yea, with strained attention, each, however, in a different way. The passers-by suspiciously wagged their heads. The executioners and the thief to the left ridiculed Him. The pharisees, scribes and chief-priests rejoiced in His downfall. Pilate, in the beginning, hesitated to pronounce the death-sentence and finally washed his hands as a sign of innocence. Herod and his wife, the adulteress, laughed. The apostles fled in terror, they could not bear the sight. Procula, the wife of Pilate, was so deeply moved and agitated, that she dreamed of the tragedy. Veronica and other pious women shed tears of compassion. Simon of Cyrene felt himself happy to have become, without his own merit, an actor in the great event. Dismas loudly proclaimed the innocence of Christ. Even an angel appeared on the scene to inspire the Divine Sufferer with courage in the performance of His awful role. Mary, the Mother of Jesus, John and Magdalene stood at the side of the Saviour, consoling Him in His last moments. Lastly, the heavenly Father received into His hands the soul of His dying Son. But, we have reason to ask, shall nature remain indifferent and look coldly on, whilst her Creator and Lord is struggling with death and whilst the Immortal One is breathing forth His soul in nameless tortures? Certainly not. The sun became darkened, the veil of the temple was torn in two, the earth trembled and quaked, the rocks were rent and the graves opened.

Let us then consider [1]

I. These wonderful events in themselves;

II. The different effects they produced upon men.

I.

These wonderful events occurred in part before the death of Christ and in part at His death.

[1] St. Matthew, xxvii., 45, 51–54; St. Luke, xxiii., 44–48.

Before the death of Christ, there occurred a total eclipse of the sun lasting three hours. This fact is historically so well substantiated that there can be no doubt about it. Three evangelists testify to it. The evangelists St. Matthew and St. Mark write: "From the sixth hour there was darkness over the whole earth, until the ninth hour." St. Luke writes: "the sun was darkened." If a historian or a newspaper correspondent wishes purposely to spread some lie broadcast over the world, he will select imaginary events which, owing to their very nature, do not happen in public, or at least such as are alleged to have happened in some remote corner of the earth. But to report, for instance, that some years ago an extraordinary eclipse of the sun happened in this town, when every body knows it to be untrue, would not occur to any one.

This eclipse of the sun[1] was, however, not a natural one. It was miraculous in every respect and that for three reasons. First it occurred at the time of the *full moon.* For this Friday was the day when, according to the Law, the Pasch should be celebrated, and this feast always occurred at the time of the full moon. Now, naturally, an eclipse of the sun can occur only at the time of the new moon, when the latter is between the sun and the earth. Then, it was miraculous because it was total *from the very beginning* and, lastly, because it remained total *for three hours.*

[1] See note 20.

In an ordinary eclipse of the sun, the moon, in the beginning, covers only a part of the sun, then gradually more, until the darkness reaches its greatest height, whereupon it again gradually decreases. This eclipse of the sun was, therefore, an extraordinary work of God, and the Holy Fathers freely apply to it the words of the prophet Amos, "And it shall come to pass in that day that the sun shall go down at mid-day, and I will make the earth dark in the day of light."[1] And, about the year 200, Tertullian, speaking of this wondrous eclipse, thus spoke to the Romans, "You yourselves have recorded this great event in your annals."

What was the meaning of this eclipse? On the part of heaven, it was the garb of mourning wherewith the sun clothed itself while the Sun of Justice was being extinguished. "Creation," says St. Chrysostom,[2] "could not bear the indignities inflicted upon the Creator." For the Saviour to Whom a loin-cloth only was left, the eclipse was a veil woven by compassionate nature to cover His nakedness. On the part of God, it was a sign of His anger. God withdrew, even from the just, the light of the sun which he ordinarily lets shine even upon the wicked. At the birth of Christ, in the middle of the night, the splendor of God's glory encircled the shepherds and brightness reigned. At His death-struggle, the sun, standing high in the heavens, became

[1] Amos, viii., 9.

[2] In Catena ex serm. de Pass. Domini.

obscured and darkness reigned. Thus also does brightness spread in the soul when Christ is born in the heart. But the gloom of night enters when He departs from the soul. Wherefore the eclipse of the sun was also an image of the blindness and obstinacy of the Jewish people.

This eclipse ended at the death of the Redeemer. Then again did the sun appear in perfect beauty. Now Divine Justice was reconciled, the sacrifice was consummated. Now the soul of Christ which had been sad unto death, was delivered from all affliction and was unspeakably happy. Now the souls of the patriarchs and saints of the Old Testament shared in the brilliancy of heavenly light and in the joys of the vision of God. Now the darkness which had hovered over the earth for four thousand years was dispelled through the death of Christ, and the new day of salvation had dawned. Now through the light of grace, all darkness was also to be driven out of the hearts of men.

To the wonderful events which happened *at* the death of Christ, belongs in the first place the tearing of the veil in the temple. As the Talmudists report, this veil was forty yards long and twenty yards wide. It was woven of gold and purple and had the thickness of an open hand. It concealed the Holy of Holies of the Temple into which the High-Priest alone was allowed to enter, and this only once a year on the feast of atonement to offer the expiatory sacrifice. Now, at the death of Christ, this veil was rent from top to bottom in two pieces. Just as Jacob of yore rent his garments in sadness, when he was told that wild-beasts had torn to pieces his son Joseph; just as Caiphas, in indignation, tore the pontifical robe, when Christ declared Himself to be the Son of God, so now the temple rent its garment both in sadness and in indignation. The tearing of the veil signified the end of the Old Law and the rejection of the Mosaic sacrifices. In future the entrance into the Holy of Holies, that is, into the Church of God, should be allowed to all men: God would no longer be the God of the Jews, but the God of all nations. All should be allowed access to the heavenly Manna concealed in the sanctuary, and the portals of the Holy of Holies, of celestial Paradise, should be open to all.

The earth quaked. This was also a sign of sadness and of indignation, owing to the crime committed against the Creator. But, more than that, as St. Ignatius remarks in his book of Exercises, it was a sign of joy and delight on account of the victory of the Crucified One and of His present glory. It is remarkable that, at this tremendous earthquake, not a single human being suffered any damage. For the might of infernal powers was broken by the death of Christ. Hell may rage and rave ever so much, it may shake the earth to its foundations, but it has lost its power over mankind, even over the bodies of men.

The rocks were rent. Hearts as hard as rocks shall now be rent; they shall become as pliable as wax and, like to wax, they shall melt before the glow of Divine Love. Now the time had finally arrived when the earth should be formed again, and when the face of the earth should be renewed.

Even the graves opened as a sign that Christ through His death had overcome death, and that all flesh should rise again on the last day. The dead, however, came forth from their graves only on Easter day and not directly after the death of Christ. It would indeed not have been fitting, if many souls had left Limbo to rejoin their bodies and dwell in Jerusalem at a time when the soul of the Redeemer honored the souls in Limbo by His presence and remained with them until the resurrection. It would also have been without purpose. For the dead were to rise in order to give testimony unto the Risen One. They were to say to the Jews, "We, who have been buried by you, have arisen; believe ye therefore in the resurrection of the Crucified." They could not give this testimony on Holy Saturday. Meanwhile the Jews and pagans had an opportunity of seeing the corpses, and this contributed not a little to remove all doubt as to the miracle of their resurrection. It is true that, to avoid defilement, the Jews did not enter the sepulchres.

Thus did both heaven and earth announce the world-moving event of the deicide. Heaven and earth arose as witnesses for the Great Dead. Even from out of the night of death there came a ray of Divine majesty. Let us now consider the different effects which these wonderful events produced upon men.

II.

As to the Mother of God and all the pious people assembled on Golgotha, these events served to confirm their faith in the Divinity of Jesus Christ and console them in their sorrow for the loss of the Departed One.

In the enemies of the Saviour, who had maliciously delivered Him to the death of the Cross, these miracles effected the awful miracle of utter blindness and obduracy. Undoubtedly, during these events, they were somewhat startled and amazed. But these terrors had hardly reached an end, when they were their former selves, and not one of them was converted.

Here we have a true type of so many infidels and of so many renegade Catholics of our day. God may show by the most fearful natural phenomena that He is great and terrible; He may darken the sun and in the dense gloom let His lightning flash and His thunder roll; He may inflict upon the infidels the most varied misfortunes, earthquakes, famine and wars; He may destroy all their machinations; nothing touches them, nothing disturbs them; they remain obdurate. They pass ridiculous resolutions of condolence, they listen to some masonic speech of beatification, they sing for the deceased a funeral serenade, and, accompanied by the strains of swelling music, they return, apparently in good cheer, to their vicious life. But, at heart, they certainly enjoy no happiness. If they do, it is the happiness of the fallen-away Catholic who said to his friends, "I would now be perfectly happy, were it not for this cursed dying." The same word applies to these hardened sinners which Holy Writ applies to the enemies of Christ, "They shall look on him whom they pierced," namely, on the last day.

It was only one class of sinners in whom, by the grace of the Crucified Saviour, these wonderful facts did not miss their salutary effects. It was those who had offended Christ not so much through malice as through weakness and ignorance. There were first of all the pagan centurion, commander of the troops, and his soldiers, who, being amazed at what was going on, exclaimed, "Indeed this was a just man. Indeed this man was the Son of God." The Catholic Church reveres this captain as a saint. Then, also many of the people, who had not taken a direct part in the crucifixion but who had merely stood around and looked on, struck their breasts and returned home with contrite feelings. We shall join in spirit these penitent sinners, strike our breasts and pray from the bottom of our hearts, "Lord, be merciful to us poor sinners."

Let us, in conclusion, cast a retrospective glance upon the wonderful proceedings which we have considered. Although they were diverse and manifold, still in their successive stages they are a true representation of the entire process of conversion. In order that the sinner may turn to God, it is above all necessary that the earth be wrapped in darkness. As long as the sinner looks complacently upon the world and its sinful pleasures, there can be no thought of serious conversion. Then the veil which hindered him from looking into his own heart must be torn in pieces: he must know his sins by means of a thorough examen of conscience. The terrible penalties of Divine Justice must move him; his sins must cause him to tremble and quake in disgust and horror, even to the marrow of his bones. The rocks, furthermore, must be rent; this heart, hard and unyielding until now, must become soft and contrite through the tears of sorrow. The graves must open; by a sincere confession, the soul must exhale the fetid odor of the grave. And after the sinner has finally risen from the grave by means of the absolution of the priest, he must, by a Christian life, give testimony everywhere to the Redeemer, risen from the grave.

After the just who had risen from their graves, had accomplished their mission and given testimony unto the risen Saviour, they returned to the sepulchres and died a painless death. Their resurrection from the grave was only a temporary one, wherefore they cannot be our models in our resurrection from the grave of sin. The only model of our spiritual resurrection is, according to Holy Writ, the risen Saviour, Who died no more and Who lives forever. Thus should we, after arising from the grave of *sin,* no more return to it. But rather, like the risen Redeemer, we should begin an entirely new, supernatural, divine life. Then, and only then, can we entertain the hope of taking part forever, after death, in the glory of the Risen Lord.

CHAPTER XXXII.

THE EVENTS IMMEDIATELY FOLLOWING THE DEATH OF CHRIST

> "The soldiers therefore came: and they broke the legs of the first, and of the other that was crucified with him. But after they were come to Jesus, when they saw that he was already dead, they did not break his legs. But one of the soldiers with a spear opened his side, and immediately there came out blood and water." (St. John, xix., 32–34.)

The next events after the death of Christ are described by St. John (xix., 31–37) as follows: "Then the Jews, that the bodies might not remain upon the cross on the Sabbath day (for that was a great Sabbath day), besought Pilate that their legs might be broken and that they might be taken away. The soldiers therefore came: and they broke the legs of the first, and of the other that was crucified with him. But after they were come to Jesus, when they saw that he was already dead, they did not break his legs. But one of the soldiers with a spear opened his side, and immediately there came out blood and water. And he that saw it hath given testimony: and his testimony is true. And he knoweth that he saith true: that you also may believe. For these things were done that the scripture might be fufilled: You shall not break a bone of him. And again another scripture saith: They shall look on him whom they pierced."

It is, therefore, two events which we are to consider, namely:

I. The breaking of the bones of the thieves and

II. The opening of the Sacred Side.

I.

Crucifixion was not only a painful and disgraceful punishment, but it was also one of long duration. It happened, at times, that the crucified hung upon the cross two or three days before dying. And, when they had finally died, the corpses, according to Roman usage, remained on the cross until the flesh had been devoured by birds of prey, or wolves and jackals. The crucified were deemed unworthy of burial. These two circumstances caused the pharisees and chief-priests no little anxiety and embarrassment. For they had remarked that, in consequence of the miraculous phenomena, some change had taken place among the people and even among the soldiers, and that a reversal of public opinion in favor of the Redeemer was imminent. Now as they perhaps even apprehended an uprising, the responsibility of which might be laid at their door, they were determined to remove from the gaze of the people the corpses of the three crucified. "Out of sight, out of mind," thought they. But for that purpose, the permission of the Roman governor was needed. They therefore sent to Pilate a committee petitioning for two favors: first, to help the three crucified to a speedy death by breaking their bones and then to be allowed to bury them. For they knew not as yet that the Redeemer had died; the executioners even did not know it. Of course the committee did not mention the real motive of the petition. But, with their usual hypocrisy, they represented to Pilate that the Mosaic Law strictly demanded the burial of executed criminals before the beginning of night; that, furthermore, it would be unbecoming and exasperating to have three criminals hanging upon the cross on the holy Paschal Sabbath; that thereby the feast would be disturbed, the people, assembled in great numbers, would be defiled and their thoughts entirely withdrawn from the paschal celebration. The committee, composed without doubt of prominent men, found a favorable hearing. And it may be that Pilate himself, who certainly felt uneasy after witnessing the violent commotion in nature, wished that the distressing business would be ended in haste.

Thereupon the executioners, armed with iron-trimmed clubs, broke the bones, and especially the knees of the two thieves. For according to the conceptions of antiquity, the real strength of a man lay in the knees, and Biblical language suggests the same idea. Many even regarded the knees as the seat of the soul. But when the soldiers came to Jesus and saw that he was already dead—and they certainly examined carefully—they did not break His bones. Jesus, then, had already died, and he surely had died so soon that His bones might not be broken. Otherwise, they hardly would have thought of opening His side, as was called for in the plan of God. The bones, then, were not broken. This was prefigured in the Old Testament; not a bone of the paschal lamb should be broken. Christ was to shed all His blood, His flesh was to be torn in pieces, but the bones were to remain intact as a sign that all the strength and power of the Divinity was inherent in the dead body. So a soldier approached and opened His side with a spear, and immediately there came out blood and water.

Let us now consider the opening of the Sacred Side.

II.

Of the four evangelists, only one narrates this incident. It is St. John, the disciple of love, he who, at the last supper, had reposed his head on this side. We ask ourselves in astonishment how it could happen that the side was opened. Is it not repulsive to every humane feeling to dishonor the body of a slain opponent? King David certainly did not act thus. When the death of King Saul, his most bitter enemy, was reported to him, he tore his garments in sadness, he wept and fasted till evening. Nor did Julius Cæsar, the

Roman general, act thus, although he was a pagan. When the head of Pompey, his opponent, was laid at his feet, he burst into a flood of tears. Even the lion looks magnanimously upon the corpse of a man whom he has overcome in combat. But Longinus, the soldier, oversteps all the bounds of humanity, and seizes the lance. Whilst therefore Holy Church speaks of the "sweet" wood of the cross and whilst, in her chant, she designates as "sweet" all the other instruments of martyrdom with which Christ, still living, was tortured, she speaks in holy indignation of the "cruel shaft" of the lance.

How, then, was it possible that Longinus should so brutally attack the Saviour, after he had, with the captain, declared his belief in the divinity of Christ only a short while before?[1] An order had just arrived from the governor to break the bones of the three crucified. To demonstrate his good will and his obedience, the soldier wielded the lance, as Christ was already dead. Or perhaps, it was merely an act of military barbarism.

The point of the lance entered the body of the Redeemer between the ribs on the right side, whence, following an oblique upward course, it pierced the heart and, perhaps, passed out on the left side. The wound on the right side must have been very large, as Thomas could lay his hand in it. Without taking into consideration the force of the thrust, the size of the wound can be fully

[1] St. Matthew, xxvii., 54.

accounted for by the shape of the Roman lance which from a long point at once extended to a considerable width.

As soon as the Sacred Heart was pierced, blood and water issued from the wound on the right side. It cannot be stated with certainty whether the blood and water flowed simultaneously or in two distinct streams, or whether the flowing water contained streaks of blood, or, again, whether blood flowed first and then water.

Neither does Holy Writ mention *how much* blood and water issued forth. However, the common belief, the discourses of many Catholic preachers which have never been discountenanced by ecclesiastical authority and especially the words of Pope Innocent VI.[1] who speaks of floods streaming from the sacred side, give credit to the idea that it was not only an issue of a few drops but that there was a copious flow of blood and water.

It is more difficult to decide the question whether the outpouring of blood and water, considered in itself, indicated some miraculous process or whether it can be explained by natural agencies.[2] It is uncertain whether St. John, in affirming that he himself had seen it; that his testimony was true; that he knew that he said true and that he gave the testimony that we might also believe, wished to confirm other miraculous incidents or had in view the death of Christ only and the fulfillment of two prophecies following it. For by

1 Decr. de festo Lanceae et Clavorum Domini.

2 See note 21.

the fact that the Redeemer's bones were not broken, as the Jews intended, but that His side was opened, two prophecies were fulfilled, "You shall not break a bone of him" and "They shall look on him whom they pierced." In any case, what St. John here so solemnly affirms is a proof that He Whose bones remained intact as if miraculously, but Whose side was opened, was the Messias and the Son of God. Forth from the ignominy and the humiliation of His bitter Passion, His lofty majesty already shone in heavenly radiance. By the reverberation of the rays of ancient prophecy which here found its fulfillment, His Cross was, so to speak, transfigured. He did not manifest the lassitude of death by a hollow rattle, but He expired with a loud, mighty shout. His death ensued not as a pitiless necessity nor as an inevitable natural process, but as a freely willed, sublime act of sacrifice. Therefore now also, in the body, suspended lifeless on the Cross, the signs of Divine glory must not be missing.

The Sacred Heart of Jesus is, then, finally opened, and from the wound in the side flows blood and water. What are the special reasons for which the Saviour permitted this last abuse of His Sacred Body?

First, through this maltreatment, the reality of His death and, consequently, the reality of His resurrection were to be placed in the most conspicuous light. It would be a refutation in advance of all the assertions of unbelievers that Christ's death was only feigned and that His resurrection was a sham. A man whose heart is pierced cannot possibly live.

Then, the opening of the Sacred Heart of Jesus was the opening of His will and testament. Christ, it is true, had at the last supper spoken to His apostles about His testament. But this communication was made in the circle of His friends and was more of a private nature. Besides, a testament is legal and valid only after the death of the testator, as before his death it can at any time be annulled. Now the pagan world, for which Christ had especially died, should also be informed what the Deceased had left to it. And His last will and testament could be found nowhere but in His heart. His heart, then, must be opened, and this was done by a soldier of the Roman emperor, by an official person, as it were, and that in the presence of all interested parties. What a splendid discovery! What a precious inheritance! "Water flowed out," says St. Ambrose,[1] "to cleanse us, and blood, to redeem us." Water flowed out of the open side to prefigure the first, and blood, to prefigure the greatest and most excellent sacrament. Water, clear water flowed out of the open side of the Redeemer to form the body of His Bride, the Holy Church, and blood, to nourish it and to give it perfection and completion. Now we understand with what right and in what sense, the Holy Fathers speak of the seven sacraments, which, like to seven streams of grace,

[1] De sacr. 1.

have flowed from the side of Christ. We understand in what sense they can say that Holy Church, the second Eve and the true Mother of the living, proceeded from the side of the Redeemer, the second Adam, whilst He lay in the sleep of death.

Lastly, the Divine Heart, the seat and fountain of all love and grace, must be opened to enable us to enter therein. "The evangelist," says St. Augustine,[1] "used a well considered word." For he did not say that the soldier *wounded* the side of Our Lord, but that he *opened* it, indicating thereby that the wound of the side should be the entrance to the Sacred Heart. Indeed, the wound of the side is the portal of the true ark of Noah. Only what enters through this portal, shall be saved from the universal destruction. The wound of the side is the golden gate of the true temple of the Lord wherein all the sick, all the beggars and all the needy obtain health and grace and mercy. It is the entrance to the true paradise, in which alone delight and peace are to be found. Thomas had no sooner put his hand on this portal than he believed and loved and said, "My Lord and my God." The Heart of Jesus is, indeed, the strength of the just, the consolation of the afflicted, the refuge of sinners. For the tempted soul, it is the cavern in the rock in which the timid dove hides itself from the hawk. To the soul which feels itself to be a

[1] Tract. in Joan, 120, 2.

parched soil, it is the fountain of living waters. To the sad and depressed soul, it is the spiritual wine-cellar in which the Divine Bridegroom gladdens His promised bride with heavenly delights. To the soul which is amazed at its coldness and dearth of love, it is the inexhaustible furnace of that fire which the Son of God brought from heaven to earth. The Catholic Church, therefore, is wise in recommending very earnestly to her children the devotion to the Sacred Heart, and in being ingenious in devising means for spreading and increasing it all over the world.

With confidence, then, let us enter into the Sacred Heart of Jesus in all our needs. In It there is room for all men. Even Longinus, the soldier, who had so cruelly wounded the Heart of Christ, received from it health and blessing. According to tradition, one of his eyes was bereft of sight. When he thrust the lance a drop of the precious Blood struck his eye, and he received his bodily and spiritual sight at the same time. He was baptized and hid himself in a fearful desert to do penance for his sins. He became a bishop and a martyr, a saint of the Catholic Church, a saint of heaven. What may we then not expect, if we not only avoid wounding the Sacred Heart by sin, but strive to honor It, to spread Its devotion, and to imitate Its virtues. Let us, then, build our dwelling in the Sacred Heart of Jesus. We shall live and die in this Heart, and be united with it forevermore.

CHAPTER XXXIII.

THE LAST EVENTS IN THE HISTORY OF THE PASSION

> "And taking him down, he (Joseph) wrapped him in fine linen, and laid him in a sepulchre, that was hewed in stone, wherein never yet any man had been laid."
>
> (St. Luke xxiii., 53.)

What the four evangelists narrate concerning the last events of the history of the Passion may be summed up as follows:[1]

After all these things, that is, after the Heart of Jesus was opened, there came a certain rich man of Arimathea, named Joseph. He went in boldly to Pilate and asked the body of Jesus. But Pilate wondered that he should be already dead. And sending for the centurion he asked him if He were already dead. And when he had understood it by the centurion, he gave the body to Joseph, and commanded that it should be delivered to him. And Nicodemus also came bringing a mixture of myrrh and aloes about an hundred pound weight. And Joseph brought linen. They took, therefore, the body of Jesus down and

[1] St. Matthew, xxvii., 57–61; St. Mark, xv. 42–47; St. Luke, xxiii., 50–56; St. John, xix., 38–42.

wound it in a clean linen cloth with the spices. Now there was in the place where he was crucified, a garden: and in the garden a new sepulchre, wherein no man yet had been laid. There they laid Jesus because of the Parasceve, that is, this circumstance caused them to select a tomb which was nigh at hand. However, they had no intention at all of depositing the body in another tomb afterwards. Joseph then rolled a great stone against the door of the monument. And the holy women, sitting over against the sepulchre, beheld where and how his body was laid. And they returned, because the Sabbath drew on, and, on the Sabbath they rested according to the commandment.

The evangelists here describe three scenes:

I. The taking down from the cross of the Sacred Body,
II. The preparation for the burial and
III. The burial itself.

I.

In the removal of the body from the cross, let us first consider the persons who took part in it. Among them, Joseph of Arimathea appears to be the most prominent. All the four evangelists have something to report of him. It seems as if they meant to express their joy that at last a wealthy and prominent man also showed interest in and sympathy for the Redeemer. For it is, indeed, beautiful and edifying to see the rich and prominent of the laity labor for Christ and for His Sacred Body, whether, as a heroic phalanx of enthusiastic warriors, they defend the mystic Body of the Lord, Holy Church, and her rights, or they bend the knee to His Sacramental Body and receive Him devoutly in Holy Communion. To return to Joseph of Arimathea, St. Matthew says that he was a rich man. St. Mark calls him a noble counsellor; St. Luke, a good and a just man who had not consented to the counsels and doings of the Sanhedrim. St. John tells of him that he was a disciple of Jesus, but secretly, for fear of the Jews. These last words do not attach any odium to Joseph. Undoubtedly it is never excusable to deny one's religious convictions, nor, in the councils of the mighty, to consent, against one's conscience and from human respect, to the impious decrees of the majority. But there are cases in which without sin one may conceal one's religious convictions, as, for instance, if a question be put by one having no right to ask it and if an answer would have bad rather than good effects. The Redeemer certainly approved of the reasons which Joseph had of not openly declaring himself for Him, otherwise He would not have recognized him as a true disciple. The other man who appeared towards evening on Golgotha was Nicodemus. Nicodemus was a pharisee, a lawyer and a teacher in Israel. He also was a secret disciple of Jesus. He had often visited the Lord at night to receive instructions in the mysteries of the faith. At a meeting of the pharisees, he with Joseph, had openly declared for Christ. At the midnight session in the house of Caiphas and at the session of the great council on the morning of Good Friday they both had been absent. For St. Mark mentions in express terms that all who were gathered there condemned Christ as being guilty of death. Formerly, then, when Christ worked miracles and all the people followed Him, Joseph and Nicodemus were His disciples secretly, for fear of the Jews. Now, however, after Christ died the shameful death of the cross, they declare themselves openly as His adherents, and all their fear has vanished. Who does not here recognize the glorious fruits of the Redeemer's death and the power of grace purchased by Christ!

The arrival of these men was a great relief to Mary and to the other women. For, if the Roman soldiers had taken down the body and buried it, it would have been very pitiable and dishonorable indeed. The body of the Saviour would have been interred with the corpses of the two thieves in the place reserved for criminals. This thought had filled with pain the heart of the dolorous Mother. Joseph therefore offered to request of Pilate the privilege of caring for the burial. It was an easy matter for him to prevail on the captain to await Pilate's decision as to the interment. Although to appear as the friend of a criminal, and that before the judge himself, required much temerity and was attendant with great risk, and although Joseph would thereby draw down upon himself the anger and even the vengeance of the

Sanhedrim, nevertheless, at Mary's desire and under her protection, as it were, he courageously went to Pilate and begged for the body of Jesus.

Pilate wondered that Jesus was already dead. For the crucified often hung upon the cross for a long time before dying. He was not satisfied with the statement of Joseph. He demanded an official declaration, for which reason he sent for the captain who had been charged with the execution. It is, then, from the lips of the captain that we also are made aware officially and in due form that Christ really died.

The petition of Joseph was granted. According to St. Anselm, he described to Pilate in touching words the woe of the Mother of Jesus, and how she would be greatly consoled if her Son, her only Son, were buried in a worthy manner. It may be that Joseph also mentioned the innocence of Jesus. Undoubtedly he also offered a large sum to Pilate whose avarice was well known. Still Pilate deemed it unworthy of an honorable man to make the sale of a criminal's corpse a source of revenue. He was high-minded enough to give Joseph the body. He therefore ordered the captain to give up the body to Joseph, for he had already abandoned it to the executioners.

Pilate little knew what he was doing. Otherwise he would have given Joseph his entire property rather than let him take that Sacred Body, the possession and consumption of which are a pledge of eternal life and which is the seed of immortality for the bodies of mortal men. But do not many Christians resemble Pilate in that they, to please others, carelessly cast away imperishable goods, the most precious of all?

After their return to Golgotha, Joseph and Nicodemus, assisted by some servants, took, with the greatest reverence, the body of Jesus down from the cross, and, after removing the crown from the head, they laid the body in the lap of His Mother. This, then, is the Sacred Body which she once bore, which she nursed and cared for, which, with motherly love, she had carried to Egypt. The Holy Face is now pale, the divine eye is dim, the divine mouth is silent and the Sacred Heart beats no more. How Mary must have gazed upon this Sacred Body and wiped away from it the drops of blood! For it was the body of her only, most beloved, divine Son; it was the body of her cruelly tortured and withal innocent Son. To whom shall I compare thee or to whom shall I liken thee to comfort thee, O holy Mother of the dead Redeemer! For great as the sea is thy sorrow. She who was queen, has become as a widow; gone is her beauty and her glory, and clouds of sadness have encompassed her brow. Her adversaries have become enriched. When the mothers of Bethlehem received in their arms the children murdered by Herod's menials, cries of woe filled the air; their lamentations and their despair might have moved to pity the rocks which echoed them. But the Mother of Jesus, although her heart was bleeding from a thousand wounds, bethought herself of the word which her Son had addressed to her from the cross. Heroically she offered up to Divine Justice the Sacred Body, which she was holding in her arms and moistening with her tears, as the redeeming price for us who are the children of her sorrow.

After the Sacred Body was taken down from the cross, preparations were begun for the burial.

II.

After the return of Joseph and of the captain from Pilate, the bodies of the two thieves, which in the meantime had been taken down from the crosses, were buried by the Roman soldiers. When the body of the Saviour had also been taken down, the three crosses with the nails and the titles of guilt were lowered into a deep excavation which was soon again filled with earth. After the soldiers had thus done their duty, the captain gave the command to return to the citadel.

Now we see on Calvary only the Mother of Jesus and a few of His friends who are taking the necessary steps to render to the dead Saviour the last honors. For He had left no instructions regarding His own burial. He knew that He would die a criminal's death, and criminals sentenced to death by a court had no right to dispose in any manner of their bodies. In the humility of His heart, Christ abided by this custom. He knew, furthermore, that He would remain in the tomb only a few hours. And to make arrangements for such a short time seemed too unimportant to Him. It may be well enough for those who must remain in their graves until the day of judgment, especially for those for whom the funeral is indeed the last honor paid to them, as in hell they are abandoned to eternal disgrace.

Joseph and Nicodemus, then, took charge of the arrangements. Nicodemus brought about a hundred pounds of a mixture of myrrh and aloes, while Joseph brought linen. In this linen they wrapped the body of Jesus along with the spices as it is customary at Jewish funerals. What would Judas have said to it? In his day it was only one pound; here there are even a hundred. But the pious men wished to show respect to the body of Him Whom they knew to be the Son of God. We also now understand the significance of the gift of myrrh brought by the pagan Kings.

The preparation of the sacred body could, however, not be carried out just now according to the regular manner, as the interment had to be finished before sun-down. Wherefore, for the time being, the spices and the sacred body were wrapped in the linens and they agreed to return to the sepulchre after the Sabbath on the morning of Easter to supply what was wanting. These men and women, with the exception, of course, of the Blessed Virgin, seemed to be so overpowered by sadness, grief and love that they took no account whatever of the fact that on the third day Christ would arise from the dead and be in the tomb no more.

We now come to the closing scene, to the burial of Jesus Christ.

III.

The preparations were, then, made, as well as time would permit. Now the funeral procession started on its way. On the one hand, it was indeed the most simple, but on the other, it was the most sacred and most holy funeral procession ever seen upon earth. The body being carried to the grave is the body of the Son of the living God. The pall-bearers are Joseph and Nicodemus, two noble laymen, with their servants. From among the clergy, the bier was accompanied by St. John, a bishop of the Catholic Church, and, according to a tradition mentioned by St. Anselm, by St. James, also a bishop of the Catholic Church, and by St. Peter, the appointed pope and prince of the apostles. These two latter had arrived on Golgotha towards evening, when the people and most of the enemies of Christ had returned to the city, and they came in time to take part in the funeral solemnity. As chief mourner, the sorrowful Mother, the Queen of heaven and earth, walked behind the bier. Then followed Magdalene and the nearest relatives of the Saviour. Lastly came some pious women singing the funeral dirge. I cannot help but imagine that along the route of the funeral procession, the trees inclined their heads and the flowers their coronas, and that the birds of heaven sang their saddest lays. Invisible in the air, the holy angels were hovering. They had seen much since the day of their creation. But they had never seen a God-Man carried as a corpse to the tomb.

Meanwhile the cortege had reached the near-by grotto in the rocks over which cypresses spread their shadows. The men entered with the body and laid the Redeemer upon His bed of stone. Outside, the blood-red sun cast its dim and quivering rays upon a group of women mutely sitting upon the ground. Great as the sea was their sorrow. "And the women," says Holy Writ, "that were come with him from Galilee were sitting over against the sepulchre, they beheld where he was laid and saw how his body was laid."

After the men had come out from the sepulchre, they closed the door and rolled before it a large stone. For if curious people, after opening the door, should forget to close it again carefully, wild beasts might find their way into the sepulchre which was by all means to be guarded against. At this moment, the sound of trumpets from the pinnacles of the temple announced the beginning of the great Sabbath, and the men and women with Mary hurried back to Jerusalem as the law required. It appears that some of the pious women had gone sooner. At least St. Luke speaks of women who were preparing spices and ointments before the beginning of the Sabbath, whereas others did this on the following evening after the Sabbath was over. At any rate, *we* may remain a moment to survey somewhat closer the sepulchre and its environment.

The sepulchre of Christ was in a garden. Our first parents had sinned in a garden. In a garden Christ had begun His passion. He had been taken captive in a garden. In a garden, therefore the history of His passion should end. In gardens, moreover, seeds are deposited in the ground. Now Christ's body was the most precious seed ever planted in the ground. It should then be deposited in a garden. Even on the holy day of Easter the most glorious fruits began to spring from this grain of seed, inasmuch as, through the power of this Sacred Body, many bodies of the departed just were raised to life, thus exemplifying in advance the general resurrection on the last day.

The sepulchre itself was in the form of a rotunda and was so high that a man could reach the top only with an extended hand. It consisted of an ante-chamber and of a small burial place destined for one person. The entrance to the sepulchre was on the east side and was very low. To the right, on the north side, at an elevation of three feet was the tomb proper. It was hollowed out, so that the sacred body reposed in a real stone coffin.

Of this grave, the evangelists record three circumstances. First, that it was hewn in a *rock*. Therefore the apostles could not possibly steal the body by constructing a subterranean passage to the tomb. Besides the corner stone must rest upon the rock.

Then they call this tomb a *new* sepulchre in

which no one had yet been buried. And indeed the respect due to the Sacred Body demanded that it be no more brought in contact with the bodies of sinners. Had it been a family vault, doubt might have been entertained on Easter day as to who the Risen One really was. And had it even been the tomb of a prophet, one might have said that the miracle of Eliseus had been repeated; that Christ had returned to life not through His own power but through contact with the body of the prophet. The sepulchre of Christ was new also in the sense that it had never had its equal. For this sepulchre was the workroom of resurrection; it was the decay and destruction of all graves; it was the tomb in which death should die the death;[1] it was the only glorious tomb.[2]

Thirdly this tomb was the tomb of another. As Christ had in life possessed nothing whereon to lay His head, He possessed nothing in death. Another's tomb! Whoever wishes to remain in a place only a few hours, will not build a house of his own there but he will seek shelter in the house of another. Another's tomb! He who dies not for his own sins but for the sins of others, has not even a right to a tomb of his own. Another's tomb! Whoever acquires a tomb of his own, thereby declares his subjection to the reign of death. Now Christ was the Lord of death. The mighty giant had become somewhat fatigued on His journey of thirty-three years. He would

[1] Serm. de Pass. Domini, inter spuria S. Athan., n. 5.
[2] Is. 53, 9, according to the Hebrew text. See note 22.

now take some rest and, on the third day, He would with a mighty arm deal death the death-blow. Another's tomb! But to whom did it belong? Whose property was it? It belonged to Joseph of Arimathea. How fortunate and enviable this man was, to have the honor of furnishing, on his own property, a resting place for the body of the God-Man. How his courage is now rewarded! How his spirit of sacrifice is now richly indemnified!

But does not the same good fortune fall to a city and to a Catholic parish which harbors the same Sacred Body under the appearance of bread on its own property, in its church? Does not a greater honor, even, redound to us, when we receive the Body of Christ in Holy Communion? Does not our heart then really become the sepulchre of the Body of Jesus Christ? If we would, then, receive in our heart the Body of the Lord, no one else should dwell therein, neither the world nor the evil one. It ought to be even free from venial sin. It ought to be as pure and immaculate as were the linen cloths. It ought to be replete, furthermore, with the costliest spices, with the good odor of all Christian virtues. And after we have devoutly received the Body of the Lord into our heart, we should not forget to close the door. We ought also to roll a large stone before that heart so that no wild beast may find it in its power to deprive us of the Redeemer.

The men and women, then, had accompanied the Blessed Virgin back to Jerusalem and, according to the commandment, they rested on the Sabbath. Nor were they in the right mood for any worldly matters. Their minds and hearts were with the crucified Redeemer. The women thought of the ointment which they would purchase after sundown and take to the sepulchre on the following day. Peter and Magdalene, however, who, on the preceding day, had shed so many bitter tears, spent the Sabbath in mourning and sorrow.

We may here recognize the best preparation for the approaching feast of Easter. Removed from the world and its tumult, let us meditate with devotion upon the sufferings of the crucified Redeemer. Let us consider what we may do for His honor. First of all, let us deplore our sins out of love for the Saviour. This is also the best preparation for that paschal feast which shall close the passion-tide of this life and which shall last not merely one day but for all eternity.

CHAPTER XXXIV.

THE WATCH AT THE TOMB

" And they departing, made the sepulchre sure, sealing the stone, and setting guards."

(St. Matthew, xxvii., 66.)

Undoubtedly some of the chief-priests and pharisees observed from a distance the burial of the Redeemer. They desired, above all, to assure themselves that the One Whom they hated was really put under ground and covered by the darkness of the tomb. Otherwise their triumph would not be complete, and they could not abandon themselves to the undisturbed festal joys of the Paschal Sabbath. The chief-priests were also much interested in knowing the exact spot where Christ had been buried. As the Redeemer's prophecy regarding His resurrection was well known to them, they probably intended to open the sepulchre after three days, show the decaying corpse to the Jews and Gentiles, and thus completely unmask the deceiver and perpetuate the triumph over the Crucified. Wherefore they found no little satisfaction in perceiving that the grave was closed and that a great stone was rolled before its entrance. They had attained their object.

Things could not have proceeded more to their liking.

One would think that now, after accomplishing their deed, the chief-priests would quietly and contentedly go home to enjoy the paschal lamb in the sacredness of the family circle and to take repose after a sleepless night and the fatigues of the day. But "there is no peace to the wicked."[1] The image of the Murdered, Whom, when He was yet in life, they had never feared, now rose suddenly like a phantom before their souls filling them with awful terrors. It was the revenge of conscience. It was the agony of the murderer who imagines that he sees his victim arise from the grave and continually follow him. The consternation and confusion of the chief-priests and pharisees was increased by their remembering the sign of the prophet Jonas, to which the Deceased had Himself once referred them. Now if Christ, like Lazarus, should in spite of all come forth from the sepulchre by means of diabolical art and show Himself in Jerusalem, their confusion and shame would be beyond all bounds.

In order, therefore, to secure themselves against the Redeemer resting in the tomb, to effectually take away from Christ the possibility of leaving it, and to defend themselves against the Dead, the chief-priests and pharisees determine to surround the sepulchre with soldiers. In this they resembled people driven to insanity by confusion and

[1] Is., xlviii., 22.

terror. "For who hath ever heard," exclaims an ancient inspired orator,[1] referring to this very incident, "that a dead man ever begins a war."

Let us now consider [2]

I. The negotiations between the chief-priests and Pilate concerning the watch at the tomb and

II. The watch over the tomb itself.

I.

An authoritative permit for the placing of a watch was the first thing required. Therefore after sundown, on the evening of Good Friday, the chief-priests and pharisees went together in great numbers to Pilate, and on this holy day they unhesitatingly entered the house which, in scrupulous punctiliousness, they had not dared to enter in the morning. For that is an erroneous opinion which maintains that the guard was procured and stationed at the tomb on Saturday morning. For in that case the enemies of Christ would surely have asserted after the resurrection that the body had been stolen by the disciples during the night of Friday, the tomb then being unguarded. But they did not wait till Saturday morning.

Without a doubt, Pilate must have been much surprised at the unexpected evening visit and even more at the unwonted salutation. "Sir," was the

[1] Amphilochius, Serm. de sepult. Domini.

[2] St. Matthew, xxvii., 62–66.

word with which the chief-priests and pharisees addressed him. How very submissive, how very polite. They in reality hated Pilate and despised him from their inmost souls as being unclean and an idolater. The mere thought that he held sway over them in the name of the emperor, the mere memory of former enactments of his, could at other times drive them into a frenzy. They had been very rough even in the morning during the trial. In anger, ay, in fury, they then had cried, "If thou release this man, thou art no friend of Cæsar." Now, however, when, in secret terror, they desire a favor of him, they appear to be suddenly metamorphosed.

They begin their address by saying, "Sir, we have remembered, that that seducer said, while he was yet alive: After three days I will rise again." This, then, is all that they remember, all that they have retained of His sermons. The good which the Saviour had done, the wonders He had worked, and the truths he had taught, they have completely forgotten. "We have remembered," they say to explain why they had not demanded the body in the afternoon to preclude all fraud. They pretend that the thought struck them only later. "That the seducer." How shameful! The sense of decorum and of humanity prompted even the pagans to say of the dead only what was good. "While he was yet alive." He is therefore dead. Accept, O ye chief-priests, our hearty thanks for this certificate of death. We shall know how to use it. "The seducer said:

After three days I will rise again.'' Well, we shall not blame you for rendering the Saviour's words incorrectly, for you are excited. For Christ really said that He would rise again *on the third day.*[1]

The chief-priests and pharisees thereupon begged Pilate to command that the tomb be guarded. Christ, then, had really been buried. The priests knew the place. They had minutely observed everything. They did not, of course, manifest the true reason of their petition, i. e., their fear of the Crucified and their anxiety lest He come forth from the tomb. Their vagaries might have caused Pilate to laugh at them as being children and fools. They, therefore, with their usual hypocrisy, spoke of their fear lest the disciples steal the body and this put them, as it were, from the frying-pan into the fire. The poor, timid disciples! What would it profit *them* to steal the body? Were Christ not to rise from the dead, *they* would be the deluded ones.

''The last error,'' the chief-priests continued in their address, ''would be worse than the first.'' By the first error they meant the doctrine of Christ's Divinity and Messianic dignity. Worse than this would be the last, that is to say, a rumor, brought about by the disciples stealing His body, that Christ had arisen. This would naturally also spread and render indestructible the first error. It would bring to Christ many new ad-

[1] See note 23.

herents. It would likewise draw down the ire of the people on themselves as well as on Pilate, and they would all have to dread the vengeance of Christ's friends on account of His execution. It might even produce a political upheaval of far greater extent than was to be feared during the life-time of the Redeemer. Command therefore, Pilate, "the sepulchre to be guarded until the third day." Again they are the obsequious servants. God grant that with many a converted sinner the last things be not worse than the first. God grant that future storms gathering over the individual or over the entire Church, may not, owing to a lack of watchfulness, be more destructive than all preceding ones! We ought also to take precautions.

The petition of the chief-priests and pharisees was graciously acceded to. Whether shrewd Pilate was moved by the reasons submitted to grant the request, may well be considered doubtful. It is more probable that he perceived the fear and dread on the part of the chief-priests in regard to this Innocent Man Whose death they had accomplished and that inwardly he laughed at and ridiculed the alleged reasons and the petitioners themselves. But, on the one hand, Pilate did not care to offend these prominent men and, on the other, he was heartily tired of the whole affair, as well because his own conduct toward the Redeemer furnished him with abundant matter for an examination of conscience that evening as because the divers and in part miraculous events of the day had depressed him and rendered him melancholy. He sought, therefore, to rid himself of his annoying visitors the best way he could, and immediately conceded what they asked for. Such is often the real sentiment underlying worldly politeness. Externally there is nothing but what is amiable, obsequious and flattering, nothing but hypocritical compliments, whilst inwardly there lie concealed aversion and contempt.

But in order not to expose himself to further entanglements and responsibilities, Pilate left the whole matter to the discretion of the chief-priests. "You have a guard," said he, "yesterday evening I placed one hundred and twenty-five soldiers at your disposal. Go and take them and guard it as you know." It was again providential that the command of the watch at the tomb was entrusted to the chief-priests. Now they could not without stultifying themselves, reproach Pilate that *his* soldiers had sold the body of the Saviour to the disciples. *They* had the supervison and any fraud or neglect that might occur would be imputed to *themselves.*

With many thanks and expressions of respect and consideration, the chief-priests and pharisees finally took leave of Pilate, both parties being filled, probably, more than ever before, with mutual contempt and disgust. What a mean, contemptible and disgusting role was played throughout the history of the Redeemer's Passion by these men, who should have been models of honorable and upright conduct! Still we may learn *one* thing from them. The prudence and zeal to which hatred for the living Saviour had impelled the chief-priests and pharisees did not depart from them even in their insane fear of the dead Saviour. Had they been used only in a *good* cause! Wherefore our prudence should be a holy prudence and our zeal, a holy zeal. Our zeal should not spring from fear of the dead Redeemer but from love for Him. The end and object of our thoughts and efforts should be the salvation of our poor souls, the general welfare of our fellow-men, the welfare and spread of the Catholic Church, the increase of the love of the Crucified Redeemer and the greater honor of the thrice holy God.

Let us now consider the watch itself of the sepulchre.

II.

Rejoicing at the favorable issue of the audience, the chief-priests and pharisees hurried from the house of Pilate to the neighboring citadel. Of the hundred and twenty-five men granted them by the governor, they, in their fear of the Dead Saviour, undoubtedly demanded quite a number. For St. Matthew expressly reports that, after the Resurrection of Christ, "several" of the guards ran to the city to announce the fact, from all of which one may conclude that a strong command was there. The commandant of the citadel hesitated. It had never yet happened that his command had been called on to protect the tomb of an executed criminal against robbery. For what did it matter if the body were indeed stolen? And the Roman soldiers who were anxious for repose, were not much pleased, either, with the command of the governor, especially as it was the doings of the Jews, whom they abominated. They scolded and cursed. But the jingling coin of the chief-priests soon allayed their excitement and elicited universal consent. Thereupon the chief-priests and pharisees went to the sepulchre with the soldiers. It was, forsooth, a remarkable procession which thus followed the Way of the Cross late in the evening of the first Good Friday.

According to credible ancient reports mentioned by the ecclesiastical writer Nicephorus,[1] the stone was first attached to the wall with iron clamps. It must be made impossible for the Dead in the tomb to roll away the stone. Neither did the chief-priests trust the Roman soldiers. And in this they were right. For men whom money can buy will also for money betray the oath of fealty they have sworn. If, then, any one should offer the soldiers more than the chief-priests had given or at least promised them, they probably would dispose of the body, and such a possibility must be prevented. Therefore, according to the narrative of Nicephorus, the priests and pharisees, like stone masons, bored with iron tools through the stone and the wall. Then through both openings they drove a large iron obtained in a neighboring

[1] Eccl. hist. i., 1, c. 32. He refers to ancient tradition; De locis sanctis inter opp. Ven. Bedae.

smithy and solidly connected both stone and wall. Furthermore, several other iron bands were passed around the stone and made fast in the wall. Their work was seasoned with sarcastic remarks addressed to the Redeemer, such as, "Now come forth, if you can," and with jeers and shouts of laughter. What the chief-priests were doing was, indeed, servile work which was strictly forbidden on the Paschal Sabbath. But, thought they, the deceiver in the tomb also worked on the Sabbath when He prepared the mud to rub on the eyes of the man born blind.

Then the tomb was sealed. This was done either by drawing a cord across the entrance stone and sealing both ends, or, if the entrance stone was held by a transverse beam, by uniting both stone and beam with a seal. The seal may have been that of the city, but more likely it was the official seal of the Sanhedrim. The Dead would certainly respect the seal of the wise Council and forbear from making any attempt at resurrection.

Finally the guard was stationed. The chief-priests to whom Pilate had entrusted the entire affair, assigned to each soldier his post. The tomb was entirely surrounded by guards. Thus, in coming out of the sepulchre, Christ would necessarily fall into the hands of a soldier. In some representations one may see a soldier occupying a position even on the top of the sepulchre. For the Saviour might possibly escape through the top. The guard had orders to make Christ a captive, in case He opened the entrance to the grave or sought an exit through some other part of the rock. O ye chief-priests! *One* prophecy still lacked its accomplishment. Saul had placed his mailed satellites before the dwelling of David whom he would destroy. Whereupon Michol showed David an egress through which he fled. Stand guard, then, ye imperial soldiers, before the grave of the Lord and see whether or not you shall succeed better than the satellites of Saul.

If ever the words of Holy Writ were accomplished, it certainly was now: "I will destroy the wisdom of the wise and the prudence of the prudent I will reject."[1] "O unfortunate and miserable Jew!" exclaims in indignation an ancient ecclesiastical writer,[2] "Who broke the chains of death, can He not break the seal on the tomb? He Who like a hero overcame hell, shall He fear the locks on the tomb? Seal the stone, place your menials, encircle the tomb with a thousand guards! Thus shalt thou render more glorious the work of Christ's Resurrection, glorious as it is in itself. For thou art placing there spectators and witnesses of His Resurrection and thou art preparing for Him servants who shall announce His wonderful works."

What this ancient writer said to the enemies of Christ, we can also say to the enemies of the Bride of Jesus Christ: "O ye impious powers of this world, ye powers of darkness, ye diabolical

[1] I. Cor., i., 19.

[2] Serm. de Pass. Domini, inter spuria S. Athan., n. 4.

powers! Concoct your plans against the Holy Catholic Church! Excogitate the most astute schemes! Exhaust all the tricks of hypocritical diplomacy, all the power and all the fraudulent methods of your secret society craft! Put in chains the Bride of the Redeemer, crucify her, bury her and surround her grave with your regiments! God, reigning in heaven, will laugh you to scorn. The sooner Good Friday arrives, the sooner our holy mother, the Catholic Church, will celebrate the feast of Easter."

After the chief-priests and pharisees had again recommended to the guard a conscientious fulfillment of their duty, and promised them a liberal reward, they returned home hurriedly and in an exuberant frame of mind. But they arrived too late for a share in the paschal lamb. There was nothing left of the Old Testament but the offal.

However, before we bid adieu to the chief-priests and pharisees, let us thank them heartily for the hint they have given us in providing a watch for the sepulchre. For indeed, our good resolutions, even if they were as solid as a rock, can be broken and crushed by the enemies of our souls. It is easy for them to tear away the seal of love which was impressed on our hearts in holy Baptism. If we would be sure that the Redeemer who dwells within us by His grace be not stolen away from us, we must place a guard around our hearts. Ye chief-priests will certainly not blame us for not calling upon *you* or *your* soldiers for this purpose. For if I am to believe what you asserted on Easter

Sunday, your guards slept instead of watching, and whilst they were asleep, the disciples stole the body, and when the guards, plunged as they were in a profound sleep, saw all that, they never even ran after the wicked disciples to take away from them their booty. No, *your* watch is not of the right sort; we cannot rely on them. When the pious women came to the tomb early on the third day, it was empty. We, therefore, turn to those of whom King David sang that God had intended them to be our guardians, and the holy angels, who together held the death-watch at the sepulchre of their Creator, will deem it an honor to defend against all enemies the Redeemer reposing in our hearts as in a tomb.

Indeed, we are not afraid of the apostles of the Lord, whom you chief-priests, pretended to fear. Ah! no! we love the holy apostles; we love them with all our heart, Peter and John and James and all the others, not forgetting Thomas, who with his hand directed us to the Divine Heart. But those we do fear are the apostles of unbelief, the apostles of immorality, those seducers, the rebellious flesh and the infernal spirits.

Hurry hither, then, ye *heavenly* spirits, ye angels of God, and take charge of the tomb. Shield the Saviour, protect Him, defend Him that He be not stolen from us. Thou especially who hast overcome Satan, Prince of the heavenly hosts, unconquered hero of God, Saint Michael! Thou Protector of the Church Militant! With thy shield and sword protect her who is, as it were, being pressed toward the tomb, the Bride of the Departed Redeemer. Enchain the unchained forces of hell, throw them back into the abyss and lead the Roman Catholic Church on to a glorious victory, to a glorious triumph. Help us also, who are the children of this Holy Mother, help us combat, help us overcome the enemy, thou who art the protector of us all. Upon thee we rely in dangers and temptations, on thee we rely in life, on thee we rely in death, in the last combat, and we shall never be confounded.

The grave, then, is locked, sealed and well guarded. We may remain without anxiety; the disciples will not rob us of the Saviour. With all peace of heart, then, and collectedness of mind, we can, by prayer and penance, prepare ourselves for the holy feast of Easter and, with the sorrowful Mother and all of the Crucified Redeemer's friends with whom we have become acquainted on the Way of the Passion, await the moment in which the cry of victory shall resound: Surrexit, non est hic! Christ is risen. He is no longer in the tomb. Alleluja.

A. M. D. G.

THE END.

NOTES

1. (page 5.)

It has been the concordant teaching of all standard theologians for many centuries past that the soul of Christ, from the moment of its creation, was in possession of the beatific vision of God. It is true that no ecumenical council has ever declared this teaching to be a dogma of faith, but it is rightly deduced from many passages of Holy Writ and from other certain truths of faith with which the former are in natural coherence. This vision of God which constitutes the essential beatitude of the saints of heaven, consists in the soul's seeing God directly, face to face, as He is, and, as a result of this clear vision, in its being drawn by unspeakable love to God, the Supreme Good, and being united to Him most intimately. From this vision and love there ought naturally to arise the greatest satisfaction and joy and the most intense delight, hence *complete happiness.* Just as naturally an intense, overflowing joy ought to dissipate all sensations of external and internal pain. Still faith teaches that Christ did suffer external and internal pains and that He was, as He said Himself, "sad unto death." Such a union of beatitude and passibility is indeed not imaginable in the saints in heaven. For, arrived at their eternal goal, they have laid aside the qualities of mundane wayfarers, and they experience henceforth only such influences coming from God as are coordinate with their beatitude. But Christ was at the same time in possession of the goal and still an earthly pilgrim; He, therefore, was in a *double state* and experienced divers influences corresponding to this twofold condition, that is to say, He experienced the Divine co-operation with His activity in accordance with this double state.

Joy and grief can co-exist in one human will if the power of *perception* is, at the same time, *impressed* by two diverse objects, an agreeable and a disagreeable one, and if it *yields* to both impressions. Now it is indeed true that the soul of Christ was immersed with all the energy and power of its activity in the infinitely attractive vision of the Divine Essence; but as the Redeemer was at the same time in the condition of an earthly pilgrim, and had assumed a passible body, God could, by granting the Divine co-operation which corresponded to this condition, maintain the soul's entire attentiveness directed to the *Passion* as well as the entire activity of the will corresponding to this attentiveness. That Christ should thus at the same time and in a *twofold* condition develop a peculiar and, in truth, most important activity, far from being an imperfection, was rather a greater perfection. Now if all this was as described, we find in Christ the sensation of pain and the natural repugnance of the will in all its strength simultaneously *with* the beatific vision. Moreover, the fact that Christ exercised the entire activity proper to one who had arrived at the goal not only did not hinder or diminish the pain and the sadness which He felt as an earthly pilgrim, but it rather increased and aggravated them. For the vision and love corresponding to the one condition also helped the other to a greater *perfection* of *perception* and of *activity of the will,* and thus the union with the Godhead not only did not render the sacred Humanity of

Christ impervious to suffering, but it increased its passibility, as it were, to an infinite degree.

With all this, the proposition stands that, according to the *natural* course of things, superabundant joy and keen suffering are incompatible. The above is offered merely as an explanation of the manner in which God maintained the compatibility of the two in the soul of Christ.

This difficult question is clearly and solidly treated in W. Wilmers', S. J., Lehrbuch der Religion II. (4th edit.), 616 sqq. Confer p. 156 sqq. Confer also Franzelin, Tract. de Verb. Inc. thes. 42, p. 433.

2. (page 25.)

The words of Jesus (St. Matthew, xxvi., 45), "Sleep ye now and take your rest," apparently contradicting the preceding words, "Watch ye and pray," and the words directly following, "Rise, let us go," are very remarkable and are differently explained. Some interpreters are of the opinion that Christ said the words, "Sleep ye now and take your rest," by way of holy irony. Sleep, that is, if ye can, now that the hostile force is nigh and their weapons are resounding. The following words, "now it is enough—rise" were said by Christ, according to them, in a more serious tone to summon the apostles to join Him in meeting the enemy. Many interpreters, however, will not concede that *irony,* no matter how well justified, proceeded from the lips of the Saviour in such a serious hour. Not a few believe with St. Augustine that, by these words, Jesus really allowed the disciples to take some sleep and that then, after some lapse of time, he ordered them to rise. But how does this opinion agree with the command immediately preceding (v. 41), "Watch ye and pray"? For this reason St. Chrysostom (in Matth. hom. 83. n. 1), believes that Jesus spoke thus because He would not plainly reproach the disciples, as He recognized the uselessness of reproach at the present moment. He saw that it would only tend to bewilder them more, and, besides, in a few moments they would take to flight. Christ needed not their help; His delivery to the enemy was a certainty at any rate. According to this explanation the word of Christ would mean, "I do not wish to chide you; sleep on if ye be so weak as that." Even in this sense, the words contain an indirect reproach, but no sarcasm. The sense is more moderate and brings the perfect resignation of the Saviour beautifully into relief, wherefore we prefer this last explanation.

Upheld by St. Luke, xxii., 46, some interpreters believe that the Saviour again summoned the disciples to prayer immediately before His capture. Then began for them in its greatest extent the danger of wavering in the faith. What then would be more natural and more necessary than the repeated summons? Besides St. Luke, xxii., 46, agrees very well with St. Matthew, xxvi., 45. Christ could have said *both*. Other interpreters, however, are of the opinion that St. Luke, who in his narrative does not distinguish different acts of prayer, merely recapitulates (xxii., 46) the chief contents of the repeated addresses. The subsequent words "adhuc eo loquente" do not contradict this explanation. According to the evangelists' manner of speaking, this expression does *not necessarily* refer to the words immediately preceding.

3. (page 53.)

The acceptation that the washing of the feet took place *before* the institution of the Bl. Eucharist, will certainly not meet with contradiction, in which case the narrative of St. John, xiii., 2-31, decides the present question. Directly after the washing of the feet (v. 12) Jesus refers to the betrayer and again, immediately, a second time (v. 21 sq.); then, without any interruption, He hands him the dipped bread (v. 26), and he "having received the morsel, went out *immediately*." In this close and concise narrative the institution of the Bl. Eucharist cannot find room; it must have occurred later. Of a truth, St. Matthew (xxvi., 25 sq.) and St. Mark, (xxiv., 18 sq.) refer it to the time *after* the traitor had heard from Christ that it was he who would betray Him. Ancient testimony is also at hand showing that Judas was not present at the institution. Thus Tatian, a disciple of the holy martyr Justin, in his Concordance of the Gospels, called Diatessaron, records the institution as taking place after the departure of Judas and properly begins its description with the words of St. John, xiii., 31: "Now is the son of man glorified, etc." Victor of Capua in his Concordance of the Gospels (Migne 1, 68, [illegible]) says the same; likewise the so called Apostolic Constitutions 5, 14. This is also the teaching of St. Hilary (Comment. in Matth. 30, 2), of St. Ephrem, of St. Cyril of Alexandria, of St. Aphraates, of Rupertus (in Jo. 6, 71), of Pope Innocent III. (De sacro altaris mysterio 4, 13) who, after giving both opinions, concludes as follows: "Quid ergo est vobis in hoc casu tenendum? Illud forte sine praeiudicio aliorum, quod Joannes insinuat, quia cum Judas accepisset bucellam panis, exiit continuo. Christus autem post alios cibos tradidit Eucharistiam."— This is also the opinion of Zacharias Chrysopolit, Peter Comestor, Salmeron, Barradius, B. Lamy, Turrianus and of the majority of more recent interpreters. Cf. R. Cornely, S. J., Historica et Critica Introductio in Libros Sacros (Parisiis 1886. Vol. III.

p. 298 sqq.), Corluy, S. J., Commentarius in Ev. St. Joannis (Gandavi 1880, p. 321–323) and J. Knabenbauer, S. J., Comment. in Matth, ii., p. 439; Comment. in Luc. p. 576; Comment. in Jo. p. 416 sq. In reply to the objection that some of the Holy Fathers are of the opposite opinion, I answer that our opponents in other questions are themselves most pronouncedly in the minority.

The narration of St. Luke (xxii., 21–23) does indeed appear to report the words concerning the betrayal as being spoken after the institution of the Bl. Eucharist. But just as St. Luke, xxi., 21, 37, 38, adds a supplementary statement to that which he has mentioned before, he could in like manner add xxii., 21–23 by way of a supplement to what had taken place during the paschal supper. He probably did not wish to disturb by a discordant note the narrative of the institution of the Bl. Sacrament, and he therefore supplied afterwards the report of what had taken place *before*. Besides, according to some commentators, St. Luke, xxii., 46 (compare note 2) and especially xxiii., 36 (comp. note 18) also deviated from the historical series of events. According to Dr. Grimm (Einheit der 4 Ev. p. 480) the dispute about rank among the disciples and the reprimand of the Saviour took place *before* the institution of the Bl. Eucharist, although St. Luke tells of them *after* mentioning the institution (xxii., 24–30). According to Dr. Grimm this scene ought most naturally to be attached chronologically to the *foot-washing* scene. Now if *this* passage is considered a supplement, then, for the reasons already mentioned, it appears even more reasonable to begin the supplement with v. 21 instead of v. 24. Furthermore the following is to be considered: according to St. Matth. xxvi., 21, and St. Mark, xiv., 18, Christ speaks of the traitor, and the disciples put their questions during the supper and *before* the institution of the Bl. Sacrament. The same is reported by St. John, who says that the Redeemer hands Judas the dipped morsel. It is manifest then, according to these narratives, that the address concerning the betrayer and the questions of the disciples occurred during the legal supper and *before* the institution of the Eucharist. Hereby the assumption is excluded that St. Luke, xxii., 21, is to be understood to mean that the *same address and the same questions* occurred a second time *after* the supper in the same manner as they had occurred *before* it. Abbot Rupert of Deutz remarks aptly: "Verba quae in priori coena Dominus de suo traditore dixit, Lucas sic praeposteravit, ut priorem paschae coenam et sequentem dominici corporis et sanguinis consecrationem narrando conjungeret et tunc demum verba quae in convivio dicta sunt continuaret." And Father Knabenbauer, in his Comment. in Jo. p. 410, after quoting this text, correctly says: "Nisi igitur, quod plane superfluum est, adstruere volueris et Christum et discipulos *bis,* i. e., inter coenandum et post spatium temporis instituta eucharistia *eadem* dixisse (Christum: Luc. 22, 22: vae etc., discipulos quaesivisse), profecto narratio apud Lucam ita concipi debet." It is not against the chronological order appealed to in favor of St. Luke that he first reports the legal supper, then the institution and that he finally adds what was stated orally before. Otherwise the passages in St. Luke, iii., 19 and xxi., 37 would also be faults against the rule: ex ordine scribere. This rule refers to events in their totality: Qui ordo ut servetur non opus est ut singulae uniuscujusque eventus conditiones et quasi partes etiam semper ordine temporis enumerentur (cf. Knabenbauer, In Luc. p. 37).

"Cibum turbae *duodenae* se dat suis manibus" that

is, suis apostolis, who are also called the twelve although they were only 11 or (Paul included) 13. Duodecim is just as fixed an official name as decemviri, centumviri, "the 40 Immortals," which names are used even if the number be not complete.

Supposing however, as some Holy Fathers and interpreters (Dr. Paul Schanz, Commentar über das Evangelium des St. Lucas, p. 509 and 510) maintain, that Judas was really present at the institution of the Bl. Sacrament, one could with good reason ask the question whether or not Judas sinned in receiving it. The law that he only who is in the state of grace may receive Holy Communion was without doubt definitely mentioned by Christ, if not proclaimed in expressed terms, when He promised the Bl. Sacrament (St. John, 6). For food and drink presupposes life. They do not give it. They maintain and strengthen it. The disciples could, then, have concluded from the words of promise that the nourishment presupposes the life of the soul, which is sanctifying grace. But, it may well be doubted that the disciples, who were slow of understanding, and whom, even after the resurrection, Christ upbraided for their indocility and lack of comprehension of even *clearly* proposed truth (v. g. that Christ would rise again), really had understood that law and drawn from the words of promise the conclusion that the reception of that food in the state of mortal sin, is a sin, even a mortal sin, a sacrilege. This applies especially to Judas, who had lost the faith before the promise was made, and who therefore was hardly capable of higher comprehension and understanding. Taken for granted, however, that Judas had rightly comprehended and understood the law, it is doubtful whether he *thought* of it. For at the last supper, the institution of the Holy Eucharist took the disciples unawares, and the invitation to partake of that food was spoken before they knew what food was really meant. Taken for granted, finally, that Judas really thought of it, then the *positive, personal urging* and *loving* invitation of Christ: Eat ye, drink ye all of this, thou also Judas, for no one is excepted, must have necessarily forced upon him the conviction that, in his dullness, he had misunderstood the words of promise, and that the law really did not exist; or that, notwithstanding his sinfulness, Christ was giving him the permission to receive communion and dispensing him from the law. In which case he would have acted in good faith in receiving Holy Communion, and he could not have sinned.

If one, nevertheless, maintained that Judas with a clear knowledge of the law deliberately committed a sacrilege, then Christ's manner of speaking and acting would be entirely inexplicable. The objection that Judas was inwardly moved by the Redeemer to renounce his treacherous design and to be contrite for it, and that on this supposition, Christ could invite him to partake of the food, is of no account, because Christ *knew that* Judas would remain obdurate.[1] Thus the Redeemer would not only have *permitted* a new crime in one whom He *knew* to be *obdurate,* but He would have *positively* invited him to sin: He even would have made this invitation *stronger* (drink ye *all* of this) after the

[1] One ought to heed, in this connection, the remarks of Barradius: If Christ gave Holy Communion to Judas, the apostles might draw the conclusion that it might be given to an unworthy person even when the latter could easily be removed. And he adds: Ordine a Joanne proposito ostendit a Christo eum potuisse facillime removeri: ergo censendum esse Christum fecisse quod quivis sacerdos facere debeat, si peccatorem sine ulla peccati manifestatione removere possit (cf. Knabenbauer, Comment. in Jo. p. 417.)

sinner had already received sacrilegiously the Body of the Lord. Had Judas been present, Christ would have formulated differently the words of invitation. But this He did not do. Therefore Judas left the hall *before* the institution of the Bl. Sacrament.

4. (page 71.)

It is on untenable grounds that many modern scientists take this young man to be St. Mark, whilst entire tradition denies that he was personally acquainted with the Lord. On account of the scanty attire of the young man it is not probable either that he had recently been in the company of the Lord or had come with Him from the city. "Naked," as the evangelist describes the fleeing young man, does not necessarily mean entirely devoid of clothing. Any one was called naked who was clad only in an undergarment or a loin-cloth. The Jews held complete nudeness in great horror. Compare Sepp, Leben Jesu VI. 330 a. 5.

5. (page 77.)

Several interpreters (Salm. Tolet. Mald. Corn. a Lap., etc.) teach that the preliminary trial, which is here described as taking place before Annas, was held before *Caiphas*. However, Father Knabenbauer, S. J., in his Comment. in Joan., published in 1898, pp. 514 and 515, refutes so thoroughly the arguments of these interpreters and so clearly solves the difficulties urged by them against the opposite opinion that we are constrained to follow his teaching, which, besides, has always had many adherents (Chrys., Aug., Thomas and others). Father Knabenbauer shows in the first place from many texts of Holy Writ (St. John, xviii., 3; xviii., 35; vii., 45; xi., 47, 56; xix., 6, xv., 21: St. Luke, iii., 2), that the high-priests kept their titles after their terms had expired and that, therefore, Caiphas the pontiff in office, need not necessarily be understood as being the one who conducted the preliminary trial. Moreover, there are several arguments demonstrating that the preliminary trial was held before Annas, whilst only the trial proper was held before Caiphas: "Quae v. 19-23 narrantur, plane non congruent cum eis quae coram Caipho fiunt, ibi Jesus privatim interrogatur de doctrina et discipulis; hic instituitur disquisitio judicialis, i. e., re adducta testes surgunt et testimonia dicunt; ibi Jesus respondet, hic tacet et solum adjuratione per Deum facta edicit quis sit; ibi nulla fertur sententia, hic reus mortis declaratur. Unde, si numc v. 24. legitur: et misit eum Annas etc., ex antecedentibus omnino suadetur, hunc versum rite poni suo loco et ordine, imo ipso suo loco rem clare definiri." To consider this verse as a subsequent supplementary addition and to translate it thus: "Annas *had* sent him bound to Caiphas the high-priest" is also improper for the reason that, in a principal sentence, the aorist is never to be taken in the sense of the pluperfect. (See Kn. loc. cit.) The apparent contradiction between the other evangelists who speak of the three denials of Peter as occurring in the courtyard of the palace of Caiphas, and St. John, who mentions that the first denial happened in the courtyard of the house of Annas, is solved by Father Knabenbauer, who clearly proves, from the narration itself of St. John, that Annas and Caiphas lived in the *same* house. For, while Christ was before Caiphas (v. 25), Peter stood at the same fire and, consequently, in the same courtyard where he had been when Christ was before Annas (v. 18). St. John, therefore, does not contradict the narratives of the other evangelists, which state that the three denials took place in the courtyard of the palace of Caipnas, but he rather completes them by showing that the first denial took place while Christ was before *Annas in the house of Caiphas.* (Kn. p. 515 and 519.)

6. (page 90.)

Regarding the history of the Sanhedrin or "Great Council" which throws such a peculiar light upon the trial of Christ, compare D. Bon. v. Haneberg's Geschichte der bibl. Offenbarung (4th ed. Ratisbon 1876), Part VI, ch. 2, p. 435. It consisted formerly of the chiefs of the tribes, of the priests and of men of all tribes who were versed in the law. It had continued throughout the time of the judges and, according to legendary data of the Rabbis, even during the time of the kings. According to the Rabbis the greater number and the greatest of the prophets, such as Josue, Samuel, Elias, Eliseus, Isaias etc. were presidents of the Sanhedrin. At any rate the Great Council was reorganized after the return of many priests and levites under Esdras. Esdras himself belonged to it as also did Aggeus, Zachary and Malachy.

7. (page 103.)

Cornelius à Lapide (St. Matthew, xxvi., 58), De ıa Palma (ch. 11), and Maszl (Vol. III., [St. Mark, xiv., 66] Vol V. [St. John, xviii., 15–18]) do not believe that the disciple who entered the courtyard of the high-priest with St. Peter was St. John, but they think that it was another, albeit a secret disciple of the Saviour; that he was perhaps of noble lineage and acquainted with Caiphas on account of his elevated position in life. Cornelius à Lapide appeals especially to the Syrian translation, "one of the other disciples." Opposed to this, however, are the Greek editions of the Bible and all the other translations, so that the text, "the other disciple," stands unshaken. The Syrian translator probably embodied his private view in the text. Now, "the other disciple" is none other than St. John. He always calls himself by this name. Later also, St. John, xx., 2; xxi., 7, 20, and in the Acts of the Apostles, John and Peter are continually found together. Like Peter, John also entered the court of Caiphas without thinking of any danger. John had less to fear for himself, as it seems that he was well thought of in the house of the high-priest. But John did not for once imagine that the entrance into that house would prove ruinous to Peter whose attachment to the Redeemer he well knew and who, a few hours before, had made so many courageous protestations. John, however, was more careful than Peter. He did not mingle among the servants and converse with them; but he went into the interior of the palace and contemplated his Saviour. Furthermore, it is very credible that he soon took his departure to inform the Bl. Virgin of the beginning of the trial. Cf. Dr. J. B. Holzammer, Handbuch zur bibl. Geschichte, II. (3d ed.), 354, note 1; J. B. Lohmann, S. J., Betrachtungen, I. (4th ed.), 265.

8. (page 133.)

Touching and beautiful is the accomplishment of the ancient prophecies to which the evangelist refers when mentioning the potter's field (St. Matth. xxvii., 9). The prophetic words quoted by him are taken partly from Zachary, xi., 12, and partly from Jeremias. The evangelist, however, mentions only the latter, because he furnishes the *chief* contents of the entire prophecy quoted as one, namely, the potter's field and its significance. The whole prophecy embraces three chief points.

1. The prophet Zachary represents the Lord as a good Shepherd expressing His indignation at the ingratitude of His flock for all the pastoral care lavished upon it. But to see whether the sheep desired the Shepherd's return or not and to make them reflect upon the benefits bestowed by Him upon them, He asks them to set a price on His labors and to indemnify Him, if it appear right to them; otherwise not to mind it. They thereupon pay Him, as a fair price for years of love and care, *thirty pieces of silver,* the price of a slave. For, according to the law (Exod. xxi., 32), that was the price to be paid to the master as an indemnity for a bond-man or a bond-woman killed by an ox. His price shows contempt for the shepherd and, at the same time, his repudiation. He can be dispensed with, and his removal is desired. Then God says to the shepherd, "Cast it to the statuary (God, the Creator), a handsome price, that I was priced at by them. And the shepherd took the thirty pieces of silver and cast them into the house of the Lord to the statuary." He also broke his second pastoral rod as he had broken the first — he ceased to be their shepherd. The good shepherd, then, who saw himself thus priced, throws the insignificant sum contemptuously upon the ground before God, the Lord of Israel, the Owner of the flock. He did this in the Temple, for there the Lord dwells, and he thereby appeals to the judgment of God. God hears the appeal and the flock shall now be abandoned to a bad shepherd. All this the evangelist now sees accomplished: the people have renounced the Messias by appreciating Him at thirty pieces of silver, and they have thus passed judgment upon themselves.

The evangelist mentions the fulfillment of this prophecy now, when he is about to narrate how the Jews delivered the Redeemer unto Pilate, the heathen.

2. But the betrayal of Judas, the appreciation of the shepherd by the flock at thirty pieces of silver, the moment, therefore, when the rejection of Israel seems to be accomplished, has as a sequel the guaranty that mercy shall not always keep her face turned away from Israel. And this guaranty is found in the "field of blood," in the *potter's field.* Whilst the siege of the Chaldeans renders Jerusalem hopeless and makes the people stand aghast at their destruction; whilst the prophet Jeremias, himself a type of the suffering Saviour in his abandonment and nudity, is serving in prison for his prophecies; the word of God comes to him to buy, in Jehovah's name, *a field* in that land "whereof they say that it is desolate, because there remaineth neither man nor beast and it is given into the hands of the enemy" (Jerem. xxxii., 43). The prophet obeys. The contract is closed with proper seals and deed, and the price of the field is paid. According to the will of God this field is to be a *pledge* that the nation shall be re-established, that it shall return and retake possession of the land. Wherefore the field is not the property of the prophet, but it was bought in the name and as the property of God.

But it is not so much temporal re-establishment, nor recuperation of external goods, nor political restoration, which are promised here. The purchase of the field is rather the pledge of a *higher, spiritual restoration,* of Messianic Salvation, of a new, eternal testament, of a new kingdom of God upon earth to be established by the death of the Redeemer. Neither external power nor earthly splendor should characterize this restoration, but rather sanctity, concord and love. (See Jerem. ch. xxxii. and xxxiii.; and also the beautiful description of the Messianic kingdom according to the sayings of the prophets in J. Knabenbauer, S. J., [Comment. in Prophet. Min. II., p. 160–168 anent Sophonias, III., 9–13].)

The fulfillment of this prophecy is the last act performed by the high-priests of Israel. In the name of the *temple,* that is, of Jehovah's dwelling therein, they buy the *potter's field.* They buy it with the money donated to the temple, with the price earned with the life and blood of the Messias, the good Shepherd; they buy it for the ridiculous price of thirty pieces of silver, by means of which He has appealed to the God of Israel and which, in the temple, He has laid at the feet of the Lord, the "statuary" of Israel.

3. In the fact that it was the field of a *potter* which was bought with the blood-money, the evangelist sees no fortuitous event, but he beholds again the fulfillment of a glorious prophecy. For according to Zachary the good shepherd significantly casts the thirty pieces of silver before the "*potter*" in the temple, that is to say before the Lord who, in a special manner, is the "statuary" of Israel. He is not only its Creator as He is the Creator of all nations, but in an incomparably more intimate manner by especial favor and through the inventive power of His love, He is its artistic, modelling Statuary, its Potter. With particular development of details, the prophet Jeremias also (ch. xviii., and xix.,) represents God to His people as a Potter, and in the name of the Lord, before the eyes of the representatives of the people, he breaks a vessel of clay to make known that as the potter breaks his vessel, so God will destroy the people and the city. But what the prophet already here (Jerem. xviii., 4) indicates,

that, namely, from the broken vessel the potter will form another more pleasing to his eyes, he also expressly promises (xxxiii., 2) when, as a pledge of the fulfillment of his promise, he offers the field bought by himself for the Lord, the Statuary of Israel. By the bringing in of the name of "Potter," the same old promise of a higher, spiritual restoration of the old testament fallen in ruins is repeated under another figure, at least by way of intimation. The purchase of the field in the name of God and with God's money (the blood-money of the Messias) is the guaranty that *now the time has arrived* when this prophecy is to be fulfilled and that the potter is to remodel gloriously the broken vessel. And this is what is remarkable in the fulfillment of the prophecy and what the evangelist wishes to bring out in relief — the field bought by the chief-priests in the name of the Lord of the temple, is the "*field of a potter.*"

Thus the evangelist has seen three prophecies accomplished simultaneously in the purchase of the potter's field, and he has therefore abridged them into one: *The God of Israel with Whose money, earned by the blood of the Messias, the field is purchased, thereby becomes the owner of the potter's field. He is Himself the Potter who at this moment rejects His people, as His people has just now rejected its Shepherd; but Who, exactly through the purchase of this field declares that He, the same Potter, will remodel the clay in His hands into a new, successful and pleasing form.* Compare Dr. J. Grimm, Die Einheit der vier Evangelien, pp. 715–724, and J. Knabenbauer, S. J., Commentarius in Prophet. Min. II, 351 sq.

9. (page 138 and 232.)

As it appears very probable from the work Hist. Revelationis Divinae N. T. (p. 234 sqq.) of J. Danko, who cites the names of many celebrated authors (p. 241) in support of his opinion, the Jews, after their return from the Babylonian captivity, or at least for a long time before the death of Christ, were wont to transfer the feast of the Passover to the Sabbath whenever it fell on a Friday. This was done in order that there might not be two successive days on which servile labor was forbidden. On the Sabbath and on the feast of reconciliation they were not allowed to work, not even to light a fire. For, considering the strictness with which the pharisees observed their feasts and Sabbaths, two such days in succession would have caused much annoyance; wherefore, on this point, they were more excusable than many Christians of our day who have a dread for ecclesiastical feasts. Such a case occurred in the year of Christ's death, for which reason the Jews ate the paschal lamb on Friday evening. But the Lord, who had come to "fulfill the law," held strictly to the requirements of the Mosaic law (Numbers ix., 12), and therefore ate the paschal lamb on Thursday evening after sundown, at the time when, according to the intimation of the evangelists (St. Luke, xxii., 7, St. Mark, xiv., 12), it should be slain, and when in olden times, the Jews actually did slay it. Thus, the indication of days as we find it in St. John, is easily explained. At the same time, by means of this fact, Divine Providence so arranged it that Christ brought about the realization of the types of the Bl. Sacrament as well as of His Sacrifice on the Cross on the same days on which these types were being celebrated in Jerusalem. He established the Bl. Eucharist in the hour in which, according to law, the paschal lamb should be eaten. (Thursday evening.) And at the hour when the true Lamb of God was taken down dead from the Cross (Friday evening), the Jews were engaged in slaying their paschal lamb. Their work, of course, was for nothing and too late, as Christ by His sacrificial death had already put an end to all the sacrifices of the law. Cf. Maldon. in Matth. cap. 26, Dr. J. Grimm, Die Einheit der vier Evangelien, p. 756 sqq.

10. (page 143.)

If one, however, lean to the first mentioned albeit more improbable opinion, that Pilate, to rid himself of the affair, actually allowed the chief-priests to execute the death-warrant without his previous investigation, then their words evidently cannot have the meaning that it was beyond their *competency.* For Pilate then would have given them permission. Neither would they say. "We may not do it *to-day* on account of the feast of the Passover," because the feast began only on that evening. Neither could the sense be: "We are not permitted to *crucify* any one. You can stone him, or decapitate him, or burn him, or hang him to a gallows."

Some interpreters who follow this explanation are of the opinion that the words of the chief-priests contain a refusal to make use of the granted permission, as though the Jews said, "Either give us back, O Pilate, all our rights and our judiciary powers in their fullest extent, or you may keep full charge of this particular case also. We shall not touch it. Either everything or nothing." But they spoke thus with the secret purpose of forcing *crucifixion* upon Christ through Pilate. Other interpreters, however, declare the sense of these words to be as follows: "We are not permitted to put Him to death, that is *to-day,* because according to our law, the execution must always be relegated to the day following the passing of the judgment. And to prevent Pilate from objecting, "What need is there of hurry? Why do you not wait with the execution until after the Paschal days?" they organized the monster massing of the people to give Pilate to understand that here was a case which brooked no delay, a death-sentence which he must make his soldiers execute without any further postponement.

In our explanation we have, from the very beginning (chap. xi., page 153), taken the standpoint that the Sanhedrin had power only to impose small penalties. A few commentators, however, think that, under the governors also, the Sanhedrin had the right to impose one of the four death-penalties mentioned above without the governor's permission, at least when there was question of crimes committed against *religion* and the *Mosaic law.* In this case, the last two explanations would be well established. The sense of Pilate's words then would be: "We Romans are not accustomed to condemn any one to death without a formal trial merely to please somebody. Now, if you have investigated the matter and found Christ guilty, and if you refuse to even lay before me the points of the accusation, why, then go and do what the law allows you. For my part, I will not meddle with it." Then the chief-priests' answer was either: We *will* not (with the intention of bringing Christ to the death of the *Cross*) or: we *may* not (meaning *to-day*).

11. (page 183.)

All that Flavius Josephus reports of Pilate is his *removal* in the year 36, on account of a slaughter of

Samaritans on Mount Garizim (Antiq. 18, 4, 2). Eusebius (H. e. II, 7) speaks of his *suicide* and cites pagan authors. Some apocryphal writers say that he died converted, while others claim that he committed suicide in Rome. Ado of Vienne († 875) is the first to narrate that Pilate was banished for life to Vienne and that the anger of the emperor C. Caligula terrorized him to such an extent that he stabbed himself to death. Cf. Chronic. 4840 (Migne P. L. CXXIII, 77). According to the chronicle of Malala, he was beheaded at Rome under the reign of Nero. There are many other tales and legends anent his person and his demise.

The gospel does not mention the name of Pilate's wife, but in tradition (in Evangelium Nicodemi, Nicephorus [H. e. I, 30] and by Malala) she is called Claudia Procula. According to the legend, she was a Jewish proselyte, as was often the case with Roman women. She is said to have been a secret disciple of Jesus. It is also mentioned by Origen (in Matth.), by St. Chrysostom and by St. Hilary that she later on became a Christian. In the Greek menology, she is venerated as a saint on the 27th day of October.

12. (page 225.)

Not a few interpreters understand the words of Christ (St. John, xix., 11): "He that hath delivered me to thee, hath the greater sin," to mean that He declared the sin of Caiphas (the Great Council) to be greater than that of Pilate. "Because thou, as judge, hast received from God especial power, thine is indeed a great sin if thou judgest not rightly. But to Caiphas no power has been given over me. He has unjustly arrogated to himself power over me, and he has also delivered me to thee impelled, as he was, by envy and hatred. *Therefore* his sin is greater than thine, if, from human respect, thou abusest thy power and condemnest me notwithstanding my innocence." The religious authorities among the Jews who maliciously surrendered to the pagan governor Him who claimed to be the Messias and by intimidation forced the governor to abuse his authority, were evidently guilty of a greater crime than the judge of weak character, who could not escape the functions of his position.

Father Knabenbauer, S. J., in his Comm. in Joan. (p. 533) prefers the foregoing opinion to all others, and he solves well the difficulty which the word "propterea" has prepared for many interpreters. As in other matters, we should also in this gladly have adopted the opinion of this excellent interpreter, if there were not one difficulty in our way. For it appears to us to be against practical prudence, even against common sense, to insinuate, by way of consolation as it were, to a man whom one wishes to caution against crime, that, even if he commit the crime, he shall not be worse, but rather better than he who misled him. Would that be really a warning against crime? Would it not rather be an encouragement to it? Now Christ, at this moment, wished nothing else than to warn Pilate, earnestly and impressively, against judicial murder, and, for the time being, this warning did not miss its effect.

We cannot understand what, under the existing circumstances, could have induced the Saviour to speak to Pilate of the *greater* sin of Caiphas. Therefore, for the present, we stand by our former interpretation, which we have taken from Toletus (in Joan. 19, 11), without, however, wishing to hinder anyone from adopting the opinion of Fr. Knabenbauer.

The opinion of a few that Christ compared the sin of Pilate with that of *Judas,* does not need a refutation. To betray and to deliver are two different acts. Judas neither executed nor intended the delivering of the Redeemer unto Pilate. He neither foresaw nor did he anticipate it.

13. (page 248.)

According to Genesis, xxii., 14, the mount on which Abraham was about to immolate his son, was Mount Moriah, the later site of the Jewish temple. On this occasion the mount was first hallowed, as well through the figure of the intended sacrifice, as by the fact that to the heroic devotion of faith which the patriarch here showed there were attached the great promises for his progeny. (Haneberg, Gesch. der bibl. Offenb. [4th ed.] p. 52.) Now the tribunal of Pilate was situated on the south side of the fortress Antonia which occupied the northwest corner of the temple court. The place of execution was just above the court-yard of the temple (Schegg-Haneberg, Evang. nach Johannes II, 441 sqq.). According to Sepp (Leben Jesu, VI, 194) Pilate did not have his court-room in the fortress Antonia, on Moriah, but in the royal palace of the Herodians, and thus Christ would have been sentenced on *Sion,* before the castle of David to which the palace of the Herodians was contiguous. Sepp and Tobler, therefore, locate the beginning of the Way of the Cross on Sion. But this opinion seems to have been successfully opposed by Schegg, Holzammer and others. The opinion of Schegg is, furthermore, entirely favored by the original local traditions of Palestine, according to which the Way of the Cross began on Moriah, in the vicinity of the temple of Solomon.

14. (page 250.)

Our description differs from the order followed in the devotion of the Way of Cross only in so far as the three falls of the Redeemer are concerned. It seems to be beyond a doubt that Christ had fallen the third time before Simon relieved Him of the Cross. Perhaps it was to avoid monotony that in the devotion of the Way of the Cross the meditations on the triple fall were separated by the introduction of other mysteries. The present Way of the Cross in Jerusalem, that is, the *direction* which it indicates, is undoubtedly correct, and the five of the fourteen stations which commemorate events not expressly mentioned in Holy Writ, are based upon ancient and venerable traditions; but, for all that, no one is bound to cling to the manner and order of representation as found in the Way of the Cross; to all of which Salmeron has already called attention.

15. (page 259)

Without in any way prejudicing the matter under consideration, one might abstract entirely from the *place* where Simon, Veronica and the weeping women met Christ. It is the almost unanimous opinion of interpreters that Simon met the Redeemer *outside* the city. As the lamentation of the pious women is mentioned by St. Luke immediately after Simon's meeting with Christ, the women probably also met Him beyond the city. According to our presentation of matters, which agrees on this point with the devotion of the Way of the Cross, the same may be said of Veronica, who seemed to have been among the lamenting women. According to others, she handed the kerchief to Christ while He was still *inside* the walls of the city. On this point certainty can no more be obtained.

16. (page 269.)

The ancient Greek interpreters of the Scriptures are wont to distinguish between the "myrrh-wine" which, according to St. Mark, Christ did not drink, and the "gall-potion," which, as St. Matthew says, Christ tasted. According to them, therefore, two different cups were offered to Christ. This interpretation, improbable in itself, arose mainly from an error in regard to the scriptural text. The old Greek editions had instead of the words, "wine with gall," the words very similar in the Greek language, "vinegar with gall." It was the object of St. Matthew to here put in relief the humiliating treatment of Jesus as a criminal and, at the same time, the fulfillment of the prophecy, "And they gave me gall for my food, and in my thirst they gave me vinegar to drink." The second part of this text of the psalm was fulfilled when, after the fifth word of Christ on the Cross, vinegar was offered Him, but the first part was fulfilled now. Thick liquids, such as milk and the like, as also wine strongly mixed with bitter herbs, can according to usage be called "food" as well as "drink."

17. (page 270.)

It appears to be a thoroughly established fact that when Christ was disrobed the loin-cloth was left Him. Not only is the statement that the Romans attached the condemned to the cross in a condition of entire nudity difficult to prove on account of the wide and varying signification of the word "nudus," but, as Schegg correctly remarks, we are "justified in making a difference between the crucifixion of a criminal, or a common slave, and the crucifixion of Jesus Christ." Surely the pronounced dread of the Jews for complete nudity and the presence of the women at the crucifixion are a guaranty that there remained to the Lord in his denudation a covering for the loins. This is also the teaching of the "Evangelium Nicodemi," which, although apocryphal and of rather late origin, seems to be supported in many of its parts by ancient traditions. If some of the Holy Fathers, thinking of sinful Adam, let the second Adam die in complete nakedness, this mystical view of the matter has been opposed by another, just as full of meaning. In Exodus, xxviii., 43, it is laid down as a "law forever" to the priests to wear the linen hip garment at divine service. And Christ, the Priest, was about to offer His sacrifice. The loin-cloth of Christ is among the sacred objects venerated at Aix-la-Chapelle. It is said that Charlemagne brought it there.

18. (page 335.)

A few interpreters apply St. Luke, xxiii., 36, to a special occurrence which must have taken place not after the fifth word, but before. In order to ridicule Christ in His thirst, the soldiers, they say, offered Him vinegar, without however letting Him have it, demanding meanwhile that He help Himself. But most interpreters apply St. Luke, xxiii., 36, to the scene of humiliation described by St. Matthew and by St. Mark after the fifth word. The description given of the mockery of Christ on the part of the soldiers, seems to be the most simple and natural adjustment of the narratives of St. Matthew, xxvii., 49, St. Mark, xv., 36, and of St. Luke, xxiii., 36. For it will not do to declare the words of St. Matthew and of St. Mark to be wholly identical. Nor is there anything which justifies the assumption that the soldier offering the vinegar was better disposed than the others and that he deprecated their derisive language. *St. Mark describes him too plainly as a participant in the scene of humiliation.* Besides the sense already given, the words of the soldiers might have one of the following meanings: a) cease your shouting lest Elias be deterred from coming. b) Cease your cries and your mockery, otherwise your tormenting will hasten His death before the arrival of Elias, and He is already very weak as I can see from close observation. c) Cease shouting and keep quiet so that we may observe with undivided attention how Elias will come to liberate Him.

Those who erroneously assume that the vinegar was handed to the crucified to hasten their death add another meaning: d) Let me hand Him the vinegar. The greater the danger of death is, the sooner will Elias come. This meaning is made more untenable by the fact that "vinegar" is here probably to be understood as meaning a sour wine, prepared from the skins of pressed grapes, which laborers were wont to drink, or the so-called "posca," the drink of the soldiers, which was composed of vinegar, water and eggs.

19. (page 337.)

Isaias, lii., 15, describes the Messias as the Chief Priest Who, after the consummation of the sacrifice, reconciles all people by means of the sacrificial blood. He also describes Him as a second Moses on the point of establishing a new testament between God and man. The prophet then, liii., 10, says in clear terms that this Messias shall offer His own life as a propitiatory sacrifice. The force of these passages is beautifully shown by J. Knabenbauer, S. J., Commentarius in Isaiam II, 319 sq.: cf. p. 308. Regarding Is., liii., 7, see ibid. p. 306, 307.

20. (page 380.)

Three of the evangelists report the wonderful darkness at the death of Christ, and they add that it existed "over the whole earth." Now it is not to be forgotten that the evangelists speak of the things which occurred in Judea where they then were, according to the direct knowledge of these things and to the extent of their knowledge of them. Therefore Origen, in his commentary on St. Matthew, remarks that there is nothing to hinder the opinion that the darkness extended only over Jerusalem and its vicinity, or, at most, over the whole of Judea, just as the tearing of the veil in the temple, the quaking of the earth, the bursting of the rocks and the opening of the graves are reported as taking place in *Jerusalem.* The expression used by the evangelists could then be translated, "over the whole land," "over the whole region," just as is understood in St. Luke, iv., 25, of the famine at the time of Elias and in many other passages of Holy Writ. Origen rightly remarks that, if this extraordinary event had taken place over the entire earth, we ought to have information of it from other sources also. This ecclesiastical writer was aware, indeed, of the statement of Phlegon of Tralles, a chronicler of the second century, who reports a solar eclipse in Bithynia and an earthquake at Nicea, both occurring about the year 29 of our calendar. This testimony is produced by Eusebius in his Chronicles, by St. Jerome in his translation of the last named work, and later on by a few Greek chroniclers. However, Origen points out that it is very uncertain whether or not Phlegon speaks of the same eclipse as the evangelists, because he fails to mention what was the most remarkable feature of it, namely, that it occurred, against the laws of nature, at the time of the full moon and that it lasted three hours. He therefore warns against placing too much reliance upon it. And indeed Phlegon seems to speak of a common, astronomical eclipse of the sun, and outside of the writers mentioned, hardly any Fathers of the Church, apologists or Church historians appeal to it. The statement of the Syrian Thallus which is mentioned, but not given verbatim, in a fragment extant of Julius Africanus, is surrounded with so much obscurity that one can conclude nothing from it with any degree of certainty. Several ancient ecclesiastical writers knew Thallus and quoted passages from him, but the very passage of such importance to them, is not mentioned by any of them. They also leave us in the dark regarding the personality of this writer and the time when he lived. To judge by the expression used in the fragment of Africanus, he also speaks of an astronomical, solar eclipse.

It is however correct that about the year 200, in proof of these miraculous events, Tertullian appealed with all confidence to the official records in the Roman archives. He undoubtedly had in view the reports of Pilate concerning the execution of Christ and the events in Palestine. With the knowledge he had of the Roman archival system, he could rightly presuppose that they were yet extant, and probably he definitely knew of their existence. Very similar to the words of Tertullian are the words which the ecclesiastical writer Rufinus, in his translation of the Church History of Eusebius (1, IX, c. 6), makes the holy martyr Lucian say about such records in the "Annals." Unfortunately, we have no clue to the source from which, almost 100 years after St. Lucian's death, Rufinus drew forth this address, which had escaped Eusebius, the contemporary of Lucian. All passages referred to here, as well as those which refer to these wonderful occurrences in the works known under the name of Dionysius the Areopagite, are grouped together in C. Baronius, Annal. Eccl. a. 34, n. 116. et 117.

St. Chrysostom and also Cornelius à Lapide believe, however, that the darkness extended over the *entire* hemisphere reached by the sun's rays, and they are followed in this belief by many prominent Catholic interpreters even to our own day. Regarding the other occurrences in nature, they are of opinion that they occurred over the whole earth. For the Lord of the whole earth was concerned, and, in His behalf, all inanimate nature arose to announce His death as the most important occurrence for the whole world.

There are many surmises as to the manner in which God's Omnipotence and Wisdom produced these phenomena. But they are naught else but surmises.

21. (page 394.)

St. John does not say *which* side was struck by the lance. The outflow of blood and water would of itself indicate the left side where the heart is. The same conclusion might be drawn from the fact that the soldier, standing opposite the cross with the spear in his right hand, would most naturally strike at the left side. Nevertheless, ancient tradition, frequent, authoritative and clearly expressed, especially in the very ancient Ethiopian translation of the Gospel, declares that it was the *right* side. According to St. Bonaventure, the stigmata of St. Francis showed the wound to be on the right side. Moreover, the Church looks upon the temple, from the right side of which, according to the vision of Ezechiel (xlvii., 1), the wonderful water flowed, as a type of the body of the Lord, and applies the words of the prophet in this sense during the paschal season. Most commentators therefore assume that the blow was aimed at the *right* side whence the point of the lance penetrated through the cavity of the breast to the left side into the heart.

As to the question whether the outflow of blood and water, *considered in itself*, indicates anything of a miraculous nature, the following may be remarked:

1. Many holy Fathers and ancient interpreters consider the flow of *blood* to be a miracle, for the reason that soon after death the blood *congeals* or, to speak more correctly, it *decomposes* into a liquid similar to water and more solid clots of blood. Naturally then, nothing else could flow out but the first mentioned aqueous fluid which, although containing minute white corpuscles of blood, invisible to the naked eye, is however by no means blood. The outflow of liquid blood, properly speaking, would therefore have been a miracle. Modern medical science, however, disputes the fact of such rapid decomposition. Jos. Bautz in the "*Katholik*" of Mayence (1886, second half, p. 585 etc.) quotes authorities who maintain that this decomposition only begins four hours after death. Only one adds the restriction that, after a prolonged agony, the blood may *perhaps sometimes* begin to coagulate at the moment of death. Many physicians here whom I have lately consulted regarding this question, have assured me that in the *human body* the blood decomposes only in from 12 to 24 hours after death, and they supported their statement with the authority of a noted physiologist of our country (J. C. Dalton, A Treatise on Human Physiology, sixth edition, Philadelphia, 1875, p. 263). Bautz himself admits, at the end of his praiseworthy article, that decomposition takes place a *considerable* time after death. Now, if this be so, then the outpouring and

even the copious outpouring of real, liquid blood can be explained naturally, especially if the lance was withdrawn with much force and quickness. Thus say the physicians.

2. That *real* water flowed out of the side of Christ, is beyond a doubt. Thus say St. Ambrose (Exposit. Ev. St. Lucae 1, 10, 135), St. Cyril of *Jerusalem* (catech. 13, 21), Origen (c. Cels.), St. Thomas (in p. 3, q. 66, art. 4 ad 3 and q. 74 art. 7 ad 3), Salmeron (1, 10 tr 45), Toletus and Cornelius à Lapide (John 19, 34), De la Palma (ch. 46) and others. Pope Innocent III. especially expressed himself very strongly against the opinion that from the side of Christ there issued not real water but "phlegma" (a thick mucus), or humor aquaticus (a thin, aqueous fluid). (lib. 3 decret. tit. 41 de celebr. Miss. c. 8): "Non aquam, sed humorem aquaticum *mentiuntur* exiisse." The above cited authorities consider the outflow of real water to be as manifest a miracle as the outflow of blood. Pope Innocent III. had, indeed, not given a decision on this question. He merely insists that it was not "humor aquaticus" but "vera aqua" which issued from the wound. But can the term "vera aqua," in the meaning of the pope, be applied to the aqueous fluid, found one hour after death in the pericardium, in the two pleurae, etc. (in the right ventricle of the heart there is then none as yet)? Or is this fluid not what he calls "humor aquaticus"? In English, it is called fluid or liquid, but not water. Let us conclude. If there was "vera aqua" in sufficient quantity in the pericardium and in the pleurae, which were pierced by the lance, a miraculous act of God was required at most to effect an abundant outflowing of the water. If real water was not contained in those parts, then Pope Innocent permits us to accept, with the above mentioned authori-

ties, a miraculous secretion of *real* water from the sacred body (the human body consists of 70% of real water in divers forms and composites) — and even a new creation, if needs be.

3. According to the opinion of physicians whom I have consulted, the fact that St. John could distinguish the blood from the water in a simultaneous outflow, was a manifest miracle. Their opinion was that the outflow should have appeared as *one* substance of the same color. Father Suarez (p. 3 q. 51, disp. 41, sec. 1) is of the same mind, and just for this as well as for other reasons, he asserts that at first blood and then water flowed out of the wound, which, perhaps, can be explained on natural grounds without the need of admitting a new miracle. Compare the article of Bautz, quoted elsewhere, p. 592.

The opinion of the English physician, William Stroud, (A Treatise on the Physical Cause of Death of Christ, London 1847), that Christ died of a *broken heart,* which opinion was adopted to some extent by physicians as well as theologians in Germany, must be rejected on theological grounds. For in this hypothesis, Christ would not have been put to death by the Jews and His death would degenerate from a freely willed sacrifice to a mere natural process. It is only when organic heart troubles pre-exist that heart rupture is occasioned by violent emotions. But there can be no thought of organic heart disease in Christ nor of any other bodily ailment. Comp. article of Bautz, p. 588.

22. (page 410.)

Commonly the words of Isaias (xi., 10), "and his sepulchre shall be glorious," are considered as a prophecy regarding the burial of the Redeemer, especially as it is beyond a doubt that in this passage there is question of the Messias. This, however, is the idea only of St. Jerome, who embodied it in his Latin translation of the Bible. The Hebrew text has it, "the people shall search for him (the glorified Messias) and his repose shall be in glory." From this text one can indeed conclude that also the *place* of His repose, the place of His dwelling, as for instance, the temple of the Old Law or the Christian Church, shall be particularly glorious, not to forget the *sepulchre* which, under such extraordinary circumstances, He selected as His especial dwelling. All this can be *deduced* from the words of the prophet but it is not *directly expressed* by them. More beautiful and clear is the prediction concerning the Saviour's sepulture by the same prophet (Is., liii., 9). It is well dilated upon in the excellent Commentarius in Isaiam Prophetam auctore J. Knabenbauer, S. J., Paris 1887, t. I, p. 1 sqq: t. II, p. 315 sq.

23. (page 417.)

Whilst Christ speaks in many passages of His resurrection *on the third day* (St. Matthew, xvi., 21; xvii., 22, xx., 19. St. Luke, ix., 22; xviii., 33. St. Mark, x., 34), He only once uses the expression that He will arise *after three days* (St. Mark, viii., 31) because in this one passage He compares Himself to Jonas. Similarly He says (St. Matth. xii., 40), again on account of the comparison, that the Son of Man will be in the heart of earth three days and three nights. Here, as well as in other passages of Holy Writ, we must have regard for the manner in which the Jews expressed themselves. In determining a time, they were wont to count entire days, months and years, if even only a small part of them, either the beginning or the end, was covered by the events spoken of. As Christ had so often very definitely determined the time of His resurrection, there could be no doubt as to how this one passage ought to be understood. The words of this passage were incorrectly given by the false witnesses. In a similar way, the latter quoted wrongly the words of Christ declaring (St. John, ii., 19) that, after His enemies had destroyed the temple of His body He would raise it up again *in* three days, i. e., within the period of three days or *before* the expiration of three days (see St. Matth. xxvi., 61).

The Two Divine Promises. Fr. Hoppe	1.25
St. Teresa of Ávila. William Thomas Walsh	18.00
Isabella of Spain—The Last Crusader. Wm. T. Walsh	16.50
Characters of the Inquisition. Wm. T. Walsh	12.00
Philip II. William Thomas Walsh. H.B.	37.50
Blood-Drenched Altars—Cath. Comment. Hist. Mexico	16.50
Self-Abandonment to Divine Providence. de Caussade	15.00
Way of the Cross. Liguorian	.75
Way of the Cross. Franciscan	.75
Modern Saints—Their Lives & Faces, Bk. 1. Ann Ball	15.00
Saint Michael and the Angels. Approved Sources	5.50
Dolorous Passion of Our Lord. Anne C. Emmerich	13.50
Our Lady of Fatima's Peace Plan from Heaven. Booklet	.75
Divine Favors Granted to St. Joseph. Pere Binet	4.00
St. Joseph Cafasso—Priest of the Gallows. St. J. Bosco	3.00
Catechism of the Council of Trent. McHugh/Callan	20.00
Padre Pio—The Stigmatist. Fr. Charles Carty	12.50
Why Squander Illness? Frs. Rumble & Carty	2.00
Fatima—The Great Sign. Francis Johnston	7.00
Heliotropium—Conformity of Human Will to Divine	11.00
Charity for the Suffering Souls. Fr. John Nageleisen	13.50
Devotion to the Sacred Heart of Jesus. Verheylezoon	12.50
Religious Liberty. Michael Davies	1.50
Sermons on Prayer. St. Francis de Sales	3.50
Sermons on Our Lady. St. Francis de Sales	9.00
Sermons for Lent. St. Francis de Sales	10.00
Fundamentals of Catholic Dogma. Ott	16.50
Litany of the Blessed Virgin Mary. (100 cards)	5.00
Who Is Padre Pio? Radio Replies Press	1.00
Child's Bible History. Knecht	4.00
The Life of Christ. 4 Vols. H.B. Anne C. Emmerich	55.00
St. Anthony—The Wonder Worker of Padua. Stoddard	3.50
The Precious Blood. Fr. Faber	11.00
The Holy Shroud & Four Visions. Fr. O'Connell	1.50
Clean Love in Courtship. Fr. Lawrence Lovasik	2.00
The Prophecies of St. Malachy. Peter Bander	4.00
The Secret of the Rosary. St. Louis De Montfort	3.00
The History of Antichrist. Rev. P. Huchede	2.50
Where We Got the Bible. Fr. Henry Graham	5.00
Hidden Treasure—Holy Mass. St. Leonard	4.00
Imitation of the Sacred Heart of Jesus. Fr. Arnoudt	13.50
The Life & Glories of St. Joseph. Edward Thompson	12.50

At your bookdealer or direct from the publisher.

Prices guaranteed through December 31, 1993.